Financial Evaluation and Risk Management of Infrastructure Projects

Kleopatra Petroutsatou
Aristotle University of Thessaloniki, Greece

Constantin Zopounidis
Technical University of Crete, Greece & Audencia Business School, France

IGI Global
PUBLISHER of TIMELY KNOWLEDGE

A volume in the Advances in Public Policy and Administration (APPA) Book Series

Published in the United States of America by
IGI Global
Information Science Reference (an imprint of IGI Global)
701 E. Chocolate Avenue
Hershey PA, USA 17033
Tel: 717-533-8845
Fax: 717-533-8661
E-mail: cust@igi-global.com
Web site: http://www.igi-global.com

Library of Congress Cataloging-in-Publication Data

Names: Petroutsatou, Kleopatra, 1972- editor. | Zopounidis, Constantin, editor.
Title: Financial evaluation and risk management of infrastructure projects / edited by Kleopatra Petroutsatou, Constantin Zopounidis.
Description: Hershey, PA : Information Science Reference, [2023] | Includes bibliographical references and index. | Summary: "This book will aim to provide relevant theoretical frameworks and the latest empirical research findings in the area. It will be written for professionals in public and private corporations, academics and students, who want to improve their understanding of the strategic role of trust at different levels of the Financial Evaluation and Risk Management of Infratsructure Projects. Also, the audience will dive into the different aspects of the decision making process with interrelated parameters under evaluation when Infrastructure Projects are the case"-- Provided by publisher.
Identifiers: LCCN 2023021793 (print) | LCCN 2023021794 (ebook) | ISBN 9781668477861 (hardcover) | ISBN 9781668477908 (paperback) | ISBN 9781668477878 (ebook)
Subjects: LCSH: Infrastructure (Economics) | Risk management. | Project management. | Decision making.
Classification: LCC HC79.C3 F5155 2023 (print) | LCC HC79.C3 (ebook) | DDC 363--dc23/eng/20230616
LC record available at https://lccn.loc.gov/2023021793
LC ebook record available at https://lccn.loc.gov/2023021794

This book is published in the IGI Global book series Advances in Public Policy and Administration (APPA) (ISSN: 2475-6644; eISSN: 2475-6652)

British Cataloguing in Publication Data
A Cataloguing in Publication record for this book is available from the British Library.

For electronic access to this publication, please contact: eresources@igi-global.com.

Advances in Public Policy and Administration (APPA) Book Series

ISSN:2475-6644
EISSN:2475-6652

MISSION

Proper management of the public sphere is necessary in order to maintain order in modern society. Research developments in the field of public policy and administration can assist in uncovering the latest tools, practices, and methodologies for governing societies around the world.

The **Advances in Public Policy and Administration (APPA) Book Series** aims to publish scholarly publications focused on topics pertaining to the governance of the public domain. APPA's focus on timely topics relating to government, public funding, politics, public safety, policy, and law enforcement is particularly relevant to academicians, government officials, and upper-level students seeking the most up-to-date research in their field.

COVERAGE

- Government
- Law Enforcement
- Political Economy
- Politics
- Public Administration
- Public Funding
- Public Policy
- Resource allocation
- Urban Planning

IGI Global is currently accepting manuscripts for publication within this series. To submit a proposal for a volume in this series, please contact our Acquisition Editors at Acquisitions@igi-global.com or visit: http://www.igi-global.com/publish/.

The Advances in Public Policy and Administration (APPA) Book Series (ISSN 2475-6644) is published by IGI Global, 701 E. Chocolate Avenue, Hershey, PA 17033-1240, USA, www.igi-global.com. This series is composed of titles available for purchase individually; each title is edited to be contextually exclusive from any other title within the series. For pricing and ordering information please visit http://www.igi-global.com/book-series/advances-public-policy-administration/97862. Postmaster: Send all address changes to above address.

Titles in this Series

For a list of additional titles in this series, please visit:
http://www.igi-global.com/book-series/advances-public-policy-administration/97862

Cognitive Governance and the Historical Distortion of the Norm of Modern Development A Theory of Political Asymmetry
Renny Rueda (American University in the Emirates, United Arab Emirates)
Information Science Reference • copyright 2024 • 310pp • H/C (ISBN: 9781668497944) • US $215.00 (our price)

Policies, Practices, and Protocols for International Commercial Arbitration
Basheer Ahmed Mohammed Khan (Supreme Court of India Bar Association, India) and Kaushal Kishore (Supreme Court of India Bar Association, New Delhi, India)
Information Science Reference • copyright 2023 • 271pp • H/C (ISBN: 9781668440407) • US $225.00 (our price)

Governmental Power Market-Ing in the VU-CHAOS World
Kittisak Jermsittiparsert (University of City Island, Cyprus) Srirath Gohwong (Universitas Muhammadiyah Sidenreng Rappang, Indonesia) Shayut Pavapanunkul (Universitas Muhammadiyah Sidenreng Rappang, Indonesia) and Nasaran Mahittichatkul (Universitas Muhammadiyah Sidenreng Rappang, Indonesia)
Information Science Reference • copyright 2023 • 296pp • H/C (ISBN: 9781668472804) • US $205.00 (our price)

Historical and Political Analysis on Power Balances and Deglobalization
Emily Brynn Stacey (Rose State College, USA)
Information Science Reference • copyright 2023 • 253pp • H/C (ISBN: 9781668456330) • US $205.00 (our price)

Juvenile Justice in African and Western Criminal Justice Systems
Simeon Peter Sungi (United States International University-Africa, Kenya) George Rugaimukamu Kakoti (Tennessee State University, USA) and Deneil D. Christian (Tennessee State University, USA)

IGI Global
PUBLISHER of TIMELY KNOWLEDGE

701 East Chocolate Avenue, Hershey, PA 17033, USA
Tel: 717-533-8845 x100 • Fax: 717-533-8661
E-Mail: cust@igi-global.com • www.igi-global.com

Table of Contents

Detailed Table of Contents

Construction projects are subject to risks and uncertainty that make the final cost of the investment difficult to predict. A life cycle cost analysis incorporating the risks involved could prove useful in the decision-making process. This analysis should be done at the start of the conception phase of the project and work itself along the project's realization. This chapter presents a specific approach for the implementation of a risk-based life cycle cost analysis. The proposed approach covers the risk-based life cycle cost analysis of a construction project, through the incorporation of well-established risk identification and risk analysis methods. The risk identification process regarding the energy-based risks of a residential construction project is performed. Finally, the proposed method is showcased on an illustrative case of a residential building with multiple different energy-based investment scenarios, and its results form the basis for the decision-making of the project.

ESG refers to environmental, social, and governance in the construction sector and can contribute to the sustainability of the companies in the construction sector. This indicates that while planning and developing a project from beginning to end, all ESG risks should be properly considered. ESG risk management and reporting are particularly significant in the construction sector. A strong ESG approach may improve supply chain efficiency, minimize health and safety concerns, reduce emissions, and encourage effective investment. Managing ESG risks is a great way for businesses engaged in the construction sector to attract investors and boost senior management expectations. This chapter aims to illustrate how a construction company may mitigate the risks faced within the use of ESG risk management. Findings illustrate that strategies based on ESG risk management can help companies in the construction sector to protect the environment and society and create long-term value for their business.

In view of the present climate around the globe, mega infrastructure developments are considered to be key catalysts driving economic development and social upliftment and transformation within the world economies today. However, the complexity of megaproject development especially when it comes to infrastructural development is a like a dual edged sword, and in recent years, the delivery of many infrastructural projects have come under scathing attack for schedule slippages, huge cost overruns, and questions over real benefits to the economic viability and sustainability it proposes to bring to the countries future DDP and GNP. This study analysed megaproject schedule challenges in transnet capital projects (TCP) in South Africa. The study employed a survey, and quantitative data were collected using a closed ended questionnaire from 191 megaproject personnel. The objective of the study was to undertake the quantitative analysis to critically assess schedule challenges.

An attempt was made to predict the cashflows of public road projects using artificial neural networks. In the context of the development of prediction models, an introduction to the financial flows, to the Greek legislation that defines them, and finally to artificial intelligence was made. Also, a literature review concerning the application of artificial intelligence in the construction industry was carried out. Neural networks were then applied based on 37 public road projects. The methodology highlighted three models for the prediction of cashflows for public road projects: a statistical exponential regression model, an artificial neural network model, and finally a hybrid model that combined the two previous ones. The hybrid model had the lowest mean absolute prediction error, followed by the model using only artificial neural networks, and lastly the statistical regression model. Finally, the conclusions of the study, the limitations that existed, suggestions for the application of the model, and ideas for future research are presented.

The purpose of this chapter is to investigate and quantify through real case studies the risks involved in time and cost overruns of infrastructure projects from the procurement to the delivery stage. Although the literature is very rich with a variety of analyses of the factors causing cost and time overruns, there is a gap in investigating the risks in the procurement phase to delivery of such projects. A holistic approach of risks identified in the procurement and construction phase of such projects is presented by using probabilistic analyses of time and cost overruns compared to contractual agreements. Three real case studies are presented with and without the risks identified, results are discussed, and conclusions are derived. This approach could enhance public authorities' processes for successful procurement and delivery. Furthermore, the quantification of these risks in terms of time and cost could pave the way for a more sustainable organization of the authorities in order to deliver successful projects within their time constraints and budget.

It is widely accepted that every project aiming at specific outcomes is unique, since it is not a routine operation. In this context it is important to identify and study certain common characteristics of an effective project manager. The aim of this research is to examine the importance of the attributes of an effective project manager by analyzing how satisfied his/her collaborators are. The study focuses on the project management of EU Operational Programs in the public sector. Based on the literature, the effective project manager should be able to understand and influence the key parameters of any project (physical, technical, scientific, etc.), such as the duration, the financial resources, the human resources, the legislation, and the operation. To analyze the degree of satisfaction and the importance of project manager characteristics, the MUSA method has been applied, which is a multiple-criteria decision-analysis approach in the field of preference disaggregation.

Foreword

Infrastructure projects are a critical driving force for domestic and international economic and social development. Several risks are encountered concerning managerial, technical, and financing issues that could threaten projects' viability. The recent economic recession resulted in an increasing need for the financial evaluation of the infrastructure projects throughout their life cycle.

This book delves into intriguing issues of infrastructure projects and explores further the mechanisms for Value for Money in the design and the procurement phases. Moreover, an analysis of the risks and uncertainties that impact on cost estimation is presented based on a well-established risk identification methodology. Environmental, Social, and Governance considerations in risk management are discussed and analyzed. Also, the wager of managing large infrastructure projects is employed by offering valuable insights into practical difficulties and opportunities in the management of such projects. Financial viability is explored using Artificial Intelligence; valuable consultation is provided for decision makers in the context of public works. Additionally, a holistic approach of the risks involved in public works from the procurement phase until the end of a project's construction is well analyzed. Finally, the competences of an effective manager in a complex and dynamic environment are examined and valuable insights are adduced.

I strongly recommend this book to all those who navigate the infrastructure projects' perplex world as a valuable point of reference; it sheds light to the issues concerning financial evaluation and risk management within infrastructures. Whether the readers are professionals, researchers or students engaged in construction management, this book addresses successfully a big array of issues concerning quantitative evaluation and multicriteria risk management techniques. Practical guidance for the financial evaluation and risk management of infrastructure projects are of utmost importance for a well-planned future.

Sergios Lambropoulos
Professor Emeritus, National Technical University of Athens, Greece

Preface

The realm of infrastructure development is a complex tapestry woven with threads of financial intricacies, risk, and the pursuit of delivering enduring value. In this edited reference book, we embark on a comprehensive exploration of the multifaceted journey from the initial conception of an infrastructure project to the meticulous curation of its service value over time. It is our privilege to present to you a compilation of knowledge, insights, and methodologies that have the potential to reshape the landscape of infrastructure project management.

The International Organization for Standardization aptly defines the life cycle cost of an infrastructure project, encapsulating the costs incurred during construction, operation, maintenance, and the eventual end-of-life phase. Each of these stages is intertwined with intricate financial calculations and is influenced by a spectrum of potential risks that can be encountered during the project's construction and service life. The accurate assessment and early mitigation of these risks stand as pillars upon which project viability rests, particularly in the wake of recent financial crises and the stringent budgetary constraints experienced in Europe and elsewhere.

In response to the evolving demands of infrastructure development and the pressing need for cost-effective projects, we recognize the critical importance of the "value for money" methodology. Its effective application is a linchpin for success in the complex world of construction.

This book emerges from a compelling need to delve deep into the world of multicriteria methodologies. Our aim is to offer a comprehensive resource that equips professionals in public and private corporations, academics, and students with the tools and knowledge necessary to navigate the intricate landscape of financial evaluation and risk management within infrastructure projects. In these pages, we bring forth theoretical frameworks and the latest empirical research findings that enrich the reader's understanding of the strategic role of trust and decision-making processes within infrastructure projects.

Our intended audience spans a diverse spectrum, encompassing professionals, researchers, and students engaged in construction management across various sectors, including public institutions, private companies, universities, and investment corporations. The insights shared within these chapters are not limited to the confines of academic discourse; they extend to support executives and decision-makers entrusted with managing infrastructure projects within a wide array of work communities and environments.

The themes explored within this book are both timely and timeless. Topics range from risk management and value engineering to the service value of assets and the cost of infrastructure projects. We journey through the fascinating intersection of behavioral finance and financial evaluation, and we venture into the world of quantitative evaluation and multicriteria risk management techniques.

As the editors of this book, we commend the dedication and expertise of our esteemed contributors who have shared their insights and experiences. Their collective wisdom and research findings serve as valuable building blocks for anyone committed to enhancing their grasp of the intricacies involved in financial evaluation and risk management within infrastructure projects.

We invite you to embark on this intellectual journey with us and explore the intricate dimensions of infrastructure projects. Whether you are a seasoned professional, a diligent researcher, or an eager student, we trust that the contents of this book will broaden your horizons, sharpen your skills, and empower you to navigate the complexities of financial evaluation and risk management in infrastructure projects.

CHAPTER OVERVIEW

Chapter 1: Exploring the Mechanisms for Value-for-Money Diffusion in the Design and Procurement of EU Public Infrastructure Projects

In this chapter, the authors delve into the intricacies of achieving Value for Money (VfM) in EU public infrastructure projects. They shed light on procurement and design options that can lead to enhanced VfM, emphasizing the significance of contractor involvement in the design phase. This chapter explores a hybrid approach that integrates open tender and Competitive Dialogue (CD) elements, offering contractors the opportunity to propose value-enhancing design variants. To address this novel approach, a Multi-Criteria Decision Making model is introduced, exemplifying its application within the context of EU procurement legislation.

Chapter 2: The Impact of Risks and Uncertainty in Life Cycle Cost Analysis of Construction Projects – The Case of Energy Analysis on Construction Projects

This chapter delves into the unpredictable nature of construction projects and how risks and uncertainties can complicate cost estimation. It introduces a risk-based Life Cycle Cost Analysis approach, emphasizing the importance of initiating this analysis at the project's inception and maintaining it throughout its realization. The authors employ well-established risk identification and analysis methods to manage energy-based risks in residential construction projects. They use an illustrative case to demonstrate how this approach informs decision-making throughout the project.

Chapter 3: ESG in Construction Risk Management – A Strategic Roadmap for Controlling Risks and Maximizing Profits

In this chapter, the focus shifts to Environmental, Social, and Governance (ESG) considerations in construction risk management. The authors explore how ESG principles can be integrated into construction projects to enhance sustainability, efficiency, safety, and long-term value creation. They highlight the role of ESG risk management in attracting investors, improving supply chain efficiency, and reducing environmental impact. The chapter provides strategic insights on how construction companies can navigate ESG risks to create a more sustainable and profitable business.

Chapter 4: Investigating Mega Project Schedule Challenges in Transnet Capital Projects

This chapter delves into the complexities of mega infrastructure projects, particularly within the context of Transnet Capital Projects in South Africa. The study analyzes the challenges associated with schedule management in these large-scale projects. By employing a quantitative approach, the authors gather data from megaproject personnel to critically assess schedule challenges. The chapter offers valuable insights into the practical difficulties and opportunities for improvement in managing large infrastructure projects.

Chapter 5: Application of Artificial Neural Networks for the Prediction of Cashflows in Public Road Works

This chapter explores the application of artificial neural networks in predicting cashflows for public road projects. The authors provide an overview of the financial flows and Greek legislation that define them, before applying neural networks to 37 public road projects. They compare different models, including a hybrid approach, to predict cashflows. The results offer a valuable foundation for decision-making within the context of public road projects and open avenues for future research.

Chapter 6: Investigating the Risks of Time and Cost Overruns in Infrastructure Projects

Chapter 6 takes a holistic approach to the investigation of risks associated with time and cost overruns in infrastructure projects, particularly in the procurement and construction phases. The authors employ probabilistic analyses to identify risks and assess their impact on project delivery. Real case studies are presented, both with and without identified risks, providing a practical understanding of the challenges and opportunities in managing time and cost in infrastructure projects.

Chapter 7: Attributes of an Effective Project Manager – The Case of European Operational Programs in the Public Sector

This chapter examines the key attributes of an effective project manager, with a focus on EU Operational Programs in the public sector. The authors explore the characteristics and competencies required for project managers to understand and influence various project parameters. Using the MUSA method, they assess the degree of satisfaction and the importance of these attributes in successful project management. The chapter offers valuable insights into the qualities that make a project manager effective in a complex and dynamic environment.

IN SUMMARY

As we draw the final curtain on this meticulously curated edited reference book, *Financial Evaluation and Risk Management of Infrastructure Projects*, we find ourselves reflecting on the remarkable journey we've undertaken alongside our esteemed contributors and readers. This book was born from a collective passion for unraveling the intricacies of infrastructure project management, financial evaluation, and risk mitigation, and it has been our privilege to guide you through its pages.

The chapters within this volume represent a diverse array of perspectives and insights from experts across the globe, each bringing a unique lens to the multifaceted world of infrastructure projects. From exploring mechanisms to achieve Value for Money (VfM) in EU public infrastructure projects to delving into the profound impact of risks and uncertainty in Life Cycle Cost Analysis, the chapters offer a comprehensive view of the field. We've ventured into the realm of Environmental, Social, and Governance (ESG) in construction risk management, investigating mega project schedule challenges, and even employed artificial neural networks to predict cashflows in public road works.

The content presented within these chapters stands as a testament to the ever-evolving nature of infrastructure project management and the intricate web of financial and risk considerations that accompany it. We have explored the nuances of decision-making, the complexities of managing large-scale projects, and the strategic importance of sustainable and responsible practices in construction.

For those navigating the world of infrastructure projects, this book serves as an invaluable resource. Whether you are a seasoned professional looking to enhance your expertise, a diligent researcher seeking fresh insights, or an eager student embarking on a learning journey, the knowledge contained herein empowers you with tools to navigate the complex landscape of financial evaluation and risk management within infrastructure projects.

We extend our heartfelt gratitude to the authors who contributed their expertise, time, and wisdom to this compilation. Your dedication to advancing the field of infrastructure project management is evident in the richness of the content you've provided.

To our readers, we hope that the chapters contained in this book have broadened your horizons, sharpened your skills, and enriched your understanding of the challenges and opportunities within the world of infrastructure projects. May the knowledge presented here fuel your passion and guide your endeavors in this dynamic field.

In closing, we are reminded that the world of infrastructure projects will continue to evolve, presenting new challenges and opportunities. It is our hope that this book will remain a timeless reference, offering valuable insights and guidance as you navigate the intricate path of financial evaluation and risk management in infrastructure projects. Thank you for joining us on this intellectual journey.

Warm regards,

Kleopatra Petroutsatou
Aristotle University of Thessaloniki, Greece

Constantin Zopounidis
Technical University of Crete, Greece & Audencia Business School, France

Chapter 1
Exploring the Mechanisms for Value-for-Money Diffusion in the Design and Procurement of EU Public Infrastructure Projects

Fani Antoniou
https://orcid.org/0000-0002-0773-5144
International Hellenic University, Greece

Marina Marinelli
https://orcid.org/0000-0002-6509-0612
National Technical University of Athens, Greece

Kleopatra Petroutsatou
https://orcid.org/0000-0003-4477-8693
Aristotle University of Thessaloniki, Greece

ABSTRACT

This chapter presents procurement and design options that can lead to public projects of higher value for money (VfM) within the currently applicable EU legislation. It particularly highlights how the timing and extent of the contractor's involvement in design enables value management/engineering and constructability reviews and maximizes project VfM. Furthermore, this chapter demonstrates how the best VfM can be achieved with the integration of features from the open tender and the Competitive Dialogue (CD). This hybrid approach gives to any contractor the option to submit value-enhancing design variants within the context of an open procedure and processes their submitted proposals as per the main principles of the CD. In

DOI: 10.4018/978-1-6684-7786-1.ch001

this context, the contracting authorities need to select specific VfM-enhancing criteria as well as an efficient and objective method to address the emerging design comparisons, evaluations, and bid rankings. The authors address this gap with a multi-criteria decision-making model and provide a detailed example in line with the EU procurement legislation.

INTRODUCTION

Infrastructure projects, typically requiring large financial investment, are crucial in promoting the socio-economic development of countries and regions by enabling transport and providing access to health, education and housing to millions of people. Therefore, the ability of European Union (EU) countries to deliver infrastructure investment priorities efficiently and effectively is crucial to achieving growth objectives, especially after taking into account that the proportion of the EU population residing in urban areas is expected to increase to 82% by 2050 (European Court of Auditors, ECA 2014). The EU legislation for public procurement is included in the Directive 2014/24/EU and its main principle is to promote the idea of creating open and fair competition among as many suppliers as possible (Torvatn & de Boer, 2017). In particular, transparency, equal treatment and non-discrimination are necessary as minimum conditions for high level competition.

Furthermore, ensuring the most efficient use of public funds and achieving Value for Money (VfM) are central objectives for governments who can define value according to their priorities, typically encompassing the project's life-cycle cost, as well as organizational, social and environmental aspects. There is no doubt that the procurement mechanisms, typically controlled by governments in public works, make an excellent opportunity for the state to incorporate VfM requirements into project design and construction. Nevertheless, delivering a public infrastructure investment program that achieves VfM returns as planned has been revealed, from relevant European Court of Auditors (ECA) audits, as a particularly difficult mission for EU countries. Indicatively, it is not uncommon for EU projects to present significant delays and cost overruns in excess of 20%, for a variety of reasons including late modifications, coordination problems, technical difficulties, and delays in making land available (European Court of Auditors, 2014). In this context, concerted efforts by the stakeholders and particularly the contracting authority (CA) are necessary to promote value and minimize cost in public works. These efforts could tremendously benefit from the implementation of the structured process of value management (VM) for the main design choices, as well as the scrutiny of the technical solutions in the light of the principles of value engineering and constructability. For those well-established methods to be effectively implemented though, the engagement of the right expertise at the right time is also required, which in turn is subject to the procurement strategy being applied. Therefore, an appropriate procurement strategy is required for the respective value priorities to be efficiently incorporated in the established procedures. This chapter aims to review the mechanisms for efficient VfM diffusion in design and procurement of public projects in relation to the available legislative options in the EU and showcase how a hybrid approach incorporating features of the competitive dialogue (CD) and the open procedure, can yield the maximum VfM benefits.

PROCUREMENT OPTIONS AND THEIR IMPLICATIONS FOR VFM

Open/Restricted Procedures and Respective Selection and Award Criteria

Public contracts in the EU can be awarded through an open or a restricted procedure, with the former representing the most usual option (Govert Heijboer & Jan Telgen, 2002) where all interested contractors are invited to submit bids following a publicly announced call. The contract is being awarded in a single stage and the process is typified by high competition. On the other hand, when the restricted procedure is selected, the process consists of two stages, starting with a prequalification stage which excludes from the bidding process contractors who do not fulfil predetermined financial and technical criteria. Such criteria can include technical competence, management capability, earlier experience, financial stability and staff qualifications (de Araújo, Alencar, & de Miranda Mota, 2017) and unavoidably the process becomes more complicated and time consuming (Lambropoulos, 2007).

Regardless of a one or two-stage procedure and according to Article 58 of the EU procurement directive (2014/24/EU), CAs may only impose on economic operators (bidders) the following selection criteria as requirements for participation in the award procedures.

(a) Suitability to pursue the professional activity;
(b) Economic and financial standing;
(c) Technical and professional ability.

These criteria are evaluated initially based on the submitted European Single Procurement Document (ESPD), which is an updated self- declaration as preliminary evidence confirming that the relevant economic operator (bidder) fulfils the selection criteria as defined in the contract documents. In addition within the ESPD the economic operator states that it is not in one of the situations referred to in Article 57 as exclusion grounds (convicted of participation in a criminal organization, corruption, fraud, terrorist offences, money laundering, child labor or human trafficking). Therefore, the evaluation of these selection criteria is on a pass/fail basis. If a bidder does not meet the selection criteria, it does not proceed to the bid evaluation phase.

Following evaluation of the selection criteria, and according to EU procurement directive (2014/24/EU), the one stage open procedure can incorporate either one or two more evaluation phases, depending on the contract award criteria. Specifically, according to article 67 of the said directive, contracting authorities shall base the award of public contracts on the most economically advantageous tender (MEAT). The MEAT from the point of view of the contracting authority shall be identified on the basis of the price or cost, using a cost-effectiveness approach, such as life-cycle costing in accordance with Article 68, and may include the best price-quality ratio, which shall be assessed on the basis of additional quality criteria that can refer to, quality, technical merit, aesthetic and functional characteristics, innovative characteristics as well as, environmental, social criteria, etc., and of course lowest price (HSPPA, 2015). In the case where the award criterion is the best price-quality ratio two evaluation phases follow. In the first evaluation phase, the technical offer as described in the tender documents is evaluated and scored passed on the defined qualitative criteria and in the second phase the financial offer is noted. The tender documents provide the rating and method of calculation of the final price-quality ratio obtained from each bidder resulting in the determination of the most economically advantageous tender."

Integrated Procurement Approaches

Constructability (or buildability), as defined by the Construction Industry Institute (CII 1986), is the optimum use of construction knowledge and experience in the conceptual planning, engineering, procurement, and field operations phases to achieve the overall project objectives. Constructability is strongly linked to a wide range of VFM-enhancing benefits, including construction cost savings, reduced design rework and shortened project duration. However, the predominant fragmented contracting sequence of the traditional project procurement system (PPS), known as Design-Bid-Build (DBB) is a major barrier to achieving VFM in construction as it impedes the effective implementation of constructability (Eriksson & Westerberg, 2011) (Ren, Shen, & Xue, 2013). On the contrary, integrated PPSs such as the Design and Build (DB), Build-Operate-Transfer (BOT), Public – Private Partnerships (PPP) and the CD procurement procedure, ensure the contractor's effective involvement (Naoum & Egbu, 2016) (Marinelli & Antoniou, 2020).

Design and Build

In the DB PPS, there is no separate bid for construction as the procurement and award of both design and construction are combined into a single stage, with a single contract. This is a strategy which has been connected to increased VfM performance resulting from fast-track delivery, design flexibility, enhanced financial certainty, improved constructability and reduced disputes (e.g. Lu, Hua, & Zhang, 2017; Park & Kwak, 2017; Naoum & Egbu, 2016; Hale, Shrestha, Gibson, & Migliaccio, 2009; Tam, 2000; Ernzen; & Cliff Schexnayder, 2000; Ernzen; & Cliff Schexnayder, 2000).

However, DB contracts present a series of disadvantages including high effort, significant resources required for the bid preparation and evaluation, as well as the fact that the required prequalification stage usually restricts the number of participants and limits competition (Park & Kwak, 2017; Naoum & Egbu, 2016; Ernzen; & Cliff Schexnayder, 2000).

Public-Private Partnerships

The ageing public infrastructure combined with the ever growing economic development makes new infrastructure plans inevitable although numerous countries experience public budget restrictions. The massive investment gap that governments have to cover has forced them to adopt complex financing schemes involving the private sector in traditionally publicly funded sectors, generally known as Public Private Partnerships (PPP). When the PPP procurement system is adopted, the client contracts with one entity that finances, designs, constructs, operates and maintains an infrastructure project for a fixed period after which the project is transferred back to the CA (Antoniou, Konstantinidis, & Aretoulis, 2016). The level of the private sector's involvement in PPPs is variable and leads to different contract types, an extensive presentation of which has been provided by Zhao & Ying (2018). The involvement of private actors enables governments to secure financing, sector-specific expertise and managerial capacity, so as to provide cost-effective infrastructure allowing for higher quality of life, economic growth and employment opportunities (Berrone et al., 2019). Furthermore, there is evidence that the percentage of PPP projects completed on time and on budget is much higher than the respective percentage of traditional contracts (Grimsey & Lewis, 2005). Nevertheless, PPPs should only be used if they provide better value for money than traditional procurement and their long-term success depends to a large degree on the choice of the best-suited private partner. Therefore, bidder qualifications and proposals must be evaluated properly to ensure the delivery of expected benefits: By suitably incorporating sustainability factors like e.g. lifecycle cost, maintenance period, environmental impact into the contract award criteria, the contracting authorities have the opportunity to maximize the potential long term sustainability performance of the project.

The disadvantage in terms of VfM of this system is that the CA is almost totally cut-out of the loop in making decisions regarding design variants. Nevertheless, it is expected that the private partner will make efficient decisions as they are responsible for long term operation and maintenance as well as design and construction.

Competitive Dialogue

A common requirement in both the open and the restricted procedures is that the CA needs to provide advanced bidding documentation in which the main features of the project are well-defined. This however, is only possible if the CA has a clear understanding of its own objectives and the means to achieve them before tendering a project. Nevertheless, it is rare for the original design documents to be so complete that the project could be built to the exact specifications (Creedy, Skitmore, & Wong, 2010), especially considering that the CAs often lack the information required to draft the tender documents, or have limited experience in organising award procedures and/or (over) ambitious project objectives to manage (Siemonsma, van Nus, & Uyttendaele, 2012). In this context, the CAs are not always able to describe what would satisfy their needs or to assess what technical, financial or legal solutions are available in the market, without prior interaction with its representatives. In response to this, the EU has also introduced the procurement procedure of the Competitive Dialogue (CD). The CD procedure is meant to allow a CA, which knows what outcome it wants to achieve in awarding a public contract (e.g., a river crossing) but does not know how best to achieve it (e.g., by a bridge or a tunnel), to discuss, in confidence, possible solutions in the dialogue phase of the tender process with shortlisted bidders before calling for final bids (Burnett, 2009). In the context of the CD procedure, any economic operator interested to participate in the process can do so. This requires them providing the information for qualitative pre-selection as defined by the CA. In the next stage, the qualified bidders and the CA engage in parallel dialogue processes, either consultative or investigative ones, with the aim to define a pool of suggested technical solutions. In the consultative approach, there is a provisionally preferred solution provided by the CA which is used as the basis for amendments and variations. In the investigative approach, there is no given technical solution and therefore, the parties proceed with different bidder-driven solutions which are competitively compared. The process starts with the CA defining its objectives and desired outcomes, and in response, the bidders submit outline solutions which subsequently become more refined during the course of the dialogue. The dialogue phase is concluded when the required solution(s) have been identified, and the respective bidders are then invited to submit a final tender for these jointly identified solution(s) (Burnett, 2009).

Disadvantages usually attributed to the CD process include the low level of competition, slow progress and legal restrictions to its use as the Article 26 of the Directive allows it only for projects involving design complexity, innovation or uncertainty. On the positive side of things though, Siemonsma et al. (2012) note that the CD process entails an optimised allocation of responsibilities and risks to the benefit of the overall expected cost and VfM of the project, no matter how complex or simple it is. They also highlight the beneficial role of the contractor's involvement in the design as this enables the CA to draft the tender documents with greater rationality. This point reflects the valuable impact of constructability achieved through the early involvement of the contractor in the process.

DESIGN CHOICES AND THEIR IMPLICATIONS FOR VFM

Making design choices which promote VfM in public works requires concerted efforts by the stakeholders and particularly the CA (Client). These efforts should be aimed at increasing value or/and decreasing cost so that the ratio between value and money improves. Value in construction is a subjective, relative, context-dependent and dynamic concept as it depends on the stakeholders' vision, it emerges from comparison, it varies according to the context where it is measured or perceived, and furthermore, changes with time (Salvatierra-Garrido & Pasquire, 2011). Efficiently capturing and implementing value in design, requires the implementation of VM for the main design choices, as well as the scrutiny of the technical solutions in the light of the principles of value engineering and constructability. A comprehensive review of the value methodologies and their variations according to the geographic context of practice have been provided by Kelly, J., Male S. and Graham (1993) and Kelly, J., Male S. and Graham (2014).

Value Management and Value Engineering

The structured process of VM aims to make explicit the functional benefits of a technical solution and appraise them consistently according to a value system determined by the client. The process incorporates a series of workshops with the participation of key representatives from both the public client and the designer, who should collectively have the necessary experience to make informed decisions. Through these meetings, the stakeholders have the opportunity to reach consensus on what constitutes 'value' for them, how this translates into specific criteria and how these criteria rank in terms of relative importance (Connaughton, J.N. and

Green, 1996). The ultimate goal of the functional value analysis conducted in VM is the identification of the design alternative which achieves maximization of the design's value for money. Detailed examples of the process can be found in ICE's guidelines (1996) while (Jay & Bowen, 2015) provide a holistic and comprehensive historical perspective of the evolution of VM over the past 100 years, highlighting its substantial contribution to innovation.

The literature presents numerous well-documented examples of VM exercises in infrastructure projects, which using functional value analysis, have highlighted how the projects' key benefits / advantages and eventually their VfM depend on aspects like safety, reduced travel time, user satisfaction, traffic capacity, flood avoidance, reliability, durability, buildability, ease of use, facilitation of maintenance and operation, recyclable material and emissions (e.g. Mao, Zhang, & AbouRizk, 2009; Yang, Baeg, & Moon, 2014; Moon, Ha, & Yang, 2012, Tang & Bittner, 2014, Mousakhani, Yavarkhani, & Sohrabi, 2017; Mousa, Hussein, & Kineber, 2022). Furthermore, the systematic review by Lin et al., 2023 identified a great range of benefits entailing from VM implementation in projects; these indicatively include cost reduction, time-savings, function optimisation, quality/ performance improvement, productivity/ efficiency enhancement, energy- saving, conflict resolution and minimisation of waste and environmental damages, amongst others.

Despite the fact that there are countries like e.g., the US, Korea and Malaysia, where governments have mandated the use of VM in design development for projects beyond a certain budget threshold, the overall worldwide awareness and implementation level is low (Lin et al., 2023). In addition, further improvement of the project's performance in the economic aspect of VfM is also possible at the stage of the design's finalization or even after this, through the process of Value Engineering (VE). VE is the organized approach aimed at eliminating unnecessary costs by finding design alternatives which can provide the necessary functions (client's requirements) at less cost compared to the approved option. VE's origins are traced back to the days of World War II, when due to material shortages, manufacturing engineers were looking for ways to achieve the same functions without compromising quality. In this context, the VE process can fully utilize the creativity of engineers towards identifying the needed functions and ensuring a systematic performance classification of all options, based on quantitative criteria for the functions defined (Tang & Bittner, 2014). Mousa et al., 2022 make a detailed presentation of the brainstorming and scoring process, focussing on the selection of the optimal structural system for a bridge project. Fathi, Taher, & Mahfouz (2020) support that there is a crucial need for a holistic VE framework integrating social and environmental criteria in this field.

Constructability Reviews

Constructability reviews aim to evaluate design options and systematically review their development with the aim to minimize future scope changes due to construction oversights and associated disputes. This is a process typically relying on the input of construction engineers in early design stages with the aim to enhance ease of construction and promote design rationalization and standardization. Conducting constructability reviews at the proper time within the design phase is imperative, as projects approaching construction become less flexible to changes, which diminishes the ability to impact cost and delivery time. Late reviews, i.e., conducted after design finalization and before construction may still detect possible oversights, but the changes at that stage would likely entail additional costs and time for the project to be completed (Stamatiadis, Sturgill, & Amiridis, 2017).

Efficient use of constructability reviews can result in improved solutions and reduced design rework, as well as cost savings, shortened project duration, increased safety and quality, improved planning and scheduling and reduced disputes (Tawiah & Russell, 2008; Gerth et al., 2013; Bakti, Majid, Zin, & Trigunarsyah, 2011; Kifokeris & Xenidis, 2017; Kim et al., 2016; Martinez, Alvear, Tommelein, & Ballard, 2015; Tan, Ong, Ong, & Choong, 2014). The constructability of infrastructure projects such as bridges, has also attracted particular research interest (e.g. Zhang & El-Diraby, 2006; Tang & Bittner, 2014; Nima, Abdul-Kadir, Jaafar, & Alghulami, 2004), highlighting the importance of appropriate construction method selection as well as the avoidance of unnecessary complexity in design.

Offsite Construction-Design Standardization

Offsite construction is defined as the manufacture and preassembly of building components, elements, or modules before installation into their final locations (Goodier & Gibb, 2007). The incorporation of offsite construction presents a widely acknowledged high value performance deriving from a significantly reduced construction programme, better quality, enhanced safety and reduced waste and as a result, it has been extensively associated to various value-promoting practices such as value management, buildability, waste minimization, and lean construction (Antoniou & Marinelli, 2020; Gerth et al., 2013; Lu et al., 2021; Marinelli, 2022). A comprehensive overview of the literature's perspectives on the benefits associated with prefabrication in construction has also been presented in the work of Goodier et al. (2019). Embracing offsite construction involves leveraging design standardization and rationalization (Antoniou and Marinelli 2020). Design rationalization refers to the minimization of materials, sizes, components, or sub-assemblies (Moore, 1996) while standardization encompasses the use of standardized components, methods, or processes that promote regularity and predictability (Gibb, 2001). Standardization allows engineers to effectively manage customer values through the development of easily understandable and complexity-free designs (Björnfot, 2008) while also holding crucial importance for the construction economy and accurate labor productivity estimation (Dikmen & Sonmez, 2011, Kim et al., 2016).

PROCUREMENT STRATEGY FOR MAXIMUM VFM

As analysed in the previous section, all the commonly used procurement procedures exhibit features which prevent the public clients from safeguarding the achievement of best VfM (Table 1). In summary, the Open Procedure, although effective in ensuring high competition, also separates design and construction, thus ruling out constructability and contractor involvement benefits. On the other hand, restricted Procedures such as the DB and the CD reduce the level of competition through a time consuming and complex preselection process but nevertheless, are able to deliver constructability benefits.

Table 1. Factors affecting the VFM performance of common procurement approaches

		DBB	DB	CD
Factors increasing VFM	High Competition	X		
	Design input from contractors		X	X
Factors decreasing VFM	Advanced bidding documentation required	X		
	Prequalification complexity	X	X	X
	Slow progression			X
	Restricted use		X	X

Proposed Procurement Procedure

The above suggest that for maximum VfM to be achieved, a procurement strategy combining high competition, objectivity and early involvement of the constructor is necessary. An example of such an approach is the one proposed in Marinelli & Antoniou, (2020), which integrates open, highly competitive bidding with value-enhancing organisational features of the CD, to efficiently implement the legislation's provision for optional variants to the subject-matter of the contract (article 45 of the Directive 2014/24/EU).

The current proposal adds to the above suggestion that the contractor selection be made through a single-stage process comprising of two distinct steps. In Step 1, the interested contractors required to submit documentation proving that they comply to the go-no go selection and exclusion criteria (ESPD and certificates of previous experience if required) and the required bid bond. The innovation of the proposed procedure is that in this step the participants are additionally invited to optionally develop and submit VfM-improving variants of the designs provided by the CA, as per the article 45 of the EU directive 2014/24/EU. All proposed variants require the submission of complete final designs since analytical calculations to justify the claimed construction cost and time savings are required. Therefore, sufficient time for this step will have to be allocated. In addition, possible monetary compensation can be offered to all designs for variants that are not adopted by the CA in order to provide additional motivation for submission of design variants. The CA will then evaluate the proposals on the basis of the VfM improvement, will incorporate the most beneficial suggestions as evaluated against the defined selection criteria and finally will amend the tender documents accordingly. In Step 2, all the contractors fulfilling the minimum selection criteria are invited to submit a bid for the final (i.e. including the variants) scope of works, no matter if they previously submitted a design variant or not. The candidates who submitted VfM-enhancing proposals, though, will receive a bonus score, reflecting the value improvement resulting from their proposals and the ranking position of each proposed variant. This bonus score can potentially become the contract award deciding factor, regardless of whether the applied award criterion is price only or the best price–quality ratio, because it ultimately adjusts the price offered by the variant proposing bidders.

Design Variant Scoring Criteria

After submission of proposed design variants, the CA will have to evaluate and provide scores based on specific criteria that are defined in the tender documents. In order to avoid confusion with the pass/fail selection criteria and the final contract award criteria, these will be called scoring criteria. The choice of scoring criteria is related to the VfM aims of the CA and could benefit from the accumulated experience in relation to the factors that affected the actual VfM performance of previously implemented public projects. These could include any construction funding constraints (upper limit construction costs, duration of funding programme etc.), as well as life-cycle cost considerations, the importance of which vary from CA to CA and time to time. Therefore, scoring criteria may be, but are not limited to the following:

Cost Criteria

1. Construction cost
2. Costs relating to land acquisition,
3. Costs relating to archaeological excavations,
4. Cost of use such as consumption of energy and other resources,
5. Maintenance costs
6. End of life costs, such as collection and recycling costs
7. Environmental sustainability costs such as cost of emissions of greenhouses gases and other climate change mitigation costs

Time Criteria

8. Required preparation time for environmental licenses
9. Required time for new land acquisition procedures
10. Required construction time

Social and Environmental Improvement Criteria

11. Disturbance to local community during construction
12. Disturbance to local community during operation
13. Improvement to worker safety conditions
14. Circular economy enhancement
15. Energy upgrading

Given the multitude and range of criteria potentially involved in the variant evaluation process, it becomes clear that the use of a Multi-criteria decision making (MCDM) technique is necessary to enable an efficient as well as accurate scoring process.

SUGGESTED METHOD FOR CRITERIA WEIGHTS ALLOCATION USING THE BEST WORST METHOD

MCDM techniques have found applications in numerous fields for solving a wide range of problems. These problems may include selecting the optimal alternative option, as demonstrated in studies by Antoniou & Aretoulis (2019) and Hasnain, Thaheem, & Ullah (2018). Additionally, MCDM techniques can be used to rank factors according to their perceived importance or impact, such as in studies by Eghbali-Zarch, Tavakkoli-Moghaddam, Dehghan-Sanej, & Kaboli (2022), Tsz Wai et al., 2021, Pan & Zhang (2021), and Antoniou (2021). According to Mi, Tang, Liao, Shen, & Lev (2019), the Analytical Hierarchy Process (AHP) is the most commonly used method for ranking alternatives. However, when there are a large number of options to be considered, using AHP can lead to inconsistent and unreliable results, as noted by Malek & Desai (2020). This is because AHP requires unstructured pairwise comparisons. To address this issue, Rezaei, (2015) introduced the Best Worst Method (BWM), which has become a popular alternative. BWM requires fewer pairwise comparisons and uses only two vectors instead of a full pairwise comparison matrix, resulting in more consistent results, as reported by Rezaei (2016). In the BWM, which is gaining popularity among researchers (Marinelli & Janardhanan, 2022), the best criterion (C_B) and worst criterion (C_W) are identified for a set of n criteria. Then, n-1 pairwise comparisons are made between each of the remaining criteria and both C_B and C_W. This approach significantly reduces the number of comparisons needed to solve MCDM problems. For example, a problem with 10 criteria would require only 17 pairwise comparisons using BWM, while AHP would require 45 comparisons (Malek & Desai, 2020). This efficiency is one of the reasons for the growing interest in BWM.

The steps of this method as given in Rezaei (2015) and Rezaei (2016) are:

Step 1. Determine a set of decision criteria.

In this step, we examine the criteria $\{c_1, c_2, ..., c_n\}$ that are relevant to making a decision.

Step 2. Identify the criteria that are considered the best (i.e., most desirable or important) and worst (i.e., least desirable or important).

Step 3. Determine the preference of the best criterion over all the other criteria using a number between 1 and 9. The resulting Best-to-Others vector, denoted as A_B, is defined as $A_B= (a_{B1}, a_{B2},...,a_{Bn})$, where a_{Bj} represents the preference of the best criterion B over criterion j.

Step 4. Determine the preference of all the criteria over the worst criterion using a number between 1 and 9. The resulting Others-to-Worst vector denoted as A_w, is defined as $A_w = (a_{1w},a_{2w},...,a_{nw})^T$, where a_{jW} represents the preference of the criterion j over the worst criterion W.

Step 5. Find the optimal weights $(w_1^*,w_2^*,...,w_n^*)$. The optimal weight for the criteria is determined by setting the weights such that $w_B/w_j=a_{Bj}$ and $w_j/w_W=a_{jW}$, for each pair of w_B/w_j and w_j/w_W.

To satisfy these conditions for all j, we should find a solution where the maximum absolute

differences $|w_B/w_j-a_{Bj}|$ and $|w_j/w_W-a_{jW}|$ for all j is minimized.

The equivalent problem to be solved, where ξ is the objective value of the model, is:

Min ξ

$|w_B/w_j - a_{Bj}| \leq \xi$, for all j

$|w_j/w_W - a_{jW}| \leq \xi$, for all j

$\Sigma w_j = 1$

$w_j \geq 0$, for all j

Then, optimal weights (w_1^*, w_2^*, …,w_n^*) and the optimal objective value of the optimization model, ξ^* can be obtained.

To evaluate the consistency level of a process, one can compute the consistency ratio (CR) using the formula CR= ξ^*/Consistency Index. The Consistency Index (CI) is a fixed value that represents the highest possible ξ value for a specific number of criteria. According to Rezaei (2016), the level of consistency in a comparison can be determined by the value of the consistency ratio (CR), with a lower CR indicating higher consistency. Rezaei further observes that if the problem being analyzed is not completely consistent (i.e., $\xi^* \neq 0$), multiple optimal solutions may arise for more than three criteria. In such cases, it is recommended to use a linear version of the method to ensure a unique ranking of the criteria and avoid the complications that can arise from multiple solutions.

The linear problem (distinguished by the index L) is the following:

Min ξ_L

$|w_B - a_{Bj} w_j| \leq \xi_L$, for all j

$|wj - a_{jW} w_W| \leq \xi_L$, for all j

$\Sigma w_j = 1$

$w_j \geq 0$, for all j

There is a unique solution to the problem, which consists of the optimal weights (w_1^*, w_2^*, ..., w_n^*) and ξ_L^*. The value of ξ_L^* can be used as an indicator of the consistency of the comparisons made, where values close to 0 indicate a high level of consistency.

Application of TOPSIS for Evaluation of Proposed Variations

A drawback of both the AHP and the BWM is that an intuitive process of transforming number values (money, duration, measurement units) to comparison ratings (on a scale of 1 to 9) must be carried out for each alternative against each criterion. For this reason, the BWM will be employed only to determine the criteria weights which is highly subjective. Previously, various methods have been employed by the authors to help this very subjective part of all MCDM methods, i.e. AHP, Simos method, goal programming, Shannon's entropy and recently the BWM (Antoniou et al., 2016; Antoniou, 2021; Petroutsatou, Ladopoulos, & Tsakelidou, 2022; Marinelli & Janardhanan, 2022; Petroutsatou, Kleopatra; Kantilierakis, 2023). In this case, the BWM, while a subset of the AHP, is considered to be efficient enough because the definition of the best and worst criterion is not arbitrarily made by the CAs but is based on years of experience of procurement of similar projects in similar funding situations.

As the alternative design variants will be evaluated against numerous scoring criteria, measured in different numerical units, the Technique for Order Preference by Similarity to Ideal Situation (TOPSIS) will be used to rank alternatives and provide their scores because it requires few user inputs. Specifically, the numerical values assigned to each evaluation of each alternative against each criteria are directly used after normalization and there is no need to carryout pairwise comparisons to assign a numerical value based on the proposed scale used by BWM and AHP. Even the verbal evaluations of alternatives (e.g. high, medium, low) can be easily transformed to a number values (e.g. 3, 2, 1). In addition, TOPSIS produces results easily as the ideal solution is defined for each criterion separately and then normalized to allow a synthesis of the results. The only subjective factors are the weights of the criteria that are directly related to the requirements of the problem. Originally proposed in 1981 by Hwang and Yoon (Hwang, C.L. and Yoon, 1981) it ranks alternatives according to their distance from the defined ideal solution. The highest-ranking delay factor is the one that has the shortest distance from the ideal solution and the greater distance from the anti-ideal solution (Ishizaka, A.; Nemery, 2013). The ideal solution is defined by selecting the maximum weighted normalized score for each criterion while the anti-ideal solution is defined by selecting the minimum weighted normalized score for each criterion. Then the distances from the ideal solution and from the anti - ideal solution are calculated using the Euclidean distance. These distances are then used to calculate the closeness coefficient, which takes values from 0 to 1. The alternatives are ranked according to descending closeness coefficients (see Figure 1).

In more detail, the TOPSIS encompasses 5 computational steps as follows:

Step 1: Normalization: The evaluations (scores) of m alternatives, or variants as in our case, against n criteria are noted in a mxn decision matrix $X = (x_{ia})$ where $i = 1, \ldots, m$ alternatives (variants) and $a = 1, \ldots n$ criteria. These are normalized to allow comparison between criteria with different units of measurement. Various methods of normalization exist such as the distributive, ideal normalization methods and the additive method (Antoniou & Aretoulis, 2019; Antoniou, 2021). The ideal normalization method, which divides each value with the ideal value is inapplicable since in some cases the ideal value is zero. Similarly, the additive method, which divides each value with the sum of all other values, may lead to a negative denominator thus altering the sign of the weighted scores. Therefore, the distributive normalization method, was chosen for application in this study. This method divides each score with the square root of the sum of squares of scores in the column.

Figure 1. Variant scoring procedure using TOPSIS

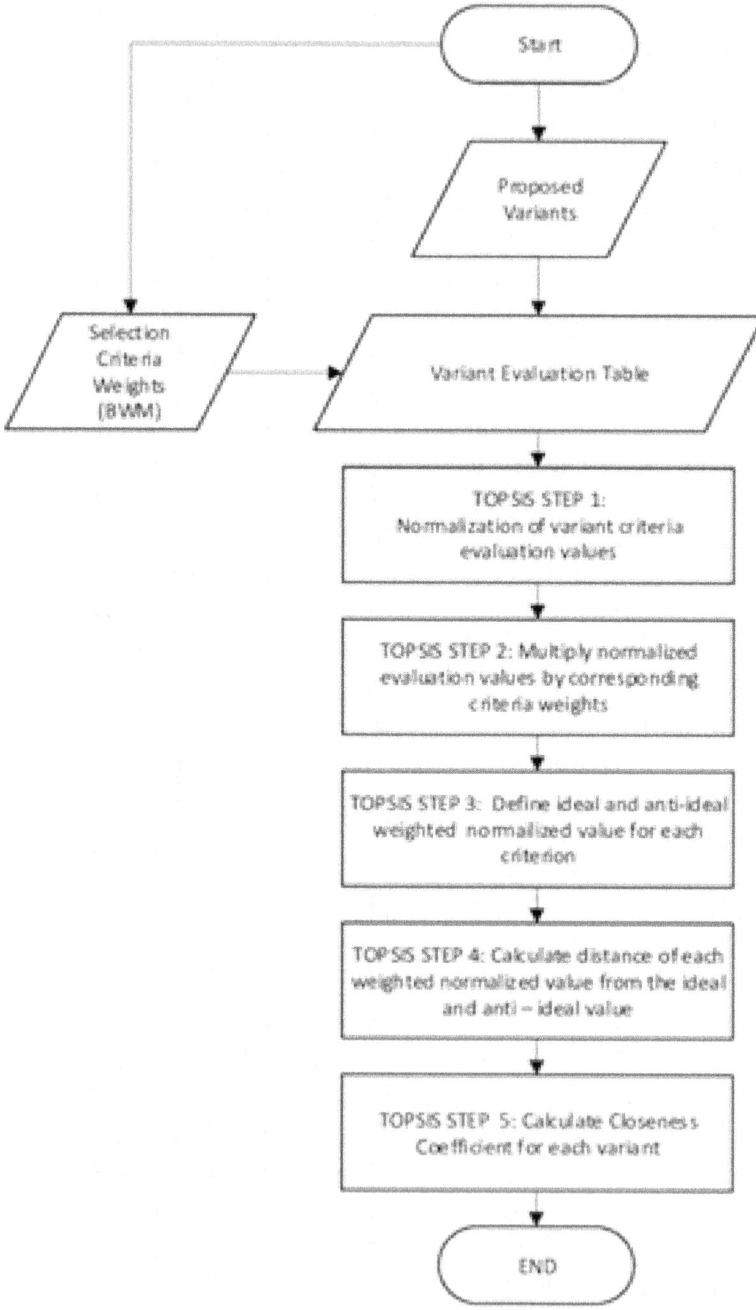

$$r_{ia} = \frac{x_{ia}}{\sqrt{\sum_{a=1}^{n} x_{ia}^{2}}} \tag{1}$$

where i = 1,….,m (SC) and a=1,….0 (alternatives)

Step 2: Weights: This step takes account of the weightings of the criteria and compiles the matrix of weighted normalized scores (X') by multiplying the normalized scores r_{ia} by the corresponding weights w_a:

$$v_{ia} = w_a r_{ia} \tag{2}$$

Step 3: Ideal and anti - ideal solution: The weighted normalized values scores are compared to the ideal and anti-ideal scores in each column by identifying the best and worst performance for each criterion in the normalized matrix.

- For the ideal solution: $A^{+} = \left(v_1^{+}, \ldots . v_m^{+}\right)$
- For the anti-ideal solution: $A^{-} = \left(v_1^{-}, \ldots . v_m^{-}\right)$

Where $v_i^{+} = \max_i \left(v_{ia}\right)$ if a criterion is to be maximized, whereas $v_i^{-} = \min_i \left(v_{ia}\right)$ if a criterion is to be minimized.

Step 4: Distance from ideal and anti-ideal solution: The distance of each delay factor from the ideal solution (d+) and the anti-ideal solution (d-) per criterion is calculated using the Euclidean distance. Eq. (3) and (4) provide the distance of each alternative (delay factor) from the ideal solution and anti-ideal solution respectively.

$$d_i^{+} = \sqrt{\sum_i \left(v_i^{+} - v_{ia}\right)^2} \tag{3}$$

$$d_i^{-} = \sqrt{\sum_i \left(v_i^{-} - v_{ia}\right)^2} \tag{4}$$

Step 5: Closeness coefficient: The closeness coefficient C_a which is calculated using eq. (9). If an alternative is closer to the ideal solution, then C_a approaches 1, otherwise, if it is closer to the non- ideal then it approaches 0.

$$C_a = \frac{d_i^-}{d_i^+ + d_i^-} \tag{5}$$

Implementation Example

The implementation example of the proposed MCDM model for incorporating VfM principles by taking advantage of the early involvement of the contractor, is based on the authors' 22 years of experience in procurement and management of highway construction contracts. The variants described have all been witnessed by the authors following the construction contract award, causing significant delays and frequent claims.

As an example, let's consider that a hypothetical original project to be tendered is a local intercity road upgrade to a highway with an overall budget of 30 million €. The project includes the construction of an interchange, the service roads, 3 underpass box structures, 3 overpasses (1 box girder and 2 voided slab decks, all cast in situ) and one ravine bridge.

Having completed all the necessary final designs, environmental license as well as the necessary expropriation procedures, the CA calls for tenders according to the two-step open procedure previously described. As part of this procurement strategy, it is defined in the tender documents that the final price offered by each candidate will be reduced by a percentage of the savings achieved by their respective proposed variant (bonus). They are also made aware that this reduced price will be the price ultimately used for bid ranking purposes, but in case they are awarded the contract, their contract price will be according to their offer.

Let's assume that in response to the procurement notice, five contractors express interest and four of them, Bidders A, B, C and D submit variants focusing on construction methods of greater cost-efficiency as shown in Table 2.

Specifically,

- Bidder A proposes a local realignment of less than 10 m horizontal displacement that includes the construction of a 500m long Cut and Cover (C&C) tunnel and the simultaneous elimination of the need for two underpasses at ch 0+500 and 1+000 since the required local road connection is restored over the new C&C tunnel.
- Bidder B hopes to take advantage of their existing precast beam formwork and proposes the replacement of the superstructure of all three overpasses and the redesign of one underpass into an overpass by realigning the local road it accommodates. All 4 overpasses decks (S3, S4, S5, and S6) are of

Table 2. Description of proposed design variants

Original Scope of Work	Proposed Design Variants	Proposed by
	New 500m C&C Tunnel after local realignment of less than 10 m horizontal displacement.	A
Underpass at ch.0+500 (S1)	Underpass at ch.0+500 eliminated and connection restored over new C&C	A
Underpass at ch. 1+000 (S2)	Underpass at ch.1+000 eliminated as unnecessary after local realignment.	A
Overpass at ch 2+000 (S3) (box girder cast in situ)	Box girder cast in situ overpass at ch 2+000 replaced with a precast prestressed beams superstructure	B
I/C underpass at ch. 5+000 (S4)	Realignment of I/C branches resulting in the replacement of the I/C underpass at ch. 5+000 with an overpass (precast prestressed beams superstructure)	B
Overpass at ch. 7+000 (S5) (with a voided slab superstructure)	Overpass at ch 7+000 replaced with a precast prestressed beams superstructure	B
Overpass at ch 9+000 (S6) (with a voided slab superstructure)	Overpass at ch 9+000 replaced with a precast prestressed beams superstructure	B
Ravine bridge (S7) (100 m) at ch 8+500	Replace ravine bridge at ch 8+500 with embankment 20m height and culvert	C
	Major realignment from ch 5+000 to 9+000 resulting in the elimination of overpasses at ch 7+000 (S5) and 9+000 (S6) in open cut construction.	D

the same geometry and therefore VfM is achieved through economy of scale and standardization by designing them all as prestressed precast beams of the same cross-section.

- Bidder C proposes the replacement of the ravine bridge (S7) at ch 8+500 with an embankment of 20m height and a culvert at its base.
- Finally, Bidder D suggests a major realignment from ch 5+000 to 9+000 resulting in the elimination of the need for overpasses S5 and S6 but requires significant new environmental licensing and land expropriation procedures.

To evaluate each of the proposed design variants, the CA defines in the tender documents the scoring criteria, their corresponding weights and the required documentation for each one of them (Table 2). For all proposed variants, the necessary final designs and resulting new bill of quantities are required to be submitted in Stage 1 by the bidders. For this reason, the extra time and cost required for the new designs is irrelevant as the design cost is borne by the bidder or can be partially compensated by the CA and are completed at the time of variant proposal.

Table 3. Scoring criteria, weights, and required documentation

Scoring Criteria	Global Weights	Global Rankings	Required Documentation
1. Construction cost savings in € (maximize)	0.256	1	Final Design, New BoQ, New project Budget
2. Maintenance cost savings in € (maximize)	0.045	8	Calculations for yearly maintenance cost savings
3. Construction time savings in months (maximize)	0.145	2	Original and new project schedule depicting construction time savings.
4. Required extra preparation time for EIA in months (minimize)	0.145	2	Estimated extra preparation time for new environmental terms and justification based on relevant legislation
5. Required extra preparation time for new expropriation procedures in months (minimize)	0.145	2	Estimated extra preparation time for new expropriation procedure and justification based on relevant legislation
6. Required extra cost for new expropriation procedures in € (minimize)	0.072	7	Estimated extra cost for new land requirements based on unit rates of existing expropriations court decisions.
7. Improvement to disturbance to local community (1-5) (maximize)	0.096	5	Detailed description of how the proposed variant reduced disturbance to local community both during construction and during operation.
8. Improvement to worker safety conditions (1-5) (maximize)	0.096	5	Detailed description of how the proposed variant improves worker safety during construction.

The weights for each scoring criterion result from the application of the BWM to rank the scoring criteria in order of importance. Obviously, the resulting weights vary according to the situation and needs of the CA at the time of tender. In this example, the scenario is that the CA's decision maker is faced with a situation where construction cost savings are considered as the most important criterion while maintenance cost savings is the least important because the authority responsible for operation and maintenance of the new highway will be able to cover these expenses from the tolls to be imposed. On the other hand, shortening of tender and construction time is of the essence due to funding deadlines. With these constraints in mind and using the BWM, the resulting weights are shown in Table 3.

The CA proceeds to the evaluation of each variant independently against each scoring criterion using the submitted designs, budgets, schedules and justifications and their own personal experience and produces a decision table (Table 4). Note that each criterion is evaluated using different scales (euros, months, Likert scale).

Table 4. Variant evaluation decision matrix

Scoring Criteria	1. constr. cost sav.€ (max)	2. maint. cost sav. € (max)	3. constr. time sav. months (max)	4. Extra time for new ET (months (min)	5. Extra time for new land (months) (min)	6. Extra cost for new land € (min)	7. Disturbance Improvement (1-5)	8. Safety Improvement (1-5)
Weights from BWM	**0.256**	**0.045**	**0.145**	**0.145**	**0.145**	**0.072**	**0.096**	**0.096**
New 1 km C&C Tunnel after realignment of less than 10 m horizontal displacement and elimination of 2 U/Ps	50k	0	3.0	3.0	3.0	50k	5	3
Box girder cast in situ overpass replaced with a precast prestressed beams superstructure	100k	-50k	3.0	0.0	0.0	0.00	5	2
Realignment of I/C branches resulting in the replacement of the I/C underpass with an overpass (precast prestressed beams superstructure)	100k	-50k	3.0	0.0	0.0	0.00	5	2
Overpass replaced with a precast prestressed beams superstructure	100k	-50k	3.0	0.0	0.0	0.00	5	2
Overpass replaced with a precast prestressed beams superstructure	100k	-50k	3.0	0.0	0.0	0.00	5	2
Replace ravine bridge with embankment 20m height and culvert	1,000k	100k	12.0	6.0	12.0	400k	1	1
Major realignment (4km) resulting in the elimination of need for underpass in open cut construction.	2,000k	100k	6.0	12.0	12.0	1,000k	5	5

As a result, to avoid the need for the decision maker to translate these values to the required rating scale (1 to 9) used in the BWM, the TOPSIS method using the distributive normalization method is applied. The resulting closeness coefficients to the ideal solutions calculated for each variant is shown in Table 5. As the closeness coefficient C is always between 0 and 1, it can correspond to a percentage which defines the bidder's share of the cost savings achieved by their accepted variant and corresponds to the 'bonus' that the bidder is entitled to in the ranking process. The resulting monetary value of the bidder's share of the savings is subtracted from their financial offer to provide the adjusted financial offer. The adjusted financial offers are then ranked and the one ranked first, wins the contract. The value of the contract though, remains equal to the value of the offer prior to the adjustment.

Table 5. Closeness coefficient of variant to ideal solution

Design Variant	C	Rank	Proposed by Bidder	Variant Accepted
New 1 km C&C Tunnel after realignment of less than 10 m horizontal displacement and elimination of U/Ps (S1) and (S2)	0.267	7	A	YES
Box girder cast in situ overpass (S3) replaced with a precast prestressed beams superstructure	0.328	3	B	YES
Realignment of I/C branches resulting in the replacement of the I/C underpass (S4) with an overpass (precast prestressed beams superstructure)	0.328	3	B	YES
Overpass (S5) replaced with a precast prestressed beams superstructure	0.328	3	B	NO
Overpass (S6) replaced with a precast prestressed beams superstructure	0.328	3	B	NO
Replace ravine bridge (S7) with embankment 20m height and culvert	0.601	1	C	YES
Major realignment from resulting in the elimination of need for underpass at ch 7+000 (S5) and 9+000 (S6) in open cut construction.	0.589	2	D	YES

As a result of the variant evaluation phase, it is found that the replacement of the ravine bridge at ch 8+500 with a 20m high embankment and culvert structure is ranked in first place yielding a coefficient of closeness to the ideal solution equal to 0.601. Since the variant in second place includes the elimination of the need for structures S5 and S6, the CA decides to accept this variant and therefore rejects bidder B's variants regarding the replacement of S5 and S6 overpasses voided slab decks to prestressed precast beams.

The construction cost savings, as these emerge from the new bill-of-quantities, can then be calculated as per Table 6. For example, the total construction cost savings resulting from all accepted proposals amounts to €3,250,000 resulting in a new tender budget of €26,750,000.

In Step 2, all the five interested contractors submit final bids for the new scope and budget of works (€26,750,000) as shown in Table 6 The lowest price is given by Bidder E (€18,725.000) corresponding to a percentage cost discount equal to 30%. However, Bidder E has not submitted any variants in Step 1. On the contrary, Bidders A, B, C and D benefit from the reduction of their offered price by the percentage defined by the resulting closeness coefficient multiplied by the construction cost savings provided by their accepted design variant. Bidder D that provided the second top ranking variant achieved C=0.589 and hence receives a bonus of 58.9%

Table 6. Evaluation of accepted variants and offers ranking

	Stage 1	Stage 2 Construction Savings Obtained From Accepted Variant	C	Stage 2 Earned Bonus	Financial Discount Offered	Financial Offer (Ci)	Initial Rank	Adjusted Financial Offer	Final Rank
OFFER A	pass	500k	0.267	13.4k	0.26	19,795.0k	4	19,781.6k	4
OFFER B	pass	200k	0.328	65.6k	0.25	20,062.5k	5	19,996.9k	5
OFFER C	pass	1,000k	0.601	601.4k	0.27	19,527.5k	3	18,926.1k	3
OFFER D	pass	500k	0.589	1,177.6k	0.28	19,260.0k	2	18,082.4k	1
OFFER E	pass	0	0.000	0	0.30	18,725.0k	1	18,725.0k	2
Original Contract Budget		30,000k							
Savings after accepted variations		3,250k							
New Contract Budget		26,750k							

x 2,000,000=1,177,592. This gives Bidder D the lowest overall price (19,260,000–1,177,592= 18,082,408< 18,725,00 offered by Bidder E) and enables them to be awarded the contract for €19,260,000 instead of the lowest bidder.

Assuming the aforementioned percentage discounts, it is evident that, had the step of submission of variants and the associated bonus been omitted and had the Bidders offered the same percentage price reduction as above, the CA would have to award the contract to Bidder E for (1-0.3) *30,000,000 = € 21,000,000. Therefore, by application of the proposed strategy for the construction of this section, the CA, first, enjoys savings of 21,000,000 – 19,260,00 = € 1,740,00 i.e., almost 5.5% of the initial budget, and second, avoids post-award changes in the project's scope and contractual budget.

CONCLUSION

Effective implementation of public procurement policy in the EU is critical in achieving VfM and efficient use of public funds in public projects delivery. This chapter highlights the impact of specific procurement choices on VfM and discusses how the implementation of VM, VE and constructability reviews can maximize project value and VfM. This chapter also builds on previous work which proposed a hybrid procurement strategy designed to enable both high economic efficiency (as in the open procedure) and the capability of the CA to discuss and optimise its proposed solution (as in the CD procedure). This is achieved by giving the bidders the option to submit value-enhancing design variants within the context of an open procedure and then, processing the submitted proposals according to the main principles of the CD. This chapter expands this procurement strategy by proposing a wide range of VfM-enhancing variant scoring criteria which include not only cost savings, but also time savings as well as social and environmental factors. Furthermore, it addresses the emerging multi-criteria design comparisons, evaluations and bid rankings through an efficient MCDM method, based on a combination of the BWM and the TOPSIS. The presented application example of the proposed strategy and decision model clarifies the practical details of the implementation process and demonstrates the VfM implications and wider sustainability benefits of the proposed strategy. Therefore, it provides a valuable tool for assisting CAs in achieving efficient public spending for the procurement of public infrastructure projects.

Further research could include interviews with procurement experts and policy makers from CAs with the aim to specify and streamline the implementation details and procedural requirements of the new procurement strategy. It could also include a questionnaire survey targeted to project managers from CAs and contractors as well as design and supervision consultants with the aim to consolidate their experiences from different kinds of projects where major design changes were accepted in the context of a value engineering exercise. This will enable the verification of the proposed scoring criteria for design variants and can form the basis for the necessary standardisation of the relevant clauses in the construction contract tender documents and the EU public procurement directive.

REFERENCES

Antoniou, F. (2021). Delay risk assessment models for road projects. *Systems*, *9*(3), 1–17. doi:10.3390ystems9030070

Antoniou, F., & Aretoulis, G. (2019). A multi-criteria decision-making support system for choice of method of compensation for highway construction contractors in Greece. *International Journal of Construction Management*, *19*(6), 492–508. do i:10.1080/15623599.2018.1452103

Antoniou, F., Konstantinidis, D., & Aretoulis, G. N. (2016). Application of the multi attribute utility theory for the selection of project procurement system for Greek highway projects. *International Journal of Management and Decision Making*, *15*(2), 83–112. doi:10.1504/IJMDM.2016.077761

Antoniou, F., & Marinelli, M. (2020). Proposal for the Promotion of Standardization of Precast Beams in Highway Concrete Bridges. *Frontiers in Built Environment*, *6*(July), 1–16. doi:10.3389/fbuil.2020.00119

Bakti, E. S., Majid, M. Z. B. A., Zin, R. M., & Trigunarsyah, B. (2011). Constructability improvement in seawater intake structure. *Engineering, Construction, and Architectural Management*, *18*(6), 595–608. doi:10.1108/09699981111180908

Berrone, P., Ricart, J. E., Duch, A. I., Bernardo, V., Salvador, J., Peña, J. P., & Planas, M. R. (2019). EASIER: An evaluation model for public-private partnerships contributing to the sustainable development goals. *Sustainability (Basel)*, *11*(8), 2339. Advance online publication. doi:10.3390u11082339

Björnfot, A. (2008). An engineering perspective on Lean Construction theory. *Proceedings of IGLC16: 16th Annual Conference of the International Group for Lean Construction*, 15–26.

Burnett, M. (2009). Using Competitive Dialogue in EU Public Procurement – Early Trends and Future Developments. *EIPAScope*, 17–22.

Connaughton, J. N., & Green, S. D. (1996). *Value management in construction: a client's guide*. CIRIA.

Creedy, G. D., Skitmore, M., & Wong, J. K. W. (2010). Evaluation of Risk Factors Leading to Cost Overrun in Delivery of Highway Construction Projects. *Journal of Construction Engineering and Management*, *136*(5), 528–537. doi:10.1061/(ASCE)CO.1943-7862.0000160

de Araújo, M. C. B., Alencar, L. H., & de Miranda Mota, C. M. (2017). Project procurement management: A structured literature review. *International Journal of Project Management*, *35*(3), 353–377. doi:10.1016/j.ijproman.2017.01.008

Eghbali-Zarch, M., Tavakkoli-Moghaddam, R., Dehghan-Sanej, K., & Kaboli, A. (2022). Prioritizing the effective strategies for construction and demolition waste management using fuzzy IDOCRIW and WASPAS methods. *Engineering, Construction, and Architectural Management*, *29*(3), 1109–1138. doi:10.1108/ECAM-08-2020-0617

Eriksson, P. E., & Westerberg, M. (2011). Effects of cooperative procurement procedures on construction project performance: A conceptual framework. *International Journal of Project Management, 29*(2), 197–208. doi:10.1016/j.ijproman.2010.01.003

Ernzen, J. J., & Schexnayder, C. (2000). One Company's Experience with Design/Build: Labor Cost Risk and Profit Potential. *Journal of Construction Engineering & Management, 126*(1), 10–14.

European Court of Auditors. (2014). *2014 Activity Report*. doi:10.2865/67808

Fathi, E. A., Taher, S. E. D., & Mahfouz, S. Y. (2020). Value engineering analysis of RC roadway bridges assimilating environmental impact. *HBRC Journal, 16*(1), 207–226. doi:10.1080/16874048.2020.1794348

Gerth, R., Boqvist, A., Bjelkemyr, M., & Lindberg, B. (2013). Design for construction: Utilizing production experiences in development. *Construction Management and Economics, 31*(2), 135–150. doi:10.1080/01446193.2012.756142

Gibb, A. G. F. (2001). Standardization and pre-assembly- distinguishing myth from reality using case study research. *Construction Management and Economics, 19*(3), 307–315. doi:10.1080/01446190010020435

Goodier, C., & Gibb, A. (2007). Future opportunities for offsite in the UK. *Construction Management and Economics, 25*(6), 585–595. doi:10.1080/01446190601071821

Goodier, C., Gibb, A., Mancini, M., Turck, C., Gjepali, O., & Daniels, E. (2019). Modularisation and offsite in engineering construction: An early decision-support tool. *Proceedings of the Institution of Civil Engineers. Civil Engineering, 172*(6), 3–14. doi:10.1680/jcien.19.00015

Grimsey, D., & Lewis, M. K. (2005). Are Public Private Partnerships value for money?: Evaluating alternative approaches and comparing academic and practitioner views. *Accounting Forum, 29*(4), 345–378. doi:10.1016/j.accfor.2005.01.001

Hale, D. R., Shrestha, P. P., Gibson, G. E. Jr, & Migliaccio, G. C. (2009). Empirical Comparison of Design/Build and Design/Bid/Build Project Delivery Methods. *Journal of Construction Engineering and Management, 135*(7), 579–587. doi:10.1061/(ASCE)CO.1943-7862.0000017

Hasnain, M., Thaheem, M. J., & Ullah, F. (2018). Best Value Contractor Selection in Road Construction Projects: ANP-Based Decision Support System. *International Journal of Civil Engineering, 16*(6), 695–714. doi:10.100740999-017-0199-2

Heijboer, G., & Telgen, J. (2002). Choosing the open or the restricted procedure: A big deal or a big deal? *Journal of Public Procurement*, *2*(2), 12–26. doi:10.1108/JOPP-02-02-2002-B002

HSPPA. (2015). *Award criteria during public procurement procedures Guideline 11*. Retrieved February 27, 2023, from https://www.eaadhsy.gr/sdg/dg.php?qid=1114

Hwang, C. L., & Yoon, K. (1981). *Multiple Attribute Decision Making: Methods and Applications*. Springer-Verlag. doi:10.1007/978-3-642-48318-9

Ishizaka, A., & Nemery, P. (2013). *Multi-Criteria Decision Analysis Methods and Software*. John Wiley and Sons Inc. doi:10.1002/9781118644898

Jay, C. I., & Bowen, P. A. (2015). Value management and innovation: A historical perspective and review of the evidence. *Journal of Engineering. Design and Technology*, *13*(1), 123–143. doi:10.1108/JEDT-03-2013-0021

Kelly, J., Male S., & Graham, D. (1993). *Value Management of Construction Projects*. Academic Press.

Kelly, J., Male, S., & Graham, D. (2014). Value Management in Design and Construction: The Economic Management of Projects (2nd ed.). Blackwell Publishing.

Kifokeris, D., & Xenidis, Y. (2017). Constructability: Outline of Past, Present, and Future Research. *Journal of Construction Engineering and Management*, *143*(8), 04017035. Advance online publication. doi:10.1061/(ASCE)CO.1943-7862.0001331

Kim, M. K., McGovern, S., Belsky, M., Middleton, C., & Brilakis, I. (2016). A Suitability Analysis of Precast Components for Standardized Bridge Construction in the United Kingdom. *Procedia Engineering*, *164*(June), 188–195. doi:10.1016/j.proeng.2016.11.609

Lambropoulos, S. (2007). The use of time and cost utility for construction contract award under European Union Legislation. *Building and Environment*, *42*(1), 452–463. doi:10.1016/j.buildenv.2005.08.002

Lin, X., Mazlan, A. N., Ismail, S., Hu, L., Kasiman, E. H., & Yahya, K. (2023). Status of value management studies in construction projects: A systematic review. *Ain Shams Engineering Journal*, *14*(1), 101820. doi:10.1016/j.asej.2022.101820

Lu, W., Hua, Y. Y., & Zhang, S. J. (2017). Logistic regression analysis for factors influencing cost performance of design-bid-build and design-build projects. *Engineering, Construction, and Architectural Management*, *24*(1), 118–132. doi:10.1108/ECAM-07-2015-0119

Lu, W., Tan, T., Xu, J., Wang, J., Chen, K., Gao, S., & Xue, F. (2021). Design for manufacture and assembly (DfMA) in construction: The old and the new. *Architectural Engineering and Design Management, 17*(1–2), 77–91. doi:10.1080/17452007.2020.1768505

Malek, J., & Desai, T. N. (2020). A systematic literature review to map literature focus of sustainable manufacturing. *Journal of Cleaner Production, 256*, 120345. doi:10.1016/j.jclepro.2020.120345

Mao, X., Zhang, X., & AbouRizk, S. M. (2009). Enhancing Value Engineering Process by Incorporating Inventive Problem-Solving Techniques. *Journal of Construction Engineering and Management, 135*(5), 416–424. doi:10.1061/(ASCE)CO.1943-7862.0000001

Marinelli, M. (2022). A DfX-based approach for incorporating sustainability in infrastructure project planning. *Built Environment Project and Asset Management, 12*(1), 20–37. doi:10.1108/BEPAM-05-2020-0083

Marinelli, M., & Antoniou, F. (2020). Improving public works' value for money: A new procurement strategy. *International Journal of Managing Projects in Business, 13*(1), 85–102. doi:10.1108/IJMPB-04-2018-0084

Marinelli, M., & Janardhanan, M. (2022). Green cement production in India: Prioritization and alleviation of barriers using the best–worst method. *Environmental Science and Pollution Research International, 29*(42), 63988–64003. doi:10.100711356-022-20217-x PMID:35469385

Martinez, E. H., Alvear, A. M., Tommelein, I. D., & Ballard, G. (2015). Formwork standardization and production flow: Lessons from an affordable housing project in Ecuador. *Proceedings of IGLC 23 - 23rd Annual Conference of the International Group for Lean Construction: Global Knowledge - Global Solutions,* 53–62.

Mi, X., Tang, M., Liao, H., Shen, W., & Lev, B. (2019). The state-of-the-art survey on integrations and applications of the best worst method in decision making: Why, what, what for and what's next? *Omega, 87*, 205–225. doi:10.1016/j.omega.2019.01.009

Moon, S., Ha, C., & Yang, J. (2012). Structured Idea Creation for Improving the Value of Construction Design. *Journal of Construction Engineering and Management, 138*(7), 841–853. doi:10.1061/(ASCE)CO.1943-7862.0000491

Moore, D. (1996). Buildability assessment and the development of an automated design aid for managing the transfer of construction process knowledge. *Engineering, Construction, and Architectural Management, 3*(1–2), 29–46. doi:10.1108/eb021021

Mousa, A. A., Hussein, M., & Kineber, A. F. (2022). Value-Engineering Methodology for the Selection of an Optimal Bridge System. *Transportation Research Record: Journal of the Transportation Research Board, 2676*(4), 483–498. doi:10.1177/03611981211062154

Mousakhani, E., Yavarkhani, M., & Sohrabi, S. (2017). Selecting an appropriate alternative for a major infrastructure project with regard to value engineering approach. *Journal of Engineering. Design and Technology, 15*(3), 395–416. doi:10.1108/JEDT-12-2015-0083

Naoum, S. G., & Egbu, C. (2016). Modern selection criteria for procurement methods in construction: A state-of-the-art literature review and a survey. *International Journal of Managing Projects in Business, 9*(2), 309–336. doi:10.1108/IJMPB-09-2015-0094

Nima, M. A., Abdul-Kadir, M. R., Jaafar, M. S., & Alghulami, R. G. (2004). Constructability Concepts in Kuala Selangor Cable-Stayed Bridge in Malaysia. *Journal of Construction Engineering and Management, 130*(3), 315–321. doi:10.1061/(ASCE)0733-9364(2004)130:3(315)

Pan, Y., & Zhang, L. (2021). Roles of artificial intelligence in construction engineering and management: A critical review and future trends. *Automation in Construction, 122*, 103517. doi:10.1016/j.autcon.2020.103517

Park, J., & Kwak, Y. H. (2017). Design-Bid-Build (DBB) vs. Design-Build (DB) in the U.S. public transportation projects: The choice and consequences. *International Journal of Project Management, 35*(3), 280–295. doi:10.1016/j.ijproman.2016.10.013

Petroutsatou, K., & Kantilierakis, D. (2023). Productivity Analysis and Associated Risks in Steel Structures. *Buildings, 13*(905), 1–18. doi:10.3390/buildings13040905

Petroutsatou, K., Ladopoulos, I., & Tsakelidou, K. (2022). Scientometric Analysis and AHP for Hierarchizing Criteria Affecting Construction Equipment Operators' Performance. *Sustainability (Basel), 14*(11), 6836. Advance online publication. doi:10.3390u14116836

Ren, Z., Shen, G. Q., & Xue, X. L. (2013). Failure Caused by Inappropriate Construction Methods: An Expensive Lesson. *Journal of Management Engineering, 29*(1), 25–34. doi:10.1061/(ASCE)ME.1943-5479.0000117

Rezaei, J. (2015). Best-worst multi-criteria decision-making method. *Omega, 53*, 49–57. doi:10.1016/j.omega.2014.11.009

Rezaei, J. (2016). Best-worst multi-criteria decision-making method: Some properties and a linear model. *Omega, 64*, 126–130. doi:10.1016/j.omega.2015.12.001

Salvatierra-Garrido, J., & Pasquire, C. (2011). Value theory in lean construction. *Journal of Financial Management of Property and Construction*, *16*(1), 8–18. doi:10.1108/13664381111116043

Siemonsma, H., van Nus, W., & Uyttendaele, P. (2012). Awarding of port PPP contracts: The added value of a competitive dialogue procedure. *Maritime Policy & Management*, *39*(1), 63–78. doi:10.1080/03088839.2011.642314

Stamatiadis, N., Sturgill, R., & Amiridis, K. (2017). Benefits from Constructability Reviews. *Transportation Research Procedia*, *25*, 2889–2897. doi:10.1016/j.trpro.2017.05.275

Tam, C. M. (2000). Design and Build on a complicated redevelopment project in Hong Kong: The Happy Valley Racecourse Redevelopment. *International Journal of Project Management*, *18*(2), 125–129. doi:10.1016/S0263-7863(99)00012-5

Tan, G. E., Ong, T. B., Ong, C. Y., & Choong, K. K. (2014). Development and standardisation of new precast concrete open spandrel arch bridge system. *Engineering for Progress, Nature and People*, 799–806. doi:10.2749/222137814814066960

Tang, P., & Bittner, R. B. (2014). Use of Value Engineering to Develop Creative Design Solutions for Marine Construction Projects. *Practice Periodical on Structural Design and Construction*, *19*(1), 129–136. doi:10.1061/(ASCE)SC.1943-5576.0000184

Tawiah, P. A., & Russell, A. D. (2008). Assessing Infrastructure Project Innovation as a Function of Procurement Mode. *Journal of Management Engineering*, *24*(3), 173–186. doi:10.1061/(ASCE)0742-597X(2008)24:3(173)

Torvatn, T., & de Boer, L. (2017). Public procurement reform in the EU: Start of a new era? *IMP Journal*, *11*(3), 431–451. doi:10.1108/IMP-09-2015-0056

Tsz Wai, C., Wai Yi, P., Ibrahim Olanrewaju, O., Abdelmageed, S., Hussein, M., Tariq, S., & Zayed, T. (2021). A critical analysis of benefits and challenges of implementing modular integrated construction. *International Journal of Construction Management*, *23*(4), 656–668. doi:10.1080/15623599.2021.1907525

Umit Dikmen, S., & Sonmez, M. (2011). An artificial neural networks model for the estimation of formwork labour. *Journal of Civil Engineering and Management*, *17*(3), 340–347. doi:10.3846/13923730.2011.594154

Yang, J., Baeg, H., & Moon, S. (2014). Utilization of contradiction for creating design alternatives in construction value engineering. *KSCE Journal of Civil Engineering*, *18*(2), 355–364. doi:10.100712205-014-0284-x

Zhang, J., & El-Diraby, T. E. (2006). Constructability Analysis of the Bridge Superstructure Rotation Construction Method in China. *Journal of Construction Engineering and Management, 132*(4), 353–362. doi:10.1061/(ASCE)0733-9364(2006)132:4(353)

Zhao, N., & Ying, F. (2018). Method selection: A conceptual framework for public sector PPP selection. *Built Environment Project and Asset Management, 9*(2), 214–232. doi:10.1108/BEPAM-01-2018-0018

Chapter 2
The Impact of Risks and Uncertainty in the Life Cycle Cost Analysis of Construction Projects:
The Case of Energy Analysis on Construction Projects

Konstantinos Kirytopoulos
National Technical University of Athens, Greece

Vasileios Sarlis
National Technical University of Athens, Greece

Dimitris Marinakis
National Technical University of Athens, Greece

Theodoros Kalogeropoulos
National Technical University of Athens, Greece

ABSTRACT

Construction projects are subject to risks and uncertainty that make the final cost of the investment difficult to predict. A life cycle cost analysis incorporating the risks involved could prove useful in the decision-making process. This analysis should be done at the start of the conception phase of the project and work itself along the project's realization. This chapter presents a specific approach for the implementation of a risk-based life cycle cost analysis. The proposed approach covers the risk-based life cycle cost analysis of a construction project, through the incorporation of well-

DOI: 10.4018/978-1-6684-7786-1.ch002

established risk identification and risk analysis methods. The risk identification process regarding the energy-based risks of a residential construction project is performed. Finally, the proposed method is showcased on an illustrative case of a residential building with multiple different energy-based investment scenarios, and its results form the basis for the decision-making of the project.

1. INTRODUCTION

Urban construction and infrastructure projects are some of the most successful businesses where investors fund substantial amounts of money, and therefore the prosperity of many nations, including Greece, is highly dependent on the size of their construction industry (Abdelkhalek et al., 2020, Antoniou, 2021). While infrastructure projects tend to be more significant to the nations' Gross Domestic Product and economies due to their larger size, urban construction projects tend to have higher profit margin (Bilal, 2019). Moreover, because of their lower initial costs they are more attainable by individual investors, compared to infrastructure projects which are typically funded by public investments (Antoniou, 2021). The large-scale urban construction projects consume massive amounts of resources and energy all throughout their life cycle, while also having significant environmental and socio-economic impacts (Georgiadou et al., 2012). Although nowadays the environmental impact of projects can be highly regulated, this is not the case with their economic evaluation which still remains a business risk (International Organization for Standardization 14001:2015). Therefore, it is important for the stakeholders of the project to have a tool which is capable of giving an answer to the project's viability and longevity. This tool is Life-cycle cost analysis (LCCA) which is able to take into consideration all of the expenses of the project, covering it from cradle to grave (Petroutsatou et al., 2021, Boussabaine & Kirham, 2008).

LCCA is a method used to assess the total cost of a project taking into consideration all the costs from its design phase, up to its disposal at the end of its life cycle. While covering the area of construction projects, it is based on Life-cycle costing (LCC) which according to ISO 15686-5:2017 can be defined as:

Methodology for systematic economic consideration of all significant and relevant initial and future costs and benefits of a whole building or structure or unit of construction works, or a system or a component or part thereof, throughout its life cycle, while fulfilling the performance requirements

At the same time according to ISO 15686-5:2017 and ISO 14040:2006:

The life cycle comprises all stages from construction, operation, and maintenance to end-of-life, including decommissioning, deconstruction and disposal.

LCCA, thanks to its holistic approach, is useful in evaluating project alternatives that fulfil similar performance requirements but differ in respect to their initial and operating costs (Plebankiewicz et al., 2016). LCCA can consider all the individual operating parameters to determine correctly and as accurately as the available information permits, the economic performance of the activity over the span of several years (Belany et al., 2021). With this information it is possible to choose the best plan for the project, by opting for the minimum total life cycle cost (Sieglinde 2016).

Moreover, LCCA is useful in building renovation and restoration, as it can easily assess and compare the effectiveness of different energy efficiency measures (EEMs) of the different renovation options and choose the most cost effective one (Di Giuseppe et al., 2017, Smith et al., 2021). Moreover, its application in the process of building retrofitting brings an innovative perspective, as it can provide trustworthy estimates of its final cost and profits, based on existing consumption development trends. Another important feature of LCCA is its ability to consider the environmental impact connected to the retrofitting or renovating activity, as the analysis provides a precise estimate of future energy and resource consumption (Belany et al., 2021).

While LCCA provides an educated and usually accurate estimate for the project's expenses, it can be enhanced by utilizing the tools of risk assessment. There have been several applications of risk analysis in other domains, such as long-term investment and commerce activities, which, if slightly altered, could fit the construction activities' framework, and be incorporated into the LCCA (Basak & Makarov, 2014, Giuffrida et al., 2021). The assessment of the project's risks and uncertainty starts with the risk identification process usually with the creation of the Risk Breakdown Structure (RBS) and the Risk Catalogues (Jepson et al., 2020). The next step is the risk analysis. In order to conduct risk analysis plenty of information is needed. The pieces of information needed can be derived either from past records or from expert opinions and are related to each risk's frequency of occurrence and to its impact on the project. With accurate information it is possible to describe the uncertainty connected to key variables of the project and describe both the probability and impact of a risk in a consistent and easy to understand manner (Savvides, 1994, Kirytopoulos, 2021). A thorough risk analysis can be coupled with a sensitivity analysis and be able to demonstrate the significance of each risk, while the experts' evaluation can provide some verbal guidance for the risks' evaluation and treatment (Merková et al., 2013). Following the accumulation of data, which should be as thorough as possible, the uncertainty and the risks can be analyzed both qualitatively and quantitatively. The qualitative and, especially, the quantitative analyses are the keys to incorporating the risk analysis into the framework of LCCA.

To make sure that risk analysis will enhance LCCA and will further verify the sustainability of a construction plan, it needs to incorporate both the uncertainty as well as the risks involved in the project, see e.g., Rostami et al. (2015). The term 'uncertainty' refers to the inherent randomness of certain actions, while the term 'risk' refers to the randomly occurring disruptive events (Kirytopoulos, 2021). These risks can affect the construction activity, but because of phenomena like optimism bias (Prater et al., 2017), risk assessment teams often neglect them. Unless there is an experienced member in the team, such risks could be ignored and be left out from the analysis and increase the project's hidden risk exposure (Tziralis et al., 2009). Furthermore, these risks can be problematic to their evaluation even after their challenging identification, and therefore, probabilistic methods, such as Monte Carlo Simulations (MCS), need to be employed to properly quantify their impact on the project (Ruffle et al., 2018, Wang et al., 2012).

During the application of LCCA, a set of input parameters and realistic predictions are required to achieve an effective assessment. While the lack of data and their associated uncertainty remain well-recognized, issues with the calculation methods of deterministic LCCA could be alleviated using several educated assumptions and MCS. Furthermore, MCS are useful in alleviating the results of LCCA from their inherent dependency on current trends of economic indices and their associated uncertainty, such as inflation and spikes in energy prices (Di Giuseppe et al., 2017). Another feature of MCS is the ability to accurately predict the future socio-economic environment where the activities will be performed and what its consequences for the project will be (Fregonara et al., 2018). Moreover, MCS can easily find its way into the analysis, as it gives a stochastic but accurate estimate for factors that would otherwise be impossible to measure as well as providing a good re-evaluation for the factors which have already been assessed (Odedairo & Olenloa, 2021). MCS provides useful data which make the incorporation of uncertainty into cash flows possible, through their stochastic nature and their ability to fill the gaps of incomplete information about a project's costs. Furthermore, MCS data can be used in conjunction with the basics of Net Present Cost (NPC) in order to create a model which can accurately assess the project viability throughout its life cycle (Bull, 2003, Shaffie & Jaaman, 2016).

This chapter aims to provide a risk-based approach of LCCA using risk identification and analysis methods and by utilizing Monte Carlo Simulations. It also provides a guide for the method proposed starting from the risk identification stage and following up to the final stages of results and the decision-making. Finally, the proposed approach is illustrated through the lens of a residential construction project of a five-storey apartment building in Greece.

The chapter is organized as follows. Section 2 presents the current literature overview over LCCA, and over the risk assessment methods and tools mainly focusing on the construction industry and highlighting some of the risks that will be analyzed in the illustrative case. Section 3 is dedicated to outlining the method proposed in order to perform the risk-based lifecycle cost analysis (LCCA-R). Section 4 presents the illustrative case of implementation of the LCCA-R on a five-storey apartment building. Finally, Section 5 provides the conclusions of the chapter and the proposed approach.

2. LIFE CYCLE COST ANALYSIS & RISK MANAGEMENT IN CONSTRUCTION

2.1. Life Cycle Cost Analysis (LCCA)

LCCA, in the construction industry, constitutes a method to estimate the total cost of a construction project from its conceptual phase following up to its disposal. The costs included in this analysis cover everything from the purchase of the property to operating expenses and disposal at the end of the life cycle. LCCA is suitable for comparing several competing proposals for project's realization from the design phase of the project, while also giving accurate results for the project's environmental impact (Smith et al., 2021). Moreover, it can be reviewed multiple times during the construction and operation phases of the project in order to provide guidance for the project's improved performance (Bull, 2003). According to Dhillon (2009), while this method can be time consuming and costly, it provides a great tool for selecting the best plan for the project and for making decision regarding renovations and replacement of equipment. It is able to provide the best course of action by minimizing the total costs of initial investment, development, supervision, maintenance, repair, and, finally, disposal/break-down (Boussabaine & Kirham, 2008). Finally, a typical LCCA for a residential building would, usually, cover the time span of 25 years (Dhillon, 2009, Wang et al., 2012).

As far as construction and infrastructure projects are concerned, a significant part of the total cost arises after their completion, in terms of maintenance and disposal. Hence, according to Petroutsatou et al. (2021), only an approach that holistically encompasses all the costs of the project can be found fruitful in facilitating the best decision-making for the stakeholders of the project. It is not uncommon for applications of LCCA in the construction sector to be far from optimal, since the costs of said projects are estimated with less detail than needed and deterministic estimations for the costs are employed, instead of opting for stochastic methods (Parra Márquez et al., 2017). Despite that, there have been applications of LCCA where the project's uncertainty has been addressed. Moretti et al. (2016) presented a life-cycle cost analysis of a highway tunnel comparing the different construction, maintenance, and lighting cost of two alternatives pavement types over the span of 30 years. Petroutsatou et al. (2021) made a life cycle-based model to estimate the cost of construction and operation of road tunnels over their 75-year long life cycle, using neural networks. Antoniou (2021) performed a risk assessment concerning the time of delivery for road projects in Greece, covering possible sources of delay from the projects' whole life cycle. Noshadravan et al. (2017) presented a method of LCCA for residential building focusing heavily on natural hazards and their impacts on such projects, while Lu et al. (2021) have used a risk based LCCA approach in order to locate the sources of safety risk in construction projects. These works have provided a holistic and risk-based approach for both infrastructure and urban construction projects, but the norm for such projects still tends to follow a deterministic LCCA approach, or more simplistic methods.

2.2. Risk Identification and Analysis Methods and Tools

Risk identification is the first stage of risk assessment of any project. At this stage the risk management team rushes in to investigate and identify the risks that affect the project's development and those risks which will arise during its operation. At this stage, there is a plethora of different methods and tools in the hands of the team. The decision of which method to follow is highly dependent on the characteristics of the project, the experience of the people responsible and, finally, the time horizon of the risk identification process. Each of these methods possesses both advantages and disadvantages, so it is quite common for risk management teams to choose a combination of them.

According to Kirytopoulos (2021) and Boussabaine & Kirham (2008), some of the most prevalent and well-known risk identification methods include: 'interviews with experts', 'brainstorming', 'Risk Breakdown Structure (RBS)' and 'Risk Catalogues'. 'Interviews with experts' is one of the most straightforward methods where people with much expertise and experience on the project's area are requested to list the risks that could have an impact on the project. A decisive factor for the effectiveness of this method is the selection of the proper experts. 'Brainstorming' involves a meeting of the risk management team along with key project stakeholders in order to exchange ideas on the project's possible threats and opportunities. The 'Risk Breakdown Structure' is a breakdown diagram consisting of several branches. In each one resides an identified source of risk and uncertainty and it is, usually, further branched out to cover more specific sources of uncertainty. This diagram provides the basis for further risk identification and the more branched out the diagram, the deeper the identification process has been performed. Finally, 'Risk Catalogues' are lists containing risks that have been identified in previous or similar projects and/or have been derived from a previously created RBS. These lists can either be related to a project of a particular sector or they can cover a broad range of projects.

During risk analysis, the risks identified in the previous stage are studied in terms of their frequency of occurrence and their impact to the project. The main concern of this stage is for the team of risk managers to correlate each risk with their severity. This will make the team able to address the more serious risks and avoid wasting resources on less important ones. The analysis of each risk can be qualitative and/or quantitative, depending on the risk's nature and its associated abundance or lack of data.

In qualitative risk analysis, the risk management team forms two scales: (i) one describing the probability of the risk's occurrence, and (ii) another one describing the level of the risk's impact on the project. These scales are expressed in verbal values (e.g., 'Low', 'Medium', ''High' referring to the probability of occurrence) and not numerical ones. The qualitative analysis of a risk can either be its definitive analysis or it can be a precursor to the risk's quantitative analysis. To carry out the quantitative risk analysis it is necessary to have documented or, at least, well-estimated numerical data concerning the probability of occurrence and the impact of the risk. Similar to the qualitative analysis, the team forms the aforementioned two scales, but in contrast to the latter, these scales are expressed in specific numerical terms (e.g., 'Once per 10 years', 'Once every year', 'Once every month', 'Once every week' when referring to the frequency of occurrence) (Kirytopoulos, 2021, Boussabaine & Kirham, 2008).

When the quantitative risk analysis is performed, the MCS presents itself as a very useful tool (Wang et al., 2012). MCS is a stochastic method used to provide a quantitative solution to non-deterministic problems (Leopoulos et al., 2006), which has found its way in a variety of areas such as financial engineering and risk management (Diamantas et al., 2007). With the MCS, a variable of the project can be chosen and then it can be described with a range of values or a mathematical distribution. Following the appropriate creation of the variables then the objective function can be created. In the case of a residential construction project, this could be 'the delay of delivery' or 'the total cost' of the project and it would be created by adding up the variables covering the project's delay or the project's costs, respectively. Then, a series of simulations is made by randomly assigning values to the variables. This process is repeated, for all the project's variables, several times (usually 5000 or more iterations) so that the distribution of the objective function is revealed. Moreover, Wang et al. (2012), in their approach to LCCA, have used MCS to calculate problematic cost values and, thus, circumvented their resource-consuming research. They, also, highlighted the impact of inaccurate input data, which can drastically decrease the model's validity and potential usefulness.

The construction industry being one of the biggest generators of revenue in the Greek and the global economy (Antoniou, 2021, Abdelkhalek et al., 2020) needs to have proper tools for optimization and risk assessment. Marinelli et al. (2018) agree that the challenges of construction projects stem from the need to maximize their perceived value, to minimize their costs and to have smooth operation and maintenance throughout their life cycle. Therefore, in order for this sector to grow and prosper, the best possible decisions need to be made for each of its projects. To reach sound and justified decision making, one must see the situations and events that arise and be able to spot the risks that lie behind them.

Based on the principles of LCCA, a construction project can be divided into 4 main stages: Planning (1), Construction (2), Maintenance and Repairs (3), and Disposal/Breakdown (4). By using the methods and tools of risk identification and based on the 4 aforementioned stages of the project's life cycle, it is possible to create an RBS. In this case, the RBS created is high level, mainly indicating potential sources of risk. Following the line of thinking of Boussabaine & Kirham (2008) and Antoniou (2021) as well as by conducting interviews with experts, it is possible to expand upon the original 4 branches and to create a more fleshed out RBS. In addition to this, it has been decided that one of the RBS branches will be dedicated to the so-called white dwarves, since their existence is often overlooked.

Figure 1. Risk breakdown structure for a residential construction activity

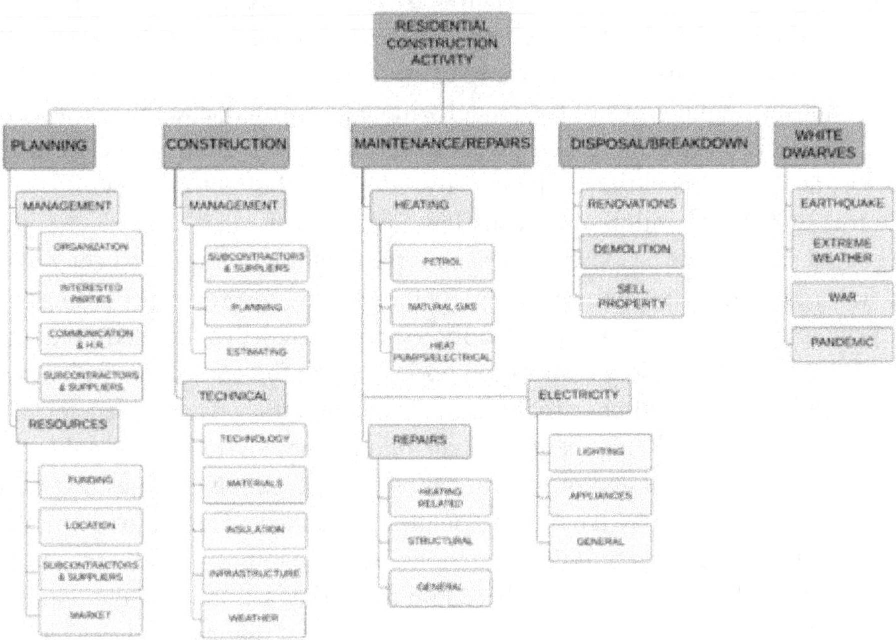

The white dwarves are risks with an extremely low probability of occurrence but with a very high impact on the project. Their importance to the risk management cannot be understated since they have been the cause of many projects' hindrance or even failure.

In parallel with the creation of the RBS (Figure 1), a brainstorming session for our illustrative case has been conducted, focusing mainly on the risks concerning the maintenance/repairs. During this session, ideas for potential energy and repair related risks were proposed. These ideas enabled the execution of a more detailed examination for this specific branch of the RBS. During this stage, more reviews with experts, from 2 well-established Greek design firms, have been conducted and a thorough examination of the energy-related risk analyses, see e.g., Georgiadou (2014), Georgiadou et al. (2012), Zhang et al. (2012) and Smith et al. (2021), has been performed. These analyses have been reviewed, and along with the RBS, formed the basis for the risk identification of the illustrative case.

3. PROPOSED APPROACH: THE RISK-BASED LIFE CYCLE COST ANALYSIS (LCCA-R)

As shown in the section 2, there are many aspects in the LCCA of a construction project that harbor risks. These risks can be categorized either as isolated disruptive events (risks) or as inherent randomness (uncertainty). The proposed approach for risk based LCCA is divided into five main steps. Firstly, the creation of a spreadsheet as per deterministic LCCA, followed by risk identification and analysis. Then, the model will be created using appropriate software to quantify all the risks involved. Finally, multiple simulations of the model will be performed, and their results will dictate the decision-making process. These steps are presented in the form of a flowchart in Figure 2 and they will be analyzed in detail directly below.

Step 1: LCCA – Creation of a Cash-flow Spreadsheet

The first stage of the proposed approach is the creation of a spreadsheet with the cash-flows containing the numerical data for the costs of the project according to the basic principles of LCCA. More specifically, a spreadsheet will be created, containing the cash-flows of the project with a time horizon up to the end of the project's life cycle. Each input and output in these cash-flows can either have a predetermined value, such as the constant payment of a loan, or it can have a fluctuating value, such as the price of heating oil and/or natural gas. At this stage, only values that have a fixed price and frequency will be placed on the spreadsheet. The rest of them, those containing fluctuating values, will not be included in the initial spreadsheet and they will be treated as risks and handled based on the following steps of the approach. This spreadsheet will form the basis for the modelling of the involved risks and the

Figure 2. Proposed approach flowchart

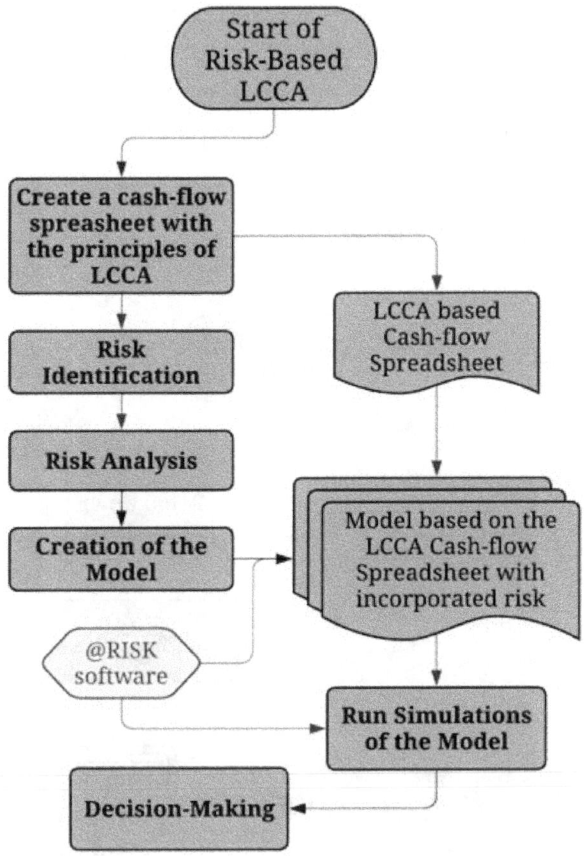

MCS. In case there is more than one scenario for the project's execution, it would be advisable to have separate spreadsheets for each one of them as it will make it easier to isolate the scenarios at the modelling stage and to compare them at the decision-making stage.

Step 2: Risk Identification

To identify the risks, the project's risk management team is advised to start looking into the literature of similar construction projects whose risk identification process has been proven fruitful and successful. This way, the team can start by conducting a brainstorming session. At the same time an RBS can be created, which will present the basis for further risk identification and the formation of a risk catalogue. However, if during the creation of the risk catalogue the team encounters a branch of the RBS or an idea that it cannot fully elaborate on, then it is paramount to conduct a number of targeted interviews with experts in order to expand upon those ideas. After cross-checking the results from all of those processes, the team should be able to judge, possessing the necessary expertise and know-how, whether or not the identification process is exhaustive enough and satisfactory. Finally, a risk catalogue with fully fleshed-out risks will be created. This process is also shown in Figure 3 in the form of a flow chart.

Figure 3. Risk identification flowchart

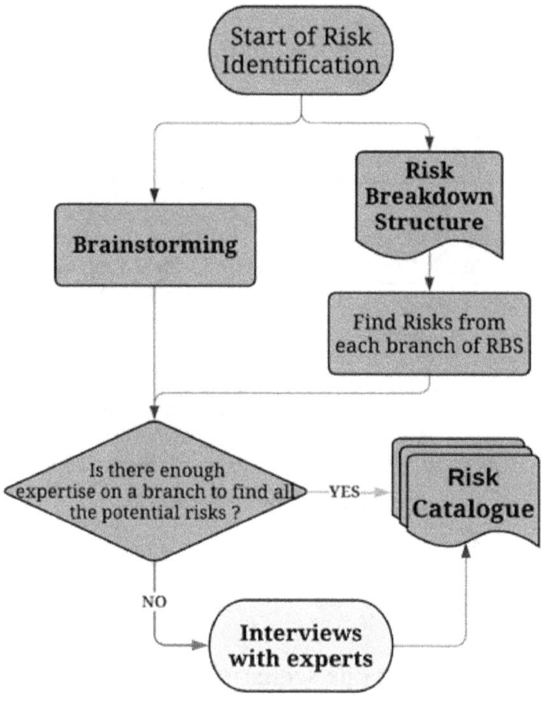

Step 3: Risk Analysis

As far as the risks' incorporation into LCCA is concerned, it is obvious that numerical data are needed, and therefore a qualitative risk analysis alone will not be sufficient. For those risks, which can be quantitatively analyzed, the team will add numerical data to their probability and their potential consequences to the project's total cost. However, for those risks whose quantitative analysis appears to be problematic the team must translate their verbal data into numerical data. This is where the MCS can be proven very useful. At the end of the analysis, a database

Figure 4. Risk analysis flowchart

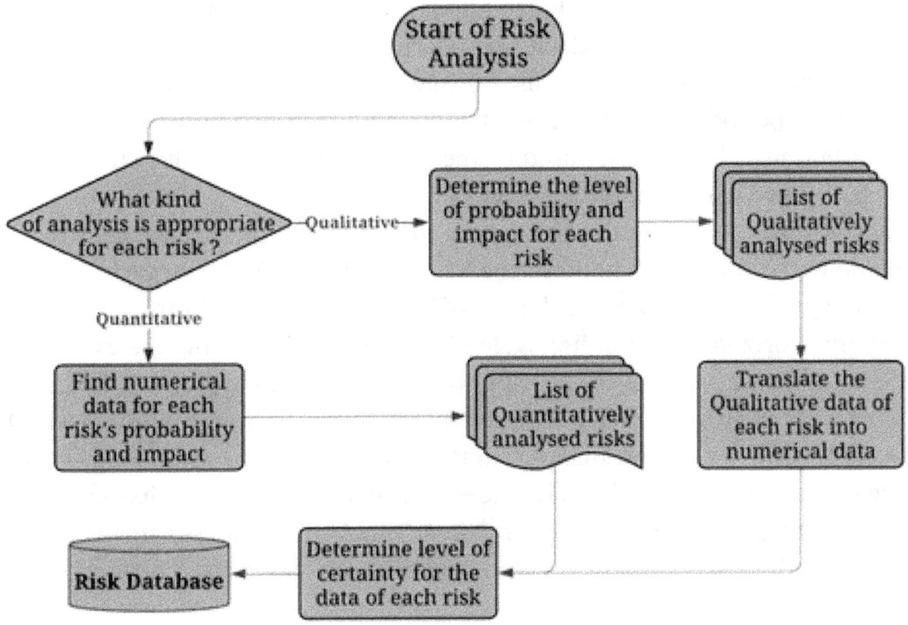

will be created containing numerical data on both the impact and the probability of each risk. This database will be utilized in the modelling stage in conjunction with the cash-flow spreadsheet. This process is, shown in the form of a flowchart in Figure 4.

Step 4: Creation of the MCS Model

In the modelling stage, the data collected from the risk analysis will be used as the basis for the approximation of each risk through a distribution curve fitting. At this stage, an MCS based software should be used to provide a variety of well-established distributions, with which the team will approximate the risks' impact and frequency. In some cases, where risks have lots of numerical data, but they do not follow any known distribution, the software package should be equipped with tools which allow the approximation of this data with the closest existing distribution (data curve fitting). This is, especially, useful when covering values which can fluctuate heavily and rapidly during certain periods of time or during the occurrence of disruptive events. The risks which fall into the category of inherent uncertainty are presented using continuous distributions. On the other hand, for individually occurring disruptive events, a Bernoulli distribution is used, based on their frequency of occurrence. At the same time, their impact is calculated using continuous distributions. The product of these two distributions gives a new distribution that accurately describes these risks. Once this process has been done for all the risks and all of the uncertainty then these distributions can be plugged into the spreadsheet with the cash-flows of the LCCA, which has been made during the first step of the proposed approach. At the end of this stage the team will have a spreadsheet containing all the cash-flows for each time period of the project containing both the fixed numerical values and the distributions which will be used by the software to perform the MCS.

Step 5: Run Model Simulations and Decision-Making

At this stage, MCS on the risk-based spreadsheet will be executed. In these simulations, the objective function is the Net Present Cost (NPC) for each investment scenario, which is calculated by the cash-flows, either deterministic or stochastic, with a time horizon up to the life cycle of the project. Following the execution of MCS, the software provides the distributions that describe the project's NPC. These distributions can provide trust-worthy estimates for project's profitability and value, allowing for better decision-making. In the case that several competing scenarios for the execution of the project are under consideration, their stochastic NPC can be estimated and compared. Therefore, the team of stakeholders can reach a more well-informed, educated, and well-grounded decision on which competing scenario to ultimately pursue.

4. ILLUSTRATIVE CASE ON THE IMPLEMENTATION OF LCCA-R

4.1. Case Description and Investment Scenarios

In this segment of the chapter, an application of the proposed approach for the risk based LCCA is presented. This application covers the case study of a five-storey apartment building currently being constructed in Greece. This building consists of a parking area (basement), a ground floor with no apartments, and 4 floors with apartments. Of the 4 floors that have apartments, the first and second floors have 4 apartments, the third one has 3 apartments and the fourth one has a single apartment. In total, there are 12 apartments in the building with a total surface of 880 m^2.

The analysis of the case study is performed using the @RISK and "4 M-K.ENA.K." software. The @RISK software has been selected as it is one of the state-of-art tools for such analyses. At the same time, the "4 M-K.ENA.K." software has been selected as it is the most advanced software for energy analysis in Greece. Moreover, it is capable of making accurate simulations of the building's shell and its associated electromechanical equipment and, thus, provide trustworthy data concerning the building's energy consumption. Finally, by comparing several competing scenarios it is able to reveal the most energy-efficient solution.

Using these computer programs, the expenses associated with the building's heating and lighting can be simulated. These energy-based expenses are considered throughout the life cycle of the project, meaning that they include the costs for all the devices installed on the property as well as the costs of its operation, maintenance, and repairs. Moreover, the analysis extends over a time span of 25 years which is typical for LCCA (Dhillon, 2009, Wang et al., 2012).

This economic analysis enables the comparison of the economic benefit or loss accompanying each investment scenario and it gives trust-worthy estimates concerning the specific route of execution that is best. The numerical data for all the different competing scenarios have been gathered, and their similarities and differences can be presented. These scenarios differ from one another in terms of their initial costs as well as their main energy source for heating. This way, along with the use of the "4 M-K.ENA.K." software, the energy consumption and expenses of each scenario can be calculated. The "4 M-K.ENA.K." software provides accurate data for the amount of thermal energy consumed as well as its source. In this case the 3 sources of energy are 'Heating Oil', 'Natural Gas', and 'Electricity' which are the most prevalent sources for heating in Greece. These values, accompanied with the costs for each respective energy source, make the calculation of the energy-expenses possible for every investment scenario. The six different investment scenarios are presented below (EER = Energy Efficiency Ratio):

a) High-End Heating Oil: This investment scenario involves using a higher-end oil burner (Efficiency = 93%, 10.000 €) with the associated pipework (10.000 €) and the heating cells (6.900 €), triple-glazing aluminum frames (120.000 €), higher-end air-conditioning units (EER = 2.7, 14.500 €), higher-end wall insulation (U = 0.357 W/m^{2}K, 65.000 €), LED light bulbs (760 €) and solar panels (2640 €).
b) Low-End Heating Oil: This investment scenario involves using a lower-end oil burner (Efficiency = 91%, 8000 €) with the associated pipework (10.000 €) and the heating cells (6.900 €), double-glazing aluminum frames (100.000 €), lower-end air-conditioning units (EER = 2.4, 8.000 €), lower-end wall insulation (U = 0.45 W/m^{2}K, 58.000 €) and regular light bulbs (1.500 €).
c) High-End Electrical Heating: This investment scenario involves using higher-end heat pumps and air-conditioning units (EER = 5.31, 55.000 €), triple-glazing aluminum frames (120.000 €), higher-end wall insulation (U = 0.357 W/m^{2}K, 65.000 €), LED light bulbs (760 €) and solar panels (2640 €).
d) Low-End Electrical Heating: This investment scenario involves using lower-end heat pumps and air-conditioning units (EER = 4.6, 45.000 €), double-glazing

aluminum frames (100.000 €), lower-end wall insulation (U = 0.45 W/m^{2}K, 58.000 €) and regular light bulbs (1.500 €)

e) High-End Natural Gas: This investment scenario involves using individual higher-end natural gas burners (Efficiency = 96%, 22.140 €) with the associated pipework (10.000 €) and the heating cells (6.900 €), triple-glazing aluminum frames (120.000 €), higher-end air-conditioning units (EER = 2.7, 14.500 €), higher-end wall insulation (U = 0.357 W/m^{2}K, 65.000 €), LED light bulbs (760 €) and solar panels (2640 €).

f) Low-End Natural Gas: This investment scenario involves using lower-end natural gas burners (Efficiency = 91%, 13.200 €) with the associated pipework (10.000 €) and the heating cells (6.900 €), double-glazing aluminum frames (100.000 €), lower-end air-conditioning units (EER = 2.4, 8.000 €), lower-end wall insulation (U = 0.45 W/m^{2}K, 58.000 €) and regular light bulbs (1.500 €).

Note: For the cost of light bulbs in each scenario, it was considered that all those, which will be used throughout the building life cycle, are purchased from the start of the project. That is the reason why regular light bulbs have a higher initial cost, since they have a shorter life expectancy (10.000 hours of use) than LED ones (50.000 hours of use), and therefore more of them will be needed.

With the use of 4 M-K.ENA. K. software the energy consumption, for each investment scenario, has been calculated and is shown in **Table 1**:

Table 1. Energy consumption per annum of each scenario broken down by its source

Scenarios		MWh per Annum		
		Heating Oil	Electricity	Natural GAS
a	HIGH-END HEATING OIL	21,1525	10,1356	0,0000
b	LOW-END HEATING OIL	30,8474	8,6373	0,0000
c	HIGH-END ELECTRICITY HEATING	0,0000	16,9220	0,0000
d	LOW-END ELECTRICITY HEATING	0,0000	18,4203	0,0000
e	HIGH-END NATURAL GAS	0,0000	9,5186	20,2711
f	LOW-END NATURAL GAS	0,0000	8,5491	31,7287

Furthermore, based on the sketches of the building there are three different kinds of lights, and their numbers go as follows:

I. Low brightness lights: There are 28 low brightness lights, all of which are located inside apartments. Their power consumption is 28W for a regular light bulb and 7W for an LED light bulb.
II. High brightness lights: There are 94 high brightness lights, of which 60 are located inside apartments, 10 are in common areas and 24 are in the parking area (basement). Their power consumption is 70W for a regular light bulb and 10W for an LED light bulb.
III. Outdoor lights: There are 49 outdoor lights, of which 39 are located on the balconies of apartments and 10 are located on the outside areas of the ground level. Their power consumption is 150W for a regular light bulb and 13W for an LED light bulb.

Finally, whenever solar panels are included in the investment scenario, there are 12 solar panels rated at 370w, which give off 4.440w, in total.

4.2. Risk Identification and Analysis

During the stage of risk identification, a risk catalogue containing the energy-related risks of the project has been created from the RBS in Figure 1. From there, the branches of "Maintenance/Repairs" and "White Dwarves" have been expanded upon, since the focus of the analysis is on the operation and the energy-based costs. This expansion started with interviews with experts from 5 well-established Greek firms, which have been conducted in two stages. Firstly, people from 2 Greek designing firms have been asked to describe the energy-related risks that they or their firm have faced in the past. Then a second phase of interviews has been conducted with people from 3 Greek construction companies and the questions asked were related to the risks' potential impact on the project's cost. Following the interviews, a more thorough review of the literature has been performed (Bull, 2003, Boussabaine and Kirham, 2008, Wang et al., 2012, Kumar et al., 2020). By cross-checking all the data gathered from these actions, the finalized risk catalogue has been created, and it is presented in Table 2.

By using @RISK, each identified risk can be modeled with a distribution and be incorporated into the simulation that will be performed afterwards. In order to model the occurrence of disruptive events, such as the breakdown of a boiler or the outbreak of a war, the use of Bernoulli distribution has been employed. Moreover, after careful examination of the prices of the Greek market for all the heating sources, which are evidently the most impactful parameters of the model, it became clear that certain events caused massive price hikes which have a 2-year effect period and follow a triangular pattern. These events mostly affect the prices of natural gas and electricity and happen roughly once every 10 years. Therefore, the creation of

Table 2. Risk catalogue of the operation, maintenance and repairs of a residential construction project

Operation, Maintenance, and Repair Risks					
1	HEATING	1.1	PETROL	1.1.1	Fluctuation in the cost of petrol
		1.2	NATURAL GAS	1.2.1	Fluctuation in the cost of natural gas
		1.3	HEAT PUMPS/ ELECTRICAL	1.3.1	Fluctuation in the cost of electricity
2	ELECTRICITY	2.1	LIGHTING	2.1.1	Not opting for the best and energy efficient methods due to high initial cost
				2.1.2	Fluctuation in lighting demand due to absence of people
		2.2	GENERAL	2.2.1	Fluctuating use of communal lighting
		2.3	SOLAR PANELS	2.3.1	Fluctuation in solar panel electricity production due to sunlight
3	REPAIRS	3.1	HEATING RELATED	3.1.1	Repairs of central heating unit (petrol)
				3.1.2	Repairs of central heating unit (natural gas)
				3.1.3	Repairs of individual heat pumps
4	WHITE DWARVES	4.1	WAR	4.1.1	War outbreak causing a huge increase in prices of energy
		4.2	GLOBAL ECONOMIC CRISIS	4.2.1	Global scale economic crisis causing a huge increase in prices of energy

a new variable called 'Peak Season' has been made. This variable indicates whether or not a price hike is occurring and, therefore, if there is an increase in the price of electricity and natural gas.

The prices for electricity and natural gas, in the Greek market, have been studied both during their price hikes and during their regular seasons. Therefore, when the price-increasing events do not occur, the prices' distributions for these sources of energy are derived from the distribution curve fitting of the data during their regular seasons. When these events do happen, instead of changing the prices' distributions, a new distribution called 'Price Increase' is added on top of the regular prices'

Table 3. Examination of the distributions used to describe each risk

1.1.1	Fluctuation in the cost of petrol	Distribution derived from data on heating oil prices. (According to reports of www.oikothermansi.gr/istoriko-diamorfosis-timwn-petrelaiou for the years 2013-2017)
1.2.1	Fluctuation in the cost of natural gas	Distribution derived from data on natural gas on regular seasons + 'Peak Season' * 'Price increase of Natural Gas' (According to the annual reports of the Regulatory Authority for Energy of Greece (P.A.E.) for the years 2019-2023)
1.3.1	Fluctuation in the cost of electricity	Distribution derived from data on electricity on regular seasons + 'Peak Season' * 'Price increase of Electricity' (According to the annual reports of the Independent Power Transmission Operator of Greece (A.Δ.M.H.E.) for the years 2019-2023)
2.1.1	Not opting for the best and energy efficient methods due to high initial cost	Since the use of the lights depends heavily on their location, the lights' distributions of use are the following (According to the interviews): a) All the lights that are in apartments follow a normal distribution with mean (μ) of 6 hours per day and standard deviation (σ) of 1 hour per day. b) All the outdoor lights that are in apartments' balconies follow a normal distribution with mean (μ) of 2 hours per day and standard deviation (σ) of 1 hour per day. c) All the lights that are in the parking area and in common areas follow a normal distribution with mean (μ) of 2 hours per day and standard deviation (σ) of 1 hour per day. d) All the outdoor lights that are in the ground level follow a normal distribution with mean (μ) of 10 hours per day and standard deviation (σ) of 1 hour per day.
2.1.2	Fluctuation in lighting demand due to absence of people	
2.2.1	Fluctuating use of communal lighting	
2.3.1	Fluctuation in solar panel electricity production due to sunlight	Regular distribution with mean (μ) of working 5 hours per day and standard deviation (σ) of 1 hour per day (According to the interviewees)
3.1.1	Repairs of central heating unit (petrol)	Happens every year with a Triangular Distribution 50-100 (According to the interviewees)
3.1.2	Repairs of central heating unit (natural gas)	Happens every year with a Triangular Distribution 50-100 (According to the interviewees)
3.1.3	Repairs of individual heat pumps	Happens every year with a Triangular Distribution 600-1200 (According to the interviewees)
4.1.1	War outbreak causing a huge increase in prices of energy	Bernoulli distribution with 20% probability of occurrence (According to the interviewees) Note: This defines the variable 'Peak Season', and for simplification of the model the '2-year effect that happens once every 10 years' has been changed to '1 year effect that happens once every 5 years'
4.2.1	Global scale economic crisis causing a huge increase in prices of energy	

distributions. The values for this 'Price Increase' distribution are calculated by subtracting the regular season's data from the price hike data. This process should be done for the prices of at least one year and a half since the event usually have a

2-year effect period. Finally, the 'Price Increase' distribution of can be created from the distribution curve fitting of these data.

Following the principles described above, along with more interviews with private experts from the Greek construction industry, every risk from table 2 has been translated into distributions in order to be incorporated into the model. These distributions are presented in Table 3 (if there is merging of cells that means that the risks are presented cumulatively by the resulting distribution):

All the distributions above, along with the data for the energy consumption and the solar panels' contribution are then added to a spreadsheet in order to perform the LCCA, as per a deterministic LCCA. Subsequently, the final cash flows for each year are calculated for the whole-time span of 25 years. At this stage the software runs several simulations for each investment scenario. Finally, using the cash flows of these simulations, the software provides the team with the stochastic distributions for the NPC of each investment scenario, allowing the team to move to the stage of decision-making.

4.3. Model Results and Decision Making

After the creation of the model, a number of 50.000 simulations were performed using the @RISK software. These runs give the numerical data to create the stochastic

Figure 5. Overlapping chart of the distributions of the NPCs of the high-end investment scenarios

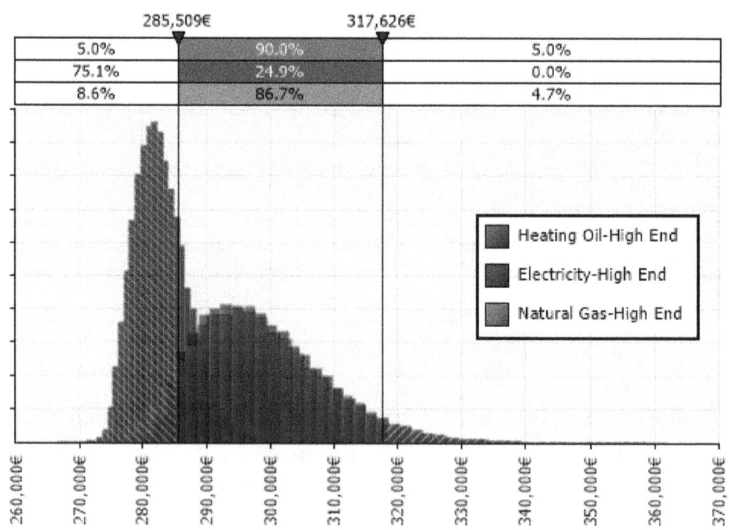

Figure 6. Overlapping chart of the distributions of the NPCs of the low-end investment scenarios

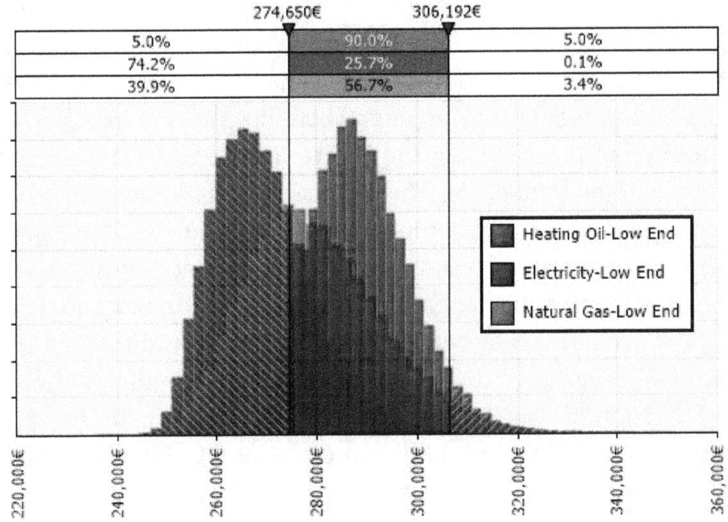

Figure 7. Overlapping chart of the distributions of the NPCs of the most competitive investment scenarios

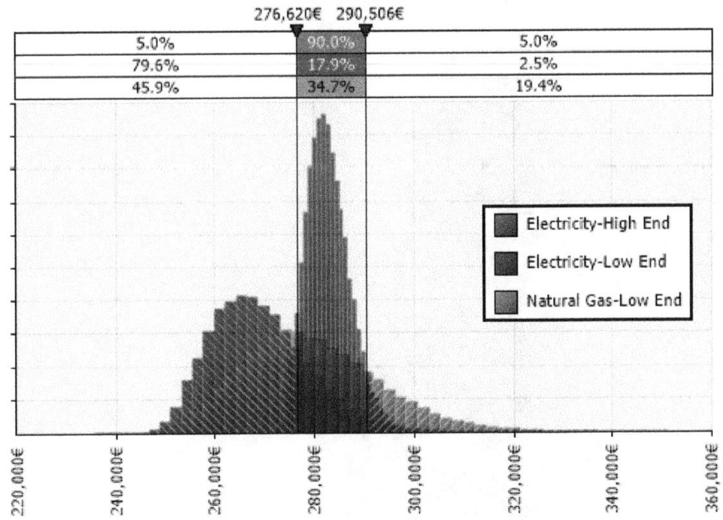

distribution for the NPC of all the investment scenarios. First comes the comparison of the NPCs of the high-end scenarios, and the results are presented in Figure 5:

Then, the comparison of the NPCs of all the low-end investment scenarios, and the results are presented in Figure 6:

From the figures above, the conclusion can be drawn that of the high-end scenarios the most competitive is the electricity-based one, since it has the lowest NPC. At the same time, in the chart of the low-end scenarios the electricity-based and the natural gas-based are highly overlapping. Therefore, the comparison of all these scenarios is needed in the same chart to determine the two most competitive that will be compared in the final stage. This comparison is shown in Figure 7:

It is obvious that the two most competitive scenarios are the low-end electricity-based and the low-end natural gas-based. However, since those two are highly overlapping it is difficult to decipher which one is better. In order to determine the probability of one scenario being better than the other, a new distribution evaluating the difference of the scenarios' NPCs needs to be created. This distribution represents the value 'NPC (Natural Gas) – NPC (Electricity)', since it can be expected that the electricity-based scenario should be more economical. This conclusion can be

Figure 8. Distribution of the NPC (natural gas) – NPC (electricity) of the low-end investment scenarios

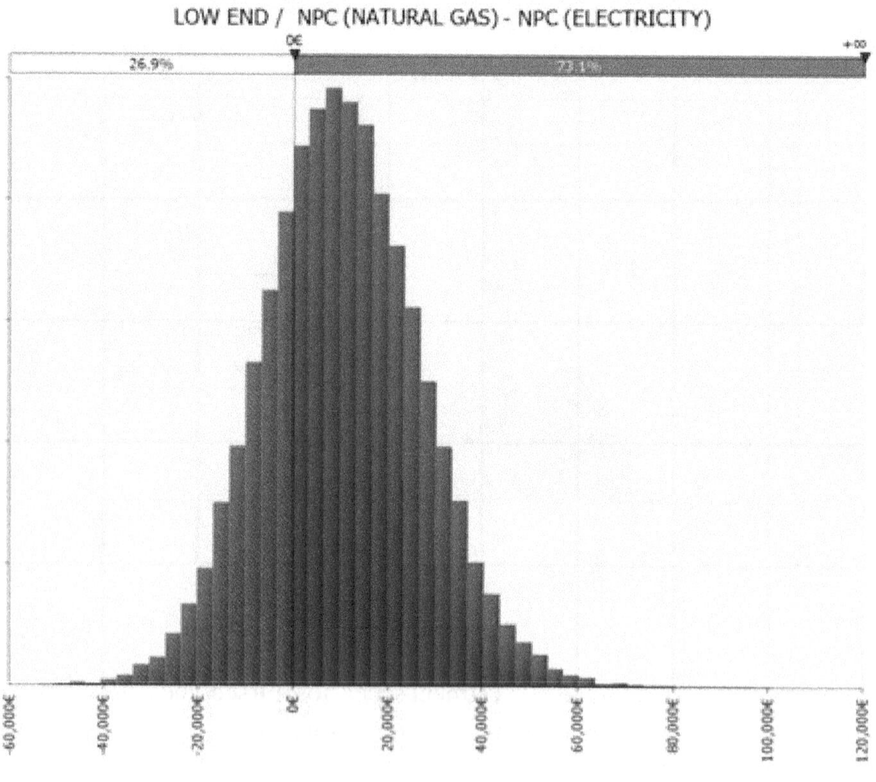

drawn because the heat pumps, which are used in the electricity-based scenarios, have much higher Coefficient of Performance (COP) than natural gas burners, thus are more energy efficient. Therefore, whenever the value of this distribution is above zero, then the natural gas-based scenario is more expensive. This distribution is presented in Figure 8.

According to Figure 8, the natural gas-based scenario is more expensive 73% of the time. Moreover, given that the initial cost of the electricity-based scenario is higher by 6.900 €, which is less than the median of the distribution (9.900 €), it can be said that the electricity-based one is a solid investment. Therefore, the results encourage the adoption of the low-end electricity-based scenario, even though it does not possess the highest efficiency. This outcome is very interesting for further research as it shows that under certain circumstances, the low-end electricity-based scenario may outperform the high-end scenario and thus make the lower investment yield a better outcome than the higher one. However, this should not be regarded as a definite conclusion and the proposed method should be followed on a case-by-case basis to indicate the proper action for each case.

5. CONCLUSION

Risk-based LCCA is not commonly used in residential construction projects. On this account, this chapter proposed an LCCA approach for such projects that incorporates the principles of risk management. Moreover, it presents the risk identification process for the construction industry, based on current literature and opinions of several experts of the industry. This process gave off an RBS (Figure 1) covering all the stages of a construction project's life cycle as well as a list of energy-related risks (Table 2). Finally, it presented an illustrative case on a residential construction project of a five-storey apartment building which is currently being built in Greece, focusing on the heating and lighting expenses throughout its life cycle, using MCS.

The findings of this chapter are useful for anyone interested in residential construction industry, since the chapter covers the previously uncharted territory of residential risk based LCCA. Firstly, the proposed approach can be implemented into a vast number of construction projects, providing the stakeholders with more tools for their decision-making. Furthermore, the RBS created for the construction industry can provide the basis for the risk identification of any construction project. Ultimately, the application of the proposed approach on the illustrative case presents a guideline for future implementation of the approach and its results give a clear picture for the best investment scenario.

The current approach is not coming without limitations. The RBS provided in this study is not exhaustive. A future study could increase the depth and width of the RBS to come up with a more detailed analysis. Moreover, future studies could examine the efficiency of the proposed approach. Risk based LCCA is very promising in the decision-making process of the construction industry, and its current development indicates that it will significantly assist future projects.

REFERENCES

Abdelkhalek, H. A., Refaie, H. S., & Aziz, R. F. (2020). Optimization of time and cost through learning curve analysis. *Ain Shams Engineering Journal, 11*(4), 1069–1082. doi:10.1016/j.asej.2019.12.007

Antoniou, F. (2021). Delay Risk Assessment Models for Road Projects. *Systems, 9*(70), 70. Advance online publication. doi:10.3390ystems9030070

Basak, S., & Makarov, D. (2014). Strategic Asset Allocation in Money Management. *The Journal of Finance, 69*(1), 179–217. doi:10.1111/jofi.12106

Belany, P., Hrabovsky, P., & Kolkova, Z. (2021). Combination of lighting retrofit and life cycle cost analysis for energy efficiency improvement in buildings. *Energy Reports, 7*, 2470–2483. doi:10.1016/j.egyr.2021.04.044

Bilal, M., Oyedele, L., Kusimo, H., Owolabi, H., Akanbi, L., Ajayi, A., Akinade, O., & Davilla Delgado, M. (2019). Investigating profitability performance of construction projects using big data: A project analytics approach. *Journal of Building Engineering, 26*, 100850. doi:10.1016/j.jobe.2019.100850

Boussabaine, A., & Kirham, R. (2008). *Whole Life-Cycle Costing: Risk and Risk Responses*. Blackwell Publishing.

Bull, J. W. (2003). *Life Cycle Costing for Construction*. John Wiley and Sons. doi:10.4324/9780203487723

Dhillon, B. S. (2009). *Life Cycle Costing for Engineers*. CRC Press.

Di Giuseppe, E., Massi, A., & D'Orazio, M. (2017). Probabilistic Life Cycle Cost Analysis of Building Energy Efficiency Measures: Selection and Characterization of the Stochastic Inputs through a Case Study. *Procedia Engineering, 180*, 491–501. doi:10.1016/j.proeng.2017.04.208

Diamantas, V., Kirytopoulos, K., & Leopoulos, V. (2007). Project's duration prediction: Traditional tools or simulation. *World Review of Entrepreneurship, Management and Sustainable Development, 3*(3), 317–333. doi:10.1504/WREMSD.2007.014049

Fregonara, E., Ferrando, D. G., & Pattono, S. (2018). Economic-environmental sustainability in building projects: Introducing risk and uncertainty in LCCE and LCCA. *Sustainability (Basel), 10*(6), 1901. doi:10.3390u10061901

Georgiadou, M. C. (2014). Future-proofed energy design approaches for achieving low-energy homes: Enhancing the code for sustainable homes. *Buildings, 4*(3), 488–519. doi:10.3390/buildings4030488

Georgiadou, M. C., Hacking, T., & Guthrie, P. (2012). A conceptual framework for future-proofing the energy performance of buildings. *Energy Policy, 47*, 145–155. doi:10.1016/j.enpol.2012.04.039

Giuffrida, M., Jiang, H., & Mangiaracina, R. (2021). Investigating the relationships between uncertainty types and risk management strategies in cross-border e-commerce logistics. *International Journal of Logistics Management, 32*(4), 1406–1433. doi:10.1108/IJLM-04-2020-0158

International Organization for Standardization. (2006*) Environmental management – Life cycle assessment – Principles and framework* (ISO No. 14040). Retrieved from https://www.iso.org/standard/37456.html

International Organization for Standardization. (2015) *Environmental management systems – Requirements with guidance for use* (ISO No. 14001). Retrieved from https://www.iso.org/standard/60857.html

International Organization for Standardization. (2017) *Building and constructed assets – Service life planning – Part 5: Life-cycle costing* (ISO No. 15686-5). Retrieved from https://www.iso.org/standard/61148.html

Jepson, J., Kirytopoulos, K., & London, K. (2020). Insights into the application of risk tools and techniques by construction project managers. *International Journal of Construction Management, 20*(8), 848–866. doi:10.1080/15623599.2018.1494673

Kirytopoulos, K. (2021). *Risk Management in Projects and Organizations* (1st ed.). Kleidarithmos.

Kumar, D., Alam, M., Zou, P. X. W., Sanjayan, J. G., & Memon, R. A. (2020). Comparative analysis of building insulation material properties and performance. *Renewable & Sustainable Energy Reviews, 131*(110038), 110038. Advance online publication. doi:10.1016/j.rser.2020.110038

Leopoulos, V. N., Kirytopoulos, K. A., & Malandrakis, C. (2006). Risk management for SMEs: Tools to use and how. *Production Planning and Control, 17*(3), 322–332. doi:10.1080/09537280500285136

Lu, Y., & Gong, P. P., Tang, Y., Sun, S., & Li, Q. (2021). BIM-integrated construction safety risk assessment at the design stage of building projects, *Automation in Construction, 124*(103553). doi:10.1016/j.autcon.2021.103553

Marinelli, M., Petroutsatou, K., Fragkakis, N., & Lambropoulos, S. (2018). Rethinking new public infrastructure value for money in recession times: The Greek case. *International Journal of Construction Management, 18*(4), 331–342. doi:10.1080/15623599.2017.1358131

Merková, M., Drábek, J., & Jelačić, D. (2013). Application of risk analysis in business investment decision-making [Primjena analize rizika u donošenju odluka o poslovnim investicijama]. *Drvna Industrija, 64*(4), 313–322. doi:10.5552/drind.2013.1317

Moretti, L., Cantisani, G., & Di Mascio, P. (2016). Management of road tunnels: Construction, maintenance and lighting costs. *Tunnelling and Underground Space Technology, 51*, 84–89. doi:10.1016/j.tust.2015.10.027

Noshadravan, A., Miller, T. R., & Gregory, J. G. (2017). A lifecycle cost analysis of residential buildings including natural hazard risk. *Journal of Construction Engineering and Management, 143*(7), 04017017. doi:10.1061/(ASCE)CO.1943-7862.0001286

Odedairo, B. O., & Olenloa, O. E. (2021). Scheduling of Post-Flood Recovery Project with Flexible Project Structure. *Journal of Engineering, Project, and Production Management, 11*(2), 118–126. doi:10.2478/jeppm-2021-0012

Parra Márquez, C., Crespo Márquez, A., González-Prida Díaz, V., Gómez Fernández, J.F., Kristjanpoller Rodríguez, F., Viveros Gunckel, P. (2017). Economic impact of a failure using life-cycle cost analysis. *Advanced Maintenance Modelling for Asset Management: Techniques and Methods for Complex Industrial Systems*, 213-243. doi:10.1007/978-3-319-58045-6_9

Petroutsatou, K., Maravas, A., & Saramourtsis, A. (2021). A life cycle model for estimating road tunnel cost. *Tunnelling and Underground Space Technology, 111*, 103858. doi:10.1016/j.tust.2021.103858

Plebankiewicz, E., Zima, K., & Wieczorek, D. (2016). Life Cycle Cost Modelling of Buildings with Consideration of the Risk. *Archives of Civil Engineering, 62*(2), 149–166. doi:10.1515/ace-2015-0071

Prater, J., Kirytopoulos, K., & Ma, T. (2017). Optimism bias within the project management context: A systematic quantitative literature review. *International Journal of Managing Projects in Business, 10*(2), 370–385. doi:10.1108/IJMPB-07-2016-0063

Rostami, A., Sommerville, J., Wong, I. L., & Lee, C. (2015). Risk management implementation in small and medium enterprises in the UK construction industry. *Engineering, Construction, and Architectural Management*, *22*(1), 91–107. doi:10.1108/ECAM-04-2014-0057

Ruffle, B., Henderson, J., Murphy-Hagan, C., Kirkwood, G., Wolf, F., & Edwards, D. A. (2018). Application of probabilistic risk assessment: Evaluating remedial alternatives at the Portland Harbor Superfund Site. *Integrated Environmental Assessment and Management*, *14*(1), 63–78. doi:10.1002/ieam.1999 PMID:29105341

Savvides, S. (1994). Risk analysis in investment appraisal. *Project Appraisal*, *9*(1), 3–18. doi:10.1080/02688867.1994.9726923

Shaffie, S. S., & Jaaman, S. H. (2016). Monte Carlo on Net Present Value for Capital Investment in Malaysia. *Procedia: Social and Behavioral Sciences*, *219*, 688–693. doi:10.1016/j.sbspro.2016.05.052

Sieglinde, F. (2016, September 19). *Life-Cycle Cost Analysis (LCCA)*. Whole Building Design Guide. https://www.wbdg.org/resources/life-cycle-cost-analysis-lcca

Smith, M., Bevacqua, A., Tembe, S., & Lal, P. (2021). Life cycle analysis (LCA) of residential ground source heat pump systems: A comparative analysis of energy efficiency in New Jersey. *Sustainable Energy Technologies and Assessments*, *47*(101364), 101364. Advance online publication. doi:10.1016/j.seta.2021.101364

Tziralis, G., Kirytopoulos, K., Rentizelas, A., & Tatsiopoulos, I. (2009). Holistic Investment Assessment: Optimization. *Risk Appraisal and Decision Making. MDE. Managerial and Decision Economics*, *30*(6), 393–403. doi:10.1002/mde.1458

Wang, N., Chang, Y. C., & El-Sheikh, A. A. (2012). Monte Carlo simulation approach to life cycle cost management. *Structure and Infrastructure Engineering*, *8*(8), 739–746. doi:10.1080/15732479.2010.481304

Chapter 3
ESG in Construction Risk Management:
A Strategic Roadmap for Controlling Risks and Maximizing Profits

Konstantina Ragazou
University of Western Macedonia, Greece

Ioannis Passas
https://orcid.org/0000-0002-1261-2878
Hellenic Mediterranean University, Greece

Alexandros Garefalakis
https://orcid.org/0000-0001-7980-3743
Hellenic Mediterranean University, Greece

Constantin Zopounidis
Technical University of Crete, Greece & Audencia Business School, France

ABSTRACT

ESG refers to environmental, social, and governance in the construction sector and can contribute to the sustainability of the companies in the construction sector. This indicates that while planning and developing a project from beginning to end, all ESG risks should be properly considered. ESG risk management and reporting are particularly significant in the construction sector. A strong ESG approach may improve supply chain efficiency, minimize health and safety concerns, reduce emissions, and encourage effective investment. Managing ESG risks is a great way for businesses engaged in the construction sector to attract investors and boost senior management expectations. This chapter aims to illustrate how a construction

DOI: 10.4018/978-1-6684-7786-1.ch003

company may mitigate the risks faced within the use of ESG risk management. Findings illustrate that strategies based on ESG risk management can help companies in the construction sector to protect the environment and society and create long-term value for their business.

INTRODUCTION

ESG broadly refers to analyzing a company's environmental, social, and governance policies, their effects, and the company's advancement compared to benchmarks. Risk management is a function of an ESG program. The performance of a company's ESG initiatives is being monitored by a wide range of stakeholders, including communities, consumers, workers, and government organizations. For instance, ESG data, such as ESG scores or ratings, may be used by lenders and investors to evaluate a company's risk exposure and potential future financial performance. To make informed advocacy and purchasing decisions, communities and consumers may be interested in learning about a company's environmental and social policies (DasGupta, 2022; Sabbaghi, 2022).

Thus, components of the environmental, social, and corporate governance (ESG) agenda have been and will continue to be a high priority for the construction business due to health and safety concerns and the industry's strong reliance on labor. Similar to this, governance has long been a hot subject in the industry due to the scale and complexity of contracts, competitive bidding procedures, and the necessity to interact with both public and private parties as well as to avoid bribery, corruption, and anticompetitive activity (Binhadab et al., 2021; Jha, 2019). All industries are focusing on the environmental issue, but buildings and construction cause 39%[1] of the world's carbon emissions. Thus, contractors must prioritize these business-critical environmental and carbon reduction measures. In the construction sector, which, like many industries, is continuing to strengthen its emphasis on ESG and convey the implications to stakeholders, these areas now represent the main pillars of their ESG agendas. Because their value in terms of growth and risk management has increased, the focus has shifted from conventional philanthropy and employee volunteerism to encouraging a more comprehensive integration of these subjects in business strategy. Corporate risk management and strategic business imperatives are increasingly supported by effective ESG programs (Baldi & Pandimiglio, 2022).

Including ESG considerations in corporate decision-making is sound risk management, regardless of the size of the business and sector. Every firm deals with a range of ESG-related problems, some of which have the potential to be significant and harm a company's finances or image. The likelihood of an ESG-related event or scandal is also enhanced for any firm that ignores environmental, social, and governance concerns. In other words, ESG risk is a common business risk, and ESG risk management should be a typical component of a company's risk management procedures. Most businesses are addressing some of these risks despite lacking an official ESG strategy (Singhania & Saini, 2022). Although the term "ESG" might sound like a hip new buzzword, a business, in the case of the construction sector, has probably been managing certain environmental, social, and corporate governance risks for a while. The urgency and method of the appeals to solve these concerns distinguish them now. More than ever, companies must define clear goals for risk reduction, use effective metrics to track their success and provide comprehensive reporting. The good news is that several services are available to assist with ESG risk management, so it need not be a burden. Particularly for medium-sized businesses, which can hardly afford to encounter a significant ESG scandal, the advantages of acting considerably outweigh the costs of in action (Galletta et al., 2023; Zhang et al., 2023).

The scope of this chapter is to highlight the importance of ESG risk management in the construction sector and to investigate the research trends in the field. Also, the chapter is organized as follows: Section 2 presents the importance of ESG in construction management, Section 3 highlights the issue of monitoring and reporting on ESG performance, Section 4 illustrates the engagement of stakeholders in ESG in Construction Risk Management, Section 5 presents the continuous improvement of companies in the construction sector based on the ESG performance, Section 6 present a set of case studies of Successful ESG Integration in Construction Risk Management. Finally, Section 7 concludes the chapter and proposes future research ideas.

1.1 ESG Risk Management vs. Traditional Enterprise Risk Management

Environmental, Social, and Governance (ESG) risk management has gained significant importance in recent years, as companies worldwide are focusing on sustainable growth and ethical practices. ESG risk management is a comprehensive approach that differs from traditional Enterprise Risk Management (ERM) in several ways (Eccles and Serafeim, 2011).

1. Scope: ESG risk management encompasses a broader scope of risks compared to ERM. While ERM is centered around financial, strategic, and operational risks that directly impact a company's bottom line, ESG risk management takes into account environmental, social, and governance risks that indirectly affect the organization's financial performance, reputation, and long-term sustainability. For instance, ESG risks include climate change, labor practices,

and corporate governance, which may not necessarily have immediate financial implications.

2. Stakeholder perspective: Traditional ERM primarily focuses on addressing the concerns of shareholders and ensuring that a company's financial performance remains robust. ESG risk management, on the other hand, considers the interests of a wider range of stakeholders, such as employees, customers, suppliers, regulators, and the communities in which a company operates. This shift in focus acknowledges that businesses have a responsibility to create value for all stakeholders, not just shareholders.
3. Time horizon: ERM usually deals with short- to medium-term risks that can directly impact a company's financial performance and stability. In contrast, ESG risk management is concerned with long-term risks that can affect a company's ability to sustain growth, maintain its social license to operate, and preserve its reputation. By addressing these long-term risks, ESG risk management contributes to a company's resilience and adaptability in a rapidly changing world.
4. Materiality assessment: ESG risk management involves a more comprehensive materiality assessment than traditional ERM. It requires companies to identify, assess, and prioritize ESG risks based on their potential impact on the organization and its stakeholders. This involves understanding and analyzing how a company's operations and value chain are linked to ESG issues, as well as monitoring and reporting on these risks.
5. Integration with strategy: ESG risk management is integrated with a company's overall strategy and is aligned with its purpose and values. Unlike traditional ERM, which is often seen as a separate function, ESG risk management is embedded across all levels of an organization, from the board of directors to front-line employees. This integration ensures that ESG risks are managed proactively and holistically, contributing to the long-term success of the organization.

In conclusion, ESG risk management represents a significant shift from traditional ERM, with an emphasis on long-term sustainability and stakeholder value creation. By adopting ESG risk management, companies can better anticipate and address risks that have far-reaching implications for their financial performance, reputation, and social license to operate (Eccles and Serafeim, 2013).

2. ESG IN CONSTRUCTION MANAGEMENT: WHY IS IT IMPORTANT FOR THE SECTOR?

Construction businesses' adoption of ESG standards is a one-way choice. Industry key players in Europe have already proceeded to significant investments in the environmental pillar sector through projects that support the European Green Deal. And they keep going. Every year, experts state that there has "never been a larger stake" for all businesses worldwide to implement ESG principles. Particularly in the construction sector, businesses have incorporated ESG concepts into their strategic planning and daily operations while also coming under increased scrutiny for their comparative performance. Construction companies and their projects must prioritize and innovate in how they define, design, implement, and demonstrate their ESG strategies to remain competitive and stay true to their commitment to a better world. This will ensure that they not only adhere to regulatory and investor requirements, but also benefit the communities in which they operate (Gangi et al., 2021).

ESG is a term that stands for environmental, social, and governance in the construction business (Passas et al., 2022) This means that all ESG risks should be considered from start to end when designing and conducting a project. ESG risk management and reporting are especially critical in the construction business. An effective ESG approach helps simplify supply chains, eliminate health and safety hazards, cut emissions, and contribute to responsible investing. Thus, managing ESG risks on the construction site is an excellent method to attract investors, acquire clients, and raise senior management expectations. Also, it may result in a safer and more efficient workplace for employees. However, ESG performance may also be linked to a financial return for the company. For several years, academics and business researchers have debated the influence of ESG performance on company value and profitability. Much research has historically focused on how corporate governance affects stock price performance. In response to the growing interest in climate change, the circular economy, and biodiversity challenges, studies investigated the relationship between environmental performance and stock price performance. With the current COVID-19 pandemic the influence of shifting demographics and societal concerns on stock returns, with a special emphasis on health, safety, and welfare, as well as human capital management challenges such as employee (Naffa and Fain, 2020)

Moreover, ESG may help a business manage risk by reducing it. This may be accomplished in the construction industry by developing risk management practices that are intended to assist businesses in the sector in coping with a variety of hazards. This spectrum mostly included financial, regulatory, or operational risks in the past. ESG risks, which address environmental, social, and governance concerns, are a new hazard category that always a main concern of the Construction Industry, and now it's even more so through the ESG. (Giese et al, 2021). For any business or organization, ESG risk management has become a crucial component of risk analysis and management. Based on the ESG risks, these cover a wide range of topics, from greenhouse gas emissions and water consumption to anti-discrimination laws, pay equity, and corporate practices. (Korinth and Lueg, (2022) The above risks are primarily divided into three categories: (i) Environment risks, which represent issues related to greenhouse gas emissions (GHG), deforestation, pollution, water consumption, biodiversity, trash, etc., (ii) Social risks that are associated with social factors, such as customer relations, human rights, labor rights, employee relations, occupational safety and health, supply chains, diversity, and inclusion and (iii) risks associated with the pillar of governance include matters like succession planning, board management practices, executive compensation diversity among board and management, corruption, fraud, data hygiene, security, equity (Giese et al., 2019)

Thus, companies in the construction industry that use ESG strategies are better able to comprehend the many risk types, manage them, and provide value through the numerous advantages that ESG in risk management may provide. One advantage of ESG risk management is that it modifies an 'organization's culture. Compared to other businesses, which might be reactive, those that place a greater emphasis on risk management tend to be more proactive. Companies in the construction sector are forced by risk management to carefully examine each of their business operations and consider what may go wrong. Moreover, companies may predict potential problems and become more proactive using this thorough what-if research. Also, businesses that heavily utilize risk management see fewer business interruptions since such issues are anticipated and resolved early on. The proactive strategy is particularly beneficial since it enables businesses in the construction sector to spot unsuccessful initiatives early on. The ongoing feedback assists businesses within the industry determine if investing more money in a failing project, would help it succeed or whether it is simply throwing good money after bad (Amel-Zadeh and Serafeim, 2018)

Additionally, with the development of ESG risk management strategies businesses in the construction sector can reduce their losses. These are the moments when badly run businesses find it difficult to survive. Contrarily, businesses that adopt ESG risk management procedures in place typically reduce their losses. Because of this, these businesses continue to be competitive. In fact, it could even become better. It is a well-known fact that businesses with superior ESG risk management procedures continue to operate and have a lot of cash on hand when unfavourable occurrences, such as recessions, occur. This explains why some businesses appear to have the additional money needed to make purchases amid a crisis. Processes for managing risks also compel active communication between various departments and stakeholders. This communication is beneficial since it makes the business more competitive. Finally, businesses with established ESG risk management strategies have superior financial management than competing firms. This is due to the fact that they frequently examine their financial data carefully and attempt to eliminate any waste. Consequently, these businesses understand their processes and budgets better. They may develop more effective budgets that allocate money in the most effective way possible to achieve the company's objectives. Budgets in these businesses don't have to be based on conjecture. The current research paper examines the contribution of ESG risk management in the construction sector and investigate the research trends within the field (Ragazou et al., 2022).

Therefore, once ESG risks have been identified, developing and implementing ESG policies and procedures is essential to address them. Effective ESG policies can help to manage risks, improve compliance, and support the company's reputation. ESG policies and procedures should be integrated into the overall risk management plan for the project and communicated to all stakeholders involved. This includes contractors, suppliers, and employees. It is also essential to ensure that all relevant regulations and standards are incorporated into ESG policies and procedures. One approach to developing ESG policies and procedures is to follow established frameworks, such as the Global Reporting Initiative (GRI) Standards, the Sustainability Accounting Standards Board (SASB), or the Task Force on Climate-related Financial Disclosures (TCFD). These frameworks guide the key sustainability issues companies should address and the metrics used to measure progress (Passas et al., 2022).

Also, it is important to involve stakeholders in developing ESG policies and procedures. Stakeholder engagement can help to identify the most significant ESG risks and ensure that policies and procedures are practical and effective. Furthermore, training programs and awareness campaigns can help to ensure that all stakeholders understand and follow ESG policies and procedures. This can include training on sustainable construction practices, waste reduction, energy efficiency, and social responsibility. Finally, ESG policies and procedures should be regularly reviewed and updated to remain relevant and effective. This includes regularly monitoring ESG performance, reviewing the impact of policies and procedures, and seeking feedback from stakeholders. Developing and implementing effective ESG policies and procedures is critical to managing ESG risks and creating value for the company. By integrating ESG policies and procedures into construction risk management, companies can improve their environmental and social impact, support compliance, and protect theirrreputation (Henriksson et al. 2019).

3. MONITORING AND REPORTING ON ESG PERFORMANCE

Monitoring and reporting ESG performance is a crucial component of ESG integration in construction risk management. By tracking ESG metrics and reporting on performance, companies can ensure they meet sustainability goals and stay accountable to stakeholders. In this chapter, we will explore best practices for monitoring and reporting ESG performance in construction, drawing on insights from recent research (Cambrea et al., 2023)

3.1 ESG Metrics and Reporting Requirements

ESG metrics are key performance indicators that companies use to measure their environmental, social, and governance impact. In construction, ESG metrics may include energy consumption, water usage, waste generation, and greenhouse gas emissions. Using standardized ESG metrics can help companies compare their performance against industry peers and track progress toward sustainability goals.

In addition to tracking ESG metrics, companies may also be required to report ESG performance to stakeholders. Regulatory requirements for ESG reporting vary by country and region, but there is a growing trend toward mandatory ESG reporting for large companies. For example, companies with more than 500 employees in the European Union must report on their ESG performance under the Non-Financial Reporting Directive. In the United States, the Securities and Exchange Commission has proposed a rule requiring public companies to disclose information about their climate-related risks and opportunities (Cruz et al, 2023).

3.2 Best Practices for Monitoring and Reporting on ESG Performance

To effectively monitor and report on ESG performance, companies should follow best practices that align with the specific risks and opportunities in the construction industry. Here are some of the best practices that have been identified in recent research:

3.2.1 Use Technology to Track ESG Metrics

The use of technology can greatly improve the accuracy and efficiency of ESG metric tracking. For example, real-time sensors can be installed on construction sites to track energy and water usage. At the same time, software can be used to analyze data and identify opportunities for improvement. By automating the collection and analysis of ESG data, companies can save time and resources while improving the accuracy of their reporting (Liu et al., 2023).

3.2.2 Engage Employees in ESG Performance Monitoring

Employees play a critical role in ESG performance monitoring, as they are often the ones who are directly responsible for energy, water, and waste management on construction sites (Ampese et al., 2022; Sahu et al., 2021; Shaheen et al., 2022). By engaging employees in ESG performance monitoring, companies can build a culture of sustainability and empower employees to identify opportunities for improvement. This can also help to improve employee morale and retention, as employees feel a sense of purpose in contributing to a more sustainable future.

3.2.3 Use ESG Reporting Frameworks to Improve Transparency

ESG reporting frameworks, such as the Global Reporting Initiative or the Sustainability Accounting Standards Board, provide a standardized way to report ESG performance. By using these frameworks, companies can improve transparency and comparability of their ESG reporting, which can help to build stakeholder trust and reduce the risk of legal and regulatory action (Tamini and Sebastianelli, 2017)

3.2.4 Provide Contextual Information in ESG Reporting

Contextual information, such as a company's sustainability strategy or specific risks and opportunities in the construction industry, can help stakeholders better understand a company's ESG performance''''. For example, a company may report on its use of sustainable materials in construction but also provide information on the availability and cost of these materials. By providing contextual information, companies can improve the relevance and usefulness of their ESG reporting to stakeholders (Gorshunov et al., 2021; Masud et al., 2022).

Concluding, monitoring, and reporting ESG performance is critical to ESG integration in construction risk management. By tracking ESG metrics and reporting on performance, companies can ensure they meet sustainability goals and stay accountable to stakeholders. Best practices for monitoring and reporting ESG performance in construction include using technology to track ESG metrics, engaging employees in ESG performance monitoring, using ESG reporting frameworks to improve transparency, and providing contextual information in ESG reporting. Effective monitoring and reporting on ESG performance can also help companies identify new sustainability and risk reduction opportunities. For example, by tracking energy usage on construction sites, companies may identify opportunities to switch to renewable energy sources or optimize energy use through building design. By engaging employees in ESG performance monitoring, companies may also identify innovations or best practices for sustainability in the construction industry. However, it is crucial to recognize that effective ESG monitoring and reporting is not a one-time event but an ongoing process. Companies should regularly review and update their ESG metrics and reporting practices to ensure that they meet the evolving needs of stakeholders and keep up with changing industry trends. Companies can better control risks and maximize profits by continuously improving ESG performance monitoring and reporting practices while contributing to a more sustainable future.

4. ENGAGING STAKEHOLDERS IN ESG IN CONSTRUCTION RISK MANAGEMENT

Engaging stakeholders, including employees, customers, and local communities, is essential to ESG in construction risk management. Companies can better understand their concerns and expectations by engaging with stakeholders and working to address them. This can help build trust and improve the company's reputation, reducing the risk of legal and regulatory action.

4.1 Engaging With Employees

Employees are an important stakeholder group in ESG in construction risk management. They are responsible for implementing ESG policies and procedures daily, and their actions can significantly impact a project's environmental and social outcomes. Engaging with employees can help to ensure that they understand the importance of ESG and are motivated to contribute to the company's sustainability goals. One way to engage employees is through training and development programs. These programs can help to raise awareness of ESG issues and provide employees with the skills and knowledge they need to implement ESG policies and procedures effectively. For example, a study by Zhang and Li (2021) found that providing ESG training to construction workers improved their knowledge of ESG and increased their motivation to engage in sustainable practices. Companies can also engage employees through employee engagement programs. These programs can involve soliciting employee feedback on ESG issues and incorporating their ideas and suggestions into the company's sustainability strategy. For example, a study by Yu, Chen, and Sun (2020) found that involving employees in developing ESG policies and procedures improved their engagement in sustainability practices (Ju et al., 2020; Lu et al., 2022).

4.2 Engaging With Customers

Customers are another important stakeholder group in ESG in construction risk management. They are increasingly interested in the environmental and social impact of the products and services they consume and are often willing to pay a premium for sustainable products and services. Engaging with customers can help build loyalty and increase sales while improving the company's reputation and reducing the risk of legal and regulatory action. One way to engage customers is through sustainability reporting. Sustainability reports can provide customers with information on the company's ESG performance and demonstrate the company's commitment to sustainability. For example, a study found that sustainability reporting improved customer loyalty and trust in the company. Companies can also engage customers through sustainable product design (Alturayeif et al., 2023). By designing environmentally and socially responsible products, companies can differentiate themselves from their competitors and appeal to sustainability-conscious customers. For example, a study by Alkhatib and Zambrano (2020) found that consumers were willing to pay more for construction materials that were certified as environmentally sustainable (Alaimo et al., 2022).

4.3 Engaging With Local Communities

Local communities are another important stakeholder group in ESG in construction risk management. They are directly affected by the environmental and social impacts of construction projects, and their support or opposition can significantly impact a project's success. Engaging with local communities can help build trust and reduce legal and regulatory action risk (Bax et al., 2023). One way to engage with local communities is through community consultation programs. These programs can involve soliciting feedback from residents on ESG issues and incorporating their ideas and suggestions into the project design and management process. For example, a study by Ali and Haidar (2019) found that community consultation improved the social sustainability of a construction project by addressing local concerns and needs. Companies can also engage with local communities through social investment programs. These programs can involve investing in local community development projects like schools, hospitals, and community centers. For example, a study by Laperriere and Zhang (2020) found that social investment improved the social sustainability of a construction project by building trust and supporting local development.

Engaging stakeholders is an essential part of ESG in construction risk management. By engaging with employees, customers, and local communities, companies can better understand their concerns and expectations and work to address them. This can help build trust and improve the company's reputation, reducing the risk of legal and regulatory action.

Employee engagement can be achieved through training and development programs that raise awareness of ESG issues and provide employees with the skills and knowledge they need to implement ESG policies and procedures effectively. Additionally, companies can engage employees through employee engagement programs that involve soliciting employee feedback on ESG issues and incorporating their ideas and suggestions into the company's sustainability strategy. Customer engagement is achieved through sustainability reporting, which provides customers with information on the company's ESG performance and demonstrates the company's commitment to sustainability (Shu & Tan, 2023; Singhania & Saini, 2022). Sustainable product design is another way to engage customers as it can help differentiate the company from its competitors and appeal to customers interested in sustainability.

Local community engagement is achieved through community consultation programs that involve soliciting feedback from residents on ESG issues and incorporating their ideas and suggestions into the project design and management process. Social investment programs are another way to engage local communities by investing in local community development projects, such as schools, hospitals, and community centers. Generally, engaging stakeholders in ESG in construction risk management is critical for improving construction projects' social and environmental outcomes. It helps build trust, improve reputation, and reduce the risk of legal and regulatory action risk. Companies that successfully engage with stakeholders on ESG issues can gain a competitive advantage, improve their financial performance, and contribute to a more sustainable future.

5. CONSTRUCTION COMPANIES SHOULD ACHIEVE CONTINUOUS IMPROVEMENT IN ESG PERFORMANCE

5.1 Importance of Continuous Improvement in ESG Performance

The construction industry is dynamic and rapidly changing; the same applies to ESG issues. Companies must adapt to new technologies, regulations, and stakeholder expectations to remain competitive and reduce their environmental and societal impact. Continuous improvement of ESG performance is critical to adapting to these changes. Continuous improvement also helps to build credibility and trust with stakeholders. As companies work to improve their ESG performance, they demonstrate a commitment to sustainable practices. They show that they are taking proactive steps to reduce their impact on the environment and society. This can increase stakeholder trust and better relationships with customers, employees, and local communities (DasGupta, 2022).

5.2 Steps Involved in Achieving Continuous Improvement in ESG Performance

There are several steps that companies can take to achieve continuous improvement in ESG performance (Figure 1):

Figure 1. Main steps to achieve continuous improvement in ESG performance

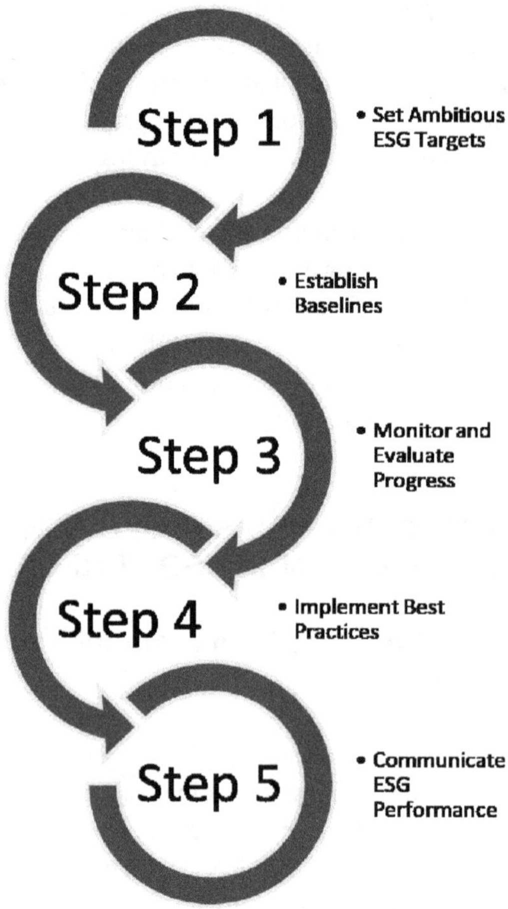

- Set Ambitious ESG Targets: The first step in achieving continuous improvement is to set ambitious ESG targets. These targets should be specific, measurable, and achievable within a reasonable timeframe. By setting ambitious targets, companies can challenge themselves to improve their ESG performance and demonstrate their commitment to sustainability (Chiu et al., 2019).
- Establish Baselines: Once ESG targets have been set, it is important to establish baselines to measure progress towards these targets. This involves collecting data on key ESG metrics, such as energy consumption, water usage, waste generation, and greenhouse gas emissions. Baseline data can be used to track progress and identify areas for improvement (Kokko et al., 2020).
- Monitor and Evaluate Progress: To achieve continuous improvement, monitoring and evaluating progress towards ESG targets is essential. This involves regularly collecting and analyzing key ESG metrics data to identify improvement areas. Companies should use this data to inform decision-making and adjust their ESG policies and procedures (Wang et al., 2019).
- Implement Best Practices: Companies should seek to implement best practices in ESG performance to achieve continuous improvement. This may involve investing in new technologies, improving supply chain management, or developing new policies and procedures to reduce environmental impact and improve social outcomes (Chiu et al., 2019).

Communicate ESG Performance: Communicating ESG performance is critical to building trust with stakeholders and demonstrating the company's commitment to sustainability. Companies should regularly report on their ESG performance, using transparent and consistent metrics, to demonstrate progress toward their ESG targets (Kokko et al., 2020).

5.3 Benefits of Continuous Improvement in ESG Performance

There are several benefits that companies can realize by achieving continuous improvement in ESG performance:

- Improved Reputation: Companies that continuously improve ESG performance can build a strong reputation for sustainability and demonstrate a commitment to reducing their impact on the environment and society (Chiu et al., 2019).
- Increased Efficiency: Companies can improve efficiency and reduce costs by implementing best practices in ESG performance. For example, reducing energy consumption or waste generation can lead to cost savings and improved operational efficiency (Kokko et al., 2020).

- Enhanced Stakeholder Engagement: By engaging stakeholders in the ESG performance improvement process, companies can build trust and improve relationships with customers, employees, and local communities. This can lead to increased support for the company and reduced risk of legal and reputational issues (Wang et al., 2019).
- Reduced Risk: Achieving continuous improvement in ESG performance can help companies to reduce risk. Companies can avoid legal and regulatory issues and reputational damage by reducing their impact on the environment and society. Companies with strong ESG performance are also more likely to be resilient in natural disasters or other disruptive events (Chiu et al., 2019).

5.4 Regulatory and Investor Support for Continuous Improvement

Achieving continuous improvement of ESG performance is not only the responsibility of companies. Regulators, investors, and other stakeholders also have an essential role in encouraging companies to improve their ESG performance (D'Hondt et al., 2021; Roy et al., 2022). Regulators can set standards and incentives to encourage sustainable practices. For example, governments can provide tax incentives or subsidies for companies that invest in renewable energy or other sustainable technologies. Regulators can also set minimum standards for ESG performance, such as requirements for reporting on greenhouse gas emissions or water usage (Wang et al., 2019). Investors can use their influence to encourage companies to improve their ESG performance. For example, investors can engage with companies on ESG issues, submit shareholder proposals, or divest from companies that do not meet their ESG standards. By using their influence, investors can encourage companies to improve their ESG performance and reduce risk (Chiu et al., 2019).

Including the above, achieving continuous improvement of ESG performance is essential for managing ESG risks and maximizing profits in the construction industry. By setting ambitious targets, establishing baselines, monitoring and evaluating progress, implementing best practices, and communicating their ESG performance to stakeholders, companies can build a strong reputation for sustainability, improve efficiency, enhance stakeholder engagement, and reduce risk. However, continuous improvement is not a one-time event and requires ongoing commitment, investment, and innovation to adapt to changing ESG issues and stakeholder expectations. Regulators and investors also have an important role to play in encouraging companies to improve their ESG performance. Companies, regulators, and investors can create a sustainable future for the construction industry by working together.

6. CASE STUDIES OF SUCCESSFUL ESG INTEGRATION IN CONSTRUCTION RISK MANAGEMENT

While ESG in construction risk management is a relatively new concept, some successful case studies of companies have already integrated ESG into their risk management practices. These companies have demonstrated that ESG can drive innovation, competitiveness, and financial performance. This chapter will explore three case studies of successful ESG integration in construction risk management.

6.1 Case Study 1: Skanska USA

Skanska USA[2], a global construction and development company, has led ESG integration in the construction industry. The company has developed a comprehensive sustainability strategy that includes goals to reduce greenhouse gas emissions, increase the use of renewable energy, and promote diversity and inclusion. Skanska has also established a green construction training program that teaches contractors how to use sustainable materials and practices (Loizia et al., 2021; Vardopoulos et al., 2021). One of Skanska's key ESG initiatives is implementing a Life Cycle Assessment (LCA) tool, which assesses the environmental impact of construction materials and processes throughout the project lifecycle. The LCA tool has helped Skanska to identify opportunities to reduce carbon emissions, waste, and water usage. For example, Skanska has used the LCA tool to develop a low-carbon concrete mix that reduces the carbon footprint of concrete production by up to 40%. Skanska has also demonstrated a commitment to social sustainability by implementing a Community Investment Program that provides funding and support to community projects in areas where the company operates. This has helped to build trust and positive relationships with local communities and stakeholders, reducing the risk of legal and regulatory action.

6.2 Case Study 2: Lendlease

Lendlease[3], an Australian construction and property management company, has been recognized as a leader in ESG integration in the construction industry. The company has developed a comprehensive sustainability strategy that includes targets to reduce greenhouse gas emissions, increase the use of renewable energy, and promote gender diversity. One of Lendlease's key ESG initiatives is using a Sustainable Design Review (SDR) process, which assesses the environmental impact of construction designs and materials. The SDR process has helped Lendlease to identify opportunities to reduce carbon emissions, waste, and water usage. For example, Lendlease has used the SDR process to develop a low-impact timber construction system that reduces the carbon footprint of building construction by up to 30%. Lendlease has also demonstrated a commitment to social sustainability by implementing a Reconciliation Action Plan that promotes Indigenous Australians' social and economic empowerment. This has helped to build positive relationships with Indigenous communities and stakeholders, reducing the risk of legal and regulatory action.

6.3 Case Study 3: Bouygues Construction

Bouygues Construction4, a French construction and engineering company, has led ESG integration in the construction industry. The company has developed a comprehensive sustainability strategy that includes targets to reduce greenhouse gas emissions, increase the use of renewable energy, and promote social inclusion. One of Bouygues' key ESG initiatives is using a Building Information Modeling (BIM) system, which uses digital models to optimize building design and construction processes. The BIM system has helped Bouygues to reduce waste, increase energy efficiency, and improve worker safety. For example, Bouygues has used the BIM system to develop a pre-fabrication process that reduces waste by up to 90% and improves worker safety by reducing on-site construction time. Bouygues has also committed to social sustainability by implementing a Social Charter that promotes fair labor practices and ethical supply chain management. This has helped to build positive relationships with workers, suppliers, and local communities, reducing the risk of legal and regulatory action.

These case studies demonstrate that ESG integration in construction risk management can improve construction companies' environmental, social, and financial performance. By identifying and mitigating ESG risks, these companies have reduced costs, improved efficiency, and built positive stakeholder relationships. They have also positioned themselves as leaders in the construction industry, attracting customers and investors who value sustainability and responsible business practices. However, ESG integration in construction risk management is not without its challenges. These challenges include the need for specialized knowledge and expertise, the cost and complexity of data collection and analysis, and the need to engage stakeholders and build partnerships across the value chain. These challenges can be overcome through collaboration, innovation, and continuous improvement.

7. CONCLUSION AND FUTURE DIRECTIONS FOR ESG IN CONSTRUCTION RISK MANAGEMENT

7.1 Conclusion

This book chapter has explored the importance of integrating environmental, social, and governance (ESG) factors into construction risk management. By addressing ESG risks, companies can control their environmental and social impact, build stakeholder trust, and create long-term value for the business. First, we discussed the importance of identifying ESG risks in construction. These risks can include environmental risks, such as resource depletion, pollution, and climate change; social risks, such as labor exploitation and community displacement; and governance risks, such as corruption and lack of transparency. Companies can develop ESG policies and procedures to address these risks by identifying them (Bontje & Zonneveld, 2019). Second, we explored the process of developing ESG policies and procedures. This involves integrating ESG risks into the overall risk management plan for the project, communicating these policies to all stakeholders involved, and ensuring that they are followed. Third, we discussed the importance of monitoring and reporting on ESG performance. This involves tracking ESG metrics such as energy consumption, water usage, waste generation, and greenhouse gas emissions. Reporting on ESG performance can also help to improve transparency and accountability, improving stakeholder trust and reducing the risk of legal and regulatory action. Fourth, we emphasized the importance of engaging stakeholders in ESG in construction risk management. This includes employees, customers, and local communities. Companies can better understand their concerns and expectations by engaging with stakeholders and working to address them. Fifth, we highlighted the need for continuous improvement of ESG performance. This involves setting ambitious sustainability targets and regularly reviewing progress towards those targets. Companies should also seek to innovate and implement new technologies and practices that can help to reduce environmental impact and improve social outcomes.

7.2 Future Directions

ESG in construction risk management is an evolving field, and there are many future directions that companies can take to improve their performance. Some potential future directions include:

7.2.1 Implementing Sustainable Building Materials

Sustainable building materials are becoming more widely available and cost-effective. Companies can integrate these materials into their projects to reduce environmental impact and improve social outcomes (Vardopoulos, 2018; Vardopoulos et al., 2021).

7.2.2 Utilizing Technology for ESG Management

New technologies, such as Building Information Modeling (BIM) and the Internet of Things (IoT), can help to improve ESG management in construction. For example, BIM can be used to analyze the energy consumption and environmental impact of a building, while IoT can be used to monitor and optimize resource usage.

7.2.3 Collaboration and Partnership

Collaboration and partnerships between companies, government agencies, and NGOs can help address complex construction industry ESG issues. By working together, stakeholders can pool resources, share knowledge and expertise, and create innovative solutions to complex ESG challenges.

7.2.4 Incorporating Social Impact Into Financial Analysis

Incorporating social impact into the financial analysis can help companies better understand their projects' social value. This can help to attract socially responsible investors, improve stakeholder trust, and create long-term value for the business (Peng & Xiong, 2022).

ESG in construction risk management is a critical issue that can significantly impact a business's environment, society, and long-term success. By addressing ESG risks, companies can control their impact and maximize their profits by building stakeholder trust and creating long-term value for the business. We have provided a strategic roadmap for integrating ESG factors into construction risk management. This includes identifying ESG risks, developing ESG policies and procedures, monitoring and reporting on ESG performance, engaging stakeholders, and seeking continuous improvement (Alkaraan et al., 2023). We have also highlighted future directions companies can take to improve their ESG performance, such as utilizing sustainable building materials, incorporating technology, collaborating and partnering, and incorporating social impact into financial analysis (Vardopoulos, 2019; Vardopoulos et al., 2018). Companies need to recognize the importance of ESG in construction risk management and take steps to address these risks. By doing so, they can protect the environment and society and create long-term value for their business.

REFERENCES

Alaimo, L. S., Ciommi, M., Vardopoulos, I., Nosova, B., & Salvati, L. (2022). The Medium-Term Impact of the COVID-19 Pandemic on Population Dynamics: The Case of Italy. *Sustainability, 14*(21), 13995. doi:10.3390/su142113995

Alkaraan, F., Elmarzouky, M., Hussainey, K., & Venkatesh, V. G. (2023). Sustainable strategic investment decision-making practices in UK companies: The influence of governance mechanisms on synergy between industry 4.0 and circular economy. *Technological Forecasting and Social Change*, *187*, 122187. Advance online publication. doi:10.1016/j.techfore.2022.122187

Alturayeif, N., Luqman, H., & Ahmed, M. (2023). A systematic review of machine learning techniques for stance detection and its applications. *Neural Computing & Applications*, *35*(7), 5113–5144. doi:10.100700521-023-08285-7 PMID:36743664

Amel-Zadeh, A., & Serafeim, G. (2018). Why and how investors use ESG information: Evidence from a global survey. *Financial Analysts Journal*, *74*(3), 87–103. doi:10.2469/faj.v74.n3.2

Ampese, L. C., Sganzerla, W. G., Di Domenico Ziero, H., Mudhoo, A., Martins, G., & Forster-Carneiro, T. (2022). Research progress, trends, and updates on anaerobic digestion technology: A bibliometric analysis. *Journal of Cleaner Production*, *331*, 130004. Advance online publication. doi:10.1016/j.jclepro.2021.130004

Baldi, F., & Pandimiglio, A. (2022). The role of ESG scoring and greenwashing risk in explaining the yields of green bonds: A conceptual framework and an econometric analysis. *Global Finance Journal*, *52*, 100711. Advance online publication. doi:10.1016/j.gfj.2022.100711

Bax, K., Sahin, Ö., Czado, C., & Paterlini, S. (2023). ESG, risk, and (tail) dependence. *International Review of Financial Analysis*, *87*, 102513. doi:10.1016/j.irfa.2023.102513

Binhadab, N., Breen, M., & Gillanders, R. (2021). Press freedom and corruption in business-state interactions. *Economic Systems*, *45*(4), 100922. Advance online publication. doi:10.1016/j.ecosys.2021.100922

Cambrea, D. R., Paolone, F., & Cucari, N. (2023). Advisory or monitoring role in ESG scenario: Which women directors are more influential in the Italian context? *Business Strategy and the Environment*, bse.3366. doi:10.1002/bse.3366

Cruz, C. A., & Matos, F. (2023). ESG Maturity: A Software Framework for the Challenges of ESG Data in Investment. *Sustainability (Basel), 15*(3), 2610. doi:10.3390u15032610

D'Hondt, C., Merli, M., & Roger, T. (2021). What drives retail portfolio exposure to ESG factors? *Finance Research Letters*. Advance online publication. doi:10.1016/j.frl.2021.102470

DasGupta, R. (2022). Financial performance shortfall, ESG controversies, and ESG performance: Evidence from firms around the world. *Finance Research Letters, 46*, 102487. Advance online publication. doi:10.1016/j.frl.2021.102487

Eccles, R. G., Serafeim, G., & Krzus, M. P. (2011). Market interest in nonfinancial information. *The Bank of America Journal of Applied Corporate Finance, 23*(4), 113–127. doi:10.1111/j.1745-6622.2011.00357.x

Eccles, R. G., Serafeim, G., Seth, D., & Ming, C. C. Y. (2013). The Performance Frontier: Innovating for a Sustainable Strategy: Interaction. *Harvard Business Review, 91*(7), 17–18.

Galletta, S., Goodell, J. W., Mazzù, S., & Paltrinieri, A. (2023). Bank reputation and operational risk: The impact of ESG. *Finance Research Letters, 51*, 103494. Advance online publication. doi:10.1016/j.frl.2022.103494

Gangi, F., Meles, A., Daniele, L. M., Varrone, N., Salerno, D., & Salerno, D. (2021). ESG criteria in alternative Investments. *The Evolution of Sustainable Investments and Finance: Theoretical Perspectives and New Challenges*, 59-99.

Giese, G., Lee, L. E., Melas, D., Nagy, Z., & Nishikawa, L. (2019). Foundations of ESG investing: How ESG affects equity valuation, risk, and performance. *Journal of Portfolio Management, 45*(5), 69–83. doi:10.3905/jpm.2019.45.5.069

Giese, G., Nagy, Z., & Lee, L. E. (2021). Deconstructing ESG ratings performance: Risk and return for E, S, and G by time horizon, sector, and weighting. *Journal of Portfolio Management, 47*(3), 94–111. doi:10.3905/jpm.2020.1.198

Gorshunov, M. A., Armenakis, A. A., Harris, S. G., & Walker, H. J. (2021). Quad-qualified audit committee director: Implications for monitoring and reducing financial corruption. *Journal of Corporate Finance, 66*, 101854. Advance online publication. doi:10.1016/j.jcorpfin.2020.101854

Henriksson, R., Livnat, J., Pfeifer, P., & Stumpp, M. (2019). Integrating ESG in portfolio construction. *Journal of Portfolio Management, 45*(4), 67–81. doi:10.3905/jpm.2019.45.4.067

Jha, C. K. (2019). Financial reforms and corruption: Evidence using GMM estimation. *International Review of Economics & Finance, 62*, 66–78. doi:10.1016/j.iref.2019.03.003

Ju, X., Ferreira, F. A. F., & Wang, M. (2020). Innovation, agile project management and firm performance in a public sector-dominated economy: Empirical evidence from high-tech small and medium-sized enterprises in China. *Socio-Economic Planning Sciences, 72*, 100779. Advance online publication. doi:10.1016/j.seps.2019.100779

Korinth, F., & Lueg, R. (2022). Corporate sustainability and risk management—The u-shaped relationships of disaggregated esg rating scores and risk in the German capital market. *Sustainability (Basel), 14*(9), 5735. doi:10.3390u14095735

Larsen, D. S., Van Stokkum, I. H. M., Vengris, M., Van Der Horst, M. A., De Weerd, F. L., Hellingwerf, K. J., & Van Grondelle, R. (2004). Incoherent manipulation of the photoactive yellow protein photocycle with dispersed pump-dump-probe spectroscopy. *Biophysical Journal, 87*(3), 1858–1872. doi:10.1529/biophysj.104.043794 PMID:15345564

Liu, X., Yang, Y., Jiang, Y., Fu, Y., Zhong, R. Y., Li, M., & Huang, G. Q. (2023). Data-driven ESG assessment for blockchain services: A comparative study in textiles and apparel industry. *Resources, Conservation and Recycling, 190*, 106837. Advance online publication. doi:10.1016/j.resconrec.2022.106837

Loizia, P., Voukkali, I., Zorpas, A. A., Navarro Pedreño, J., Chatziparaskeva, G., Inglezakis, V. J., Vardopoulos, I., & Doula, M. (2021). Measuring the level of environmental performance in insular areas, through key performed indicators, in the framework of waste strategy development. *The Science of the Total Environment, 753*, 141974. doi:10.1016/j.scitotenv.2020.141974 PMID:32906046

Lu, Y., Wang, L., & Zhang, Y. (2022). Does digital financial inclusion matter for firms' ESG disclosure? Evidence from China. *Frontiers in Environmental Science, 10*, 1029975. Advance online publication. doi:10.3389/fenvs.2022.1029975

Masud, M. A. K., Rahman, M., & Rashid, M. H. U. (2022). Anti-Corruption Disclosure, Corporate Social Expenditure and Political Corporate Social Responsibility: Empirical Evidence from Bangladesh. *Sustainability (Basel), 14*(10), 6140. Advance online publication. doi:10.3390u14106140

Naffa, H., & Fain, M. (2020). Performance measurement of ESG-themed megatrend investments in global equity markets using pure factor portfolios methodology. *PLoS One, 15*(12), e0244225. doi:10.1371/journal.pone.0244225 PMID:33351834

Passas, I., Ragazou, K., Zafeiriou, E., Garefalakis, A., & Zopounidis, C. (2022). ESG Controversies: A Quantitative and Qualitative Analysis for the Sociopolitical Determinants in EU Firms. *Sustainability (Basel)*, *14*(19), 12879. doi:10.3390u141912879

Peng, W., & Xiong, L. (2022). Managing financing costs and fostering green transition: The role of green financial policy in China. *Economic Analysis and Policy*, *76*, 820–836. Advance online publication. doi:10.1016/j.eap.2022.09.014

Ragazou, K., Passas, I., & Garefalakis, A. (2022). It Is Time for Anti-Bribery: Financial Institutions Set the New Strategic "Roadmap" to Mitigate Illicit Practices and Corruption in the Market. *Administrative Sciences*, *12*(4), 1–25. doi:10.3390/admsci12040166

Roy, P. P., Rao, S., & Zhu, M. (2022). Mandatory CSR expenditure and stock market liquidity. *Journal of Corporate Finance*, *72*, 102158. Advance online publication. doi:10.1016/j.jcorpfin.2022.102158

Sabbaghi, O. (2022). The impact of news on the volatility of ESG firms. *Global Finance Journal*, *51*, 100570. Advance online publication. doi:10.1016/j.gfj.2020.100570

Sahu, A. K., Padhy, R. K., Das, D., & Gautam, A. (2021). Improving financial and environmental performance through MFCA: A SME case study. *Journal of Cleaner Production*, *279*, 123751. Advance online publication. doi:10.1016/j.jclepro.2020.123751

Shaheen, S. M., Antoniadis, V., Shahid, M., Yang, Y., Abdelrahman, H., Zhang, T., Hassan, N. E. E., Bibi, I., Niazi, N. K., Younis, S. A., Almazroui, M., Tsang, Y. F., Sarmah, A. K., Kim, K. H., & Rinklebe, J. (2022). Sustainable applications of rice feedstock in agro-environmental and construction sectors: A global perspective. *Renewable & Sustainable Energy Reviews*, *153*, 111791. Advance online publication. doi:10.1016/j.rser.2021.111791

Shu, H., & Tan, W. (2023). Does carbon control policy risk affect corporate ESG performance? *Economic Modelling*, *120*, 106148. Advance online publication. doi:10.1016/j.econmod.2022.106148

Singhania, D. M., & Saini, D. N. (2022). Systems approach to environment, social and governance (ESG): Case of Reliance industries. *Sustainable Operations and Computers*, *3*, 103–117. doi:10.1016/j.susoc.2021.11.003

Tamimi, N., & Sebastianelli, R. (2017). Transparency among S&P 500 companies: An analysis of ESG disclosure scores. *Management Decision*, *55*(8), 1660–1680. doi:10.1108/MD-01-2017-0018

Vardopoulos, I. (2018). Multi-Criteria Decision-Making Approach for the Sustainable Autonomous Energy Generation through Renewable Sources. Studying Zakynthos Island in Greece. *Journal of Environment and Sustainable Development*, *7*(1), 52. Advance online publication. doi:10.5296/emsd.v7i1.12110

Vardopoulos, I. (2019). Critical sustainable development factors in the adaptive reuse of urban industrial buildings. A fuzzy DEMATEL approach. *Sustainable Cities and Society*, *50*, 101684. Advance online publication. doi:10.1016/j.scs.2019.101684

Vardopoulos, I., Falireas, S., Konstantopoulos, I., Kaliora, E., & Theodoropoulou, E. (2018). Sustainability assessment of the agri-environmental practices in Greece. Indicators' comparative study. *International Journal of Agricultural Resources, Governance and Ecology*, *14*(4), 368–399. doi:10.1504/IJARGE.2018.098024

Vardopoulos, I., Konstantopoulos, I., Zorpas, A. A., Limousy, L., Bennici, S., Inglezakis, V. J., & Voukkali, I. (2021). Sustainable metropolitan areas perspectives through assessment of the existing waste management strategies. *Environmental Science and Pollution Research International*, *28*(19), 24305–24320. Advance online publication. doi:10.100711356-020-07930-1 PMID:32072414

Zhang, N., Zhang, Y., & Zong, Z. (2023). Fund ESG performance and downside risk: Evidence from China. *International Review of Financial Analysis, 86.*

ENDNOTES

1. WGBC: New report: the building and construction sector can reach net zero carbon emissions by 2050, https://worldgbc.org/article/new-report-the-building-and-construction-sector-can-reach-net-zero-carbon-emissions-by-2050 / Retrieved: 03/05/23
2. Skanska USA. (2019). 2019 Sustainability Report. Retrieved from https://www.skanska.com/globalassets/us/sustainability/sustainability-reports/skanska-usa-2019-sustainability-report.pdf
3. Lendlease. (2019). 2019 Annual Report. Retrieved from https://www.lendlease.com/-/media/llcom/investor-centre/annual-reports/2019-annual-report-lendlease-group.ashx
4. Bouygues Construction. (2018). 2018 Annual Report. Retrieved from https://www.bouygues-construction.com/sites/default/files/rapport_annuel/2018/rapport_annuel_2018_eng.pdf

Chapter 4
Investigating Mega Project Schedule Challenges in Transnet Capital Projects

Vannie Naidoo
https://orcid.org/0000-0001-8435-4348
University of KwaZulu-Natal, South Africa

Rajen Chetty
University of KwaZulu-Natal, South Africa

ABSTRACT

In view of the present climate around the globe, mega infrastructure developments are considered to be key catalysts driving economic development and social upliftment and transformation within the world economies today. However, the complexity of megaproject development especially when it comes to infrastructural development is a like a dual edged sword, and in recent years, the delivery of many infrastructural projects have come under scathing attack for schedule slippages, huge cost overruns, and questions over real benefits to the economic viability and sustainability it proposes to bring to the countries future DDP and GNP. This study analysed megaproject schedule challenges in transnet capital projects (TCP) in South Africa. The study employed a survey, and quantitative data were collected using a closed ended questionnaire from 191 megaproject personnel. The objective of the study was to undertake the quantitative analysis to critically assess schedule challenges.

DOI: 10.4018/978-1-6684-7786-1.ch004

INTRODUCTION

Literature expounds that in the last few decades, society has started to measure progress in terms of the quality of life usually associated with large investments in infrastructure such as housing, transportation, manufacturing, and health services. Mega-infrastructure projects in recent years have been considered to be major drivers of economic growth, job creation, and sustainable communities. Naidoo (2022) posits that many theorists writing in the area of mega-projects outlined different views and perceptions of what to their understanding are mega-projects. Mega-projects do not exist in isolation but they are closely integrated and aligned to socio-economic requirements Mega-projects are crucial as they strive to provide infrastructural development and support the growth and sustainability of a country's economy. Scheduling is an integral part of mega-projects, and special attention needs to be given to the planning of this activity. Investors in mega projects both in the private and public sectors continue to push the boundaries of development in an attempt to satisfy society's appetite and remain competitive. However, large-scale projects have come under intense scrutiny and criticism for poor delivery, overruns in project costs, and failure to meet promises of scheduled delivery. As a result of project performance and reports of failures, project practitioners appear to adopt a defensive stance whilst stakeholders remain skeptical. It is estimated that in Transnet's capital-intensive Rail Freight Business, 55% of projects have failed with detrimental impacts on its business strategy (Xaba: 2011). Further reports indicate that Transnet's projects are failing with challenges in project delivery and concomitant major schedule slippages, (Le Guerm: 2013). Transnet's situation is not isolated as an international study by Merrow (2011) that reports that 65% of mega-industrial projects have failed with dire consequences for operations and long-term sustainability. Merrow expounds further that 28% of these failed projects did not meet their scheduled delivery dates. Mega project schedules are considered a crucial factor in commitments made to stakeholders and shareholder value.

BACKGROUND TO THE STUDY

Transnet, is the backbone of South Africa's rail, port, and pipeline transport network (Transnet, 2014:6). Transnet consists of five main operating divisions namely Transnet National Ports Authority (TNPA), Transnet Port Terminals (TPT), Transnet Freight Rail (TFR), Transnet Rail Engineering (TRE), and Transnet Pipelines (TPL). The study is on Transnet Capital Projects, which is a state-owned company, that has a direct impact on the lives of all South Africans. Transnet Capital projects are involved in many different mega-projects in their various divisions. Transnet Capital Projects is a specialist wing of the Transnet Corporate office which is mandated to deliver infrastructure projects on behalf of Transnet's Divisions (Transnet, 2015). Transnet Capital Projects plays a critical role in ensuring that Transnet achieves its capital infrastructure strategy through the investment and delivery of infrastructure in the port, rail, and pipeline business sectors. Some mega-projects under execution were the new manganese export terminal; new railway lines from Kimberly to Ngqura; new deep-water quay walls at the Durban Container Terminal; a new Waterberg railway line; new quay walls at Maydon Wharf; a new tippler project in Saldanha; and the new multi-purpose product pipeline from Durban to Johannesburg (Transnet, 2015).

In order for Transnet Capital Projects to survive and grow in a challenging market environment, as well as capitalize on global opportunities on the African continent in particular, it is crucial that the company wisely invests in the efficiently executed high-value mega projects. Maintaining the current status quo on mega projects may lead to failed business initiatives with potentially detrimental consequences on operational efficiencies and financial well-being. Further negative impacts will also be felt by Transnet's Capital Projects customers and the national logistics platforms as well. This study was undertaken to establish and critically assess the scheduling challenges facing Transnet's Capital Projects mega projects.

The objectives of this study are to critically assess the underlying factors that are driving the poor performance of mega projects in Transnet Capital Projects whilst focussing on challenges related to mega project schedules. Against this background, a theoretical assessment is undertaken to determine factors contributing to mega project schedule challenges and critical relationships between these project factors. Hence empirical data received from project personnel in Transnet Capital Projects are systematically analysed and processed to unravel strengths, weaknesses, and challenges contributing to megaproject failures.

This study aims to contribute valuable information and data for Transnet Capital Projects to strategically improve its mega projects techniques and processes in its efforts to capitalize on its infrastructure investments, lower the costs of logistics and deliver capacity in the timeframes communicated to its customers. It further aims to contribute valuable learnings from Transnet Capital Projects to the African continent and the project management fraternity as a whole.

LITERATURE REVIEW

Various themes were investigated and discussed below in the literature review.

Economic Implication of Megaprojects

He et al(2019) argue that mega-infrastructure projects are a type of national strategic projects which have a profound impact on politics, the economy, science and technology, society, the environment, and other fields. Adama (2018) indicates that mega-projects are important ways and mean to improve the economic carrying capacity of cities, which can not only catalyse urban development but also lead to an improvement of local planning systems and building planning capacity. Ibrahim et al. (2020) define megaprojects as large-scale investment projects with colossal use of resources including financial, human, and equipment.

The Accelerated Shared Growth Initiative (AsgiSA) was launched in 2006 by the South African government as a major initiative for economic growth and subsequent improvements in the quality of life for all South Africans (Department of Trade and Industry: 2011). As a state-owned entity, Transnet has extensively contributed to economic development and transformation in South Africa Its R300bn Market Demand Strategy (MDS) infrastructure program is currently being executed and is aimed at delivering job creation, skills development, and socio-economic benefits to South Africa and the African continent with its mega-infrastructure expansions in ports, railway infrastructure, logistics platforms, and major capacity improvement in petroleum pipelines (Transnet: 2014).

Indications are that overall global growth continues to increase steadily with the changes in areas of production and consumption and that there are opportunities for nations to capitalize on these trends. (World Bank: 2015). There are further studies that demonstrate that this increase in growth is the key driver for the mega-infrastructure boom and is further exacerbated by migrations of populations to major cities in search of a better quality of life (PriceWaterhouseCoopers: 2015). In its global review, (McKinsey: 2016) reports that the high demand for mega infrastructure requires major upgrades to housing, transportation, and health services, particularly driven by the demand in Asian countries including India and China, as well as developing countries in South America and Africa. This movement in economic growth and related infrastructure requirements is predicted to continue over the next few decades, thus supporting the requirements for mega-infrastructure projects in ports, rail, and cities (PriceWaterhouseCoopers: 2015).

However, project management bodies such as APM (2016) concede that even with the best tools, software, techniques, and ongoing improvements in practices, project managers continue to be challenged in delivering projects and, in most cases, fail to complete them. Kerzner (2013) cautions that the field of project management is relatively new to many organizations. In order for organizations to be successful in project delivery, there needs to be a culture of analysing project challenges and continuous research to adapt processes to deliver projects on time, within investment-cost budgets and quality requirements. In an effort to support positive outcomes and success stories in upcoming project endeavours, it is critical to determine project challenges in Transnet Capital Projects.

Project Success and Failure

As recently as the last decade, scholars appear to agree that project successes and challenges are indeed difficult to frame; however, scholars emphasize that project schedules, budgets, and quality dimensions are relevant descriptors as posed in the 'iron triangle' of project management (Han, Yusof, Ismail, & Aun: 2012). In his review, Dalcher (2012) goes further to iterate that success needs to be expanded from a view of planning and controlling to include views of clients, contractors, and stakeholders which are generally neglected. Wells (2012) adds that recent thinking is moving toward understanding the influence of project-personnel attributes including skills, experience, and behaviour, and their impacts on project success. This notion is reinforced by APM (2016) which indicates that studies reveal that the competency of project professionals and the capability of the project teams are highly critical success factors in addition to traditional factors such as project processes and the external environment.

Focusing at a granular level in his study of industrial megaprojects, Merrow (2011) reveals the top seven reasons for project failure can be summarised as investment imbalances, compressed schedules, insufficient upfront detailed planning, insufficient funding for upfront planning, cost cutting, passing risks onto contractors and dismissal or loss of key project personnel. Stemming from their study on international project development, Ika & Hodgson (2014) agree with Merrow's results that project failure occurs when planned schedules, costs, scope, and quality required are not met. The Standish Group's (2014) CHAOS report reveals that the rate of IT project failures is increasing and that the top three failures can be attributed to user involvement, lack of executive support, and unclear statement of requirements. Parvaneh and El-Saegh (2016) agree with the view that deliverables not meeting the 'iron triangle of time, cost, and quality' can be regarded as a failure, but demonstrate further that there is no agreed set of standards that can be used to measure or describe project successes or failures.

Project Schedule

The schedule of projects consists of a series of activities with start and completion dates for each activity required to complete the project (Graham & Englund: 2004). The schedules are developed by the project team with specialist leads developing the disciplines, and work packages, and endorsing the activities as well as the length of time that is required to execute to completion each of the activities (TILOS: 2012). PMI (2013) alludes to the approved schedule as the 'baseline schedule' that is used in controlling schedule processes. Marks & Ellis (2013) add that delays are described as the over-run of time beyond the agreed date of completion as contained in the contract between parties. Hazini, Dehghan, & Ruwanpura,:2014) indicate that project schedules also contain information on the sequence of activities, interdependencies among activities, and the duration of each activity. According to Varajao, Dominguez, Ribeiro, and Paiva (2014), construction projects have been severely criticized for delays and they conclude that project managers must allocate appropriate resources to ensure effective schedule development, management, and recovery with the purpose of adhering to committed completion dates.

Schedule Management

Usually, reliance is placed on the performance of the past similar project and their activities to determine the duration of time required as inputs for the activities in a new project (Sawyer: 2012). On the other hand, Sawyer (2012) also cautions that this approach may be risky or untrustworthy if reliable forecasting techniques and statistics are not adopted. TEAC (time estimation at completion), SV (schedule variation), SPI (schedule performance index) are widely used formula illustrated by PMI (2013) for reviewing schedule performance and determining the estimated project completion date based on information at the time of review. Norouzi, Heydari, Noori, and Bagherpour (2015) point out that 'unless reliable and timely reporting is established', schedule updates will produce 'false forecasts of schedules and costs'. They, therefore, recommend the use of 'dynamic scheduling' to predict the trustworthy completion of projects.

Slippage in Schedules

Merrow (2011) in a study of 318 mega industrial projects involving primarily onshore industrial processing plants, reveals that poor engineering and associated quality control are the chief contributors to slippages in project schedules. He explains that long lead items such as bulk-engineered material are severely impacted by major cost overruns. Marks and Ellis (2013) add that schedule risks are often compounded as a result of project teams compressing time-sensitive projects and overlapping activities in an attempt to achieve earlier project completion. They caution that compressing schedules often results in higher costs and that the project team needs to weigh up the benefits of accelerating schedules against costs and risks. In addition, Haznini et al. (2014) explain that further slippages and cost increases may result if inappropriate tactics are applied with subjective strategies hence resulting in a loss-making endeavor. Wilkinson (2015) adds that schedule slippages occur as a result of changing project requirements stemming from incomplete integration of stakeholders in the early stages of project planning. Andersen, Samset, and Welde (2016,) argue that the complexity of mega projects often leads to schedule slippages. Narbaev and De Marco (2013) recommend that project teams consider the application of "genetic algorithms" for addressing the time-cost trade-off, as genetic algorithms are capable of running complex problems in a short period.

After discussing the major themes in the literature review the methodology employed in the study will be discussed below.

METHODOLOGY

In order to understand the complex nature of megaproject schedules in Transnet Capital Projects, the study adopted a quantitative research stance utilizing a survey-based research design (Sekaran & Bougie, 2019). Focussing on a cross-sectional survey sample, the study applied a descriptive paradigm using scientific methods for diligence and accuracy to ensure replicability (Sekaran & Bougie, 2019; Zhang & Fan, 2013).

Sample and Data Collection

In order to investigate the challenges in mega-project schedules, it was necessary to select personnel in Transnet Capital Projects who are involved in the execution of mega-projects. The participants targeted in this study were all persons in the population of 324 persons consisting of project directors, senior project managers, project managers, engineers, project control managers, quantity surveyors, procurement and contract managers, environmental managers, and quality managers. The survey sample in this case was the same as the targeted population and the targeted participants could easily be reached since their email addresses were available in Transnet Capital Projects.

Data Collection

A 5-point Likert-scale type questionnaire with an ordinal scale was used to collect primary data from Transnet Capital Projects personnel. There were two parts to the questionnaire with the first part seeking information on the respondents and the second part posing statements related to Transnet Capital Projects' mega-project schedules. The questionnaire was securely loaded onto an electronic platform 'Survey Monkey' and distributed to participants in geographically-remote offices.

Completed questionnaires were received from 191 respondents thus meeting the requirements for achieving a confidence level of 95% and 5% margin of error, according to guidelines provided by Krejcie and Morgan (1970).

Data Analysis. Field data were analyzed using the Statistical Package for Social Scientists for all multiple-choice questions. A pilot test was applied to test the validity of the questionnaire before its distribution to participants. The internal consistency of the main questionnaire produced a Cronbach's alpha coefficient of 0,895 which was within the accepted range of 0,7 and 1,0 recommended by scholars. The Cronbach's alpha test demonstrated that the data collected was reliable for further analysis. Inferential statistics was undertaken to test the hypotheses questions put forward.

In order to ascertain whether the data followed a normal distribution, a Normality Test was undertaken for the schedule management dimension before proceeding with any further analysis. Since the Kolmogorov-Smirnov test indicated that the overall scores for the dimension were not normally distributed, inferential testing using non-parametric tests was undertaken. Non-parametric testing, namely the Mann-Whitney Test, was performed on the data whereby the medians of the two groups were compared to determine any significant relationships amongst the selected constructs.

DISCUSSION OF THE EMPIRICAL STUDY

In this section, the authors will outline in detail the descriptive and inferential statists reflected in the empirical study.

Descriptive Analysis

Gender: Sixty-nine percent of the respondents were male and females made up 31% of the participants. The gender data indicates that whilst males dominate teams, there is strong evidence of female participation in Transnet Capital Projects mega-projects. The results in this study are closely aligned with Transnet's report of 70,1% of males in the company (Transnet, 2017)

Age: The findings reveal that almost a quarter (24,7%) of all participants are less than thirty years of age whilst the majority of participants (33,5%) are in the 30-40-year age group. Nearly 29,4% are in the 41-50-year age group and the over 50-year age group makes up 12,4%. The results indicate that virtually a quarter of all participants are a fairly young group of individuals probably with limited exposure and experience in mega-projects. There appears to be a link to age analysis of the younger group and experience as the study further discloses that almost half (47%) of all respondents disagreed that personnel on mega-projects in Transnet Capital

Projects possess the correct skill sets hence raising concerns. This concern may pose further risk to Transnet Capital Projects delivering mega projects on time since the inferential statistics analysis in this study indicates that there is a strong relationship between the availability of the correct skill sets in the company and the completion of mega-projects on time. However, the bulk of the participants being in the middle to older age groups presents opportunities through effective training and coaching programs for the younger group to grow in their jobs and enhance value to Transnet.

Marital Status: Most (62%) of participants are married whilst 32% are single. Four percent of participants are divorced and 2% chose other as a status. The results show that all participants irrespective of marital status had a chance to participate in this survey. The results are additionally suggestive that TCP may be in a stronger position as a result of one-third of respondents being single to deploy project staff to remote geographical locations for the execution of its port, pipeline, and rail megaprojects.

Level of Education: Nearly 40,9% of participants have an undergraduate qualification while the majority (59,7%) of participants possess a postgraduate qualification. The study results reveal that apart from a basic undergraduate qualification, most Transnet Capital Project personnel have had opportunities to fulfill the requirements of postgraduate qualifications. The findings also support the company's strategy of acquiring and promoting qualified staff in its project teams. Upon further investigation, Kulkarni, Lengnicj-Hall, and Martinez (2015) relate that increased competition in the labour market has led new graduates to acquire further qualifications to compensate for their deficiencies in work experience. Thus, it would be worthwhile to assess job fit at the company due to perceptions of disagreement from almost half (47%) of respondents that the right skill sets are available on Transnet Capital Project's mega-project teams.

Nationality: Ninety-nine percent of all participants are of South African nationality while 1% of the participants in this survey consisted of foreign nationalities. Evidence from the study demonstrates that TCP has created opportunities for foreign nationals to complement its megaproject execution teams. The JIPSA Report (2016) and Transnet's Sustainability Report (Transnet, 2015) highlight a shortage of skills pertaining to the project and operations environment. As an interim measure, there may be opportunities for the company is to source foreign nationals possessing the correct skills and experience to supplement its mega project teams. However, Nesheim and Smith (2015) caution that differences in education and training systems in various nationalities may be impediments and that high levels of maturity, respect, acceptance of differences, and common project goals are key success factors.

Inferential Statistics

In this section, the hypotheses were tested and a discussion of the results is presented below.

Hypotheses: Hypotheses were formulated to test the influence of key variables amongst the various dimensions.

Null Hypothesis 1: There is no relationship between the development of realistic schedules and mega project completion on time.

Table 1. Correlation between the development of realistic schedules and mega project completion on time

Correlations				
			Mega Projects Are Completed on Time	**A Realistic Schedule Is Developed**
Spearman's rho	Mega projects are completed on time	Correlation Coefficient	1.000	.401**
		Sig. (2-tailed)		.000
		N	191	191
	A realistic schedule is developed	Correlation Coefficient	.401**	1.000
		Sig. (2-tailed)	.000	
		N	191	191
**. Correlation is significant at the 0.01 level (2-tailed).				

Since the data were not normally distributed, Spearman's rho test was conducted to determine the relationship between variables. It was found that a moderate but significant relationship exists between a realistic schedule being developed and mega projects being completed on time ($r=0.401$, $p<0.01$). Therefore, the null hypothesis is rejected.

Transnet Capital Projects results are aligned with the views of Narbaev and De Marco (2013) as well as Berg and Karlsen (2014) who agree that the level of detail of activities and the accuracy of the estimation of the duration of activity schedules all contribute significantly to the management of schedules and successful project completion. Merrow (2013) further contributes to this notion in his review of mega-industrial projects when he clarifies that the completion of successful mega-projects is associated with detailed planning at the early phases of the project.

Table 2. The correlation between effective change-control processes and mega project completion on time

Correlations				
			Mega Projects Are Completed on Time	**Change-Control Processes Are Effective**
Spearman's rho	Mega projects are completed on time	Correlation Coefficient	1.000	.236**
		Sig. (2-tailed)	.	.001
		N	191	191
	Change-control processes are effective	Correlation Coefficient	.236**	1.000
		Sig. (2-tailed)	.001	.
		N	191	191
**. Correlation is significant at the 0.01 level (2-tailed).				

Null Hypothesis 2: There is no relationship between effective change-control processes and mega project completion on time

The relationship between effective change-control processes and mega project completion on time was found to have a low positive but significant relationship (r=0.236, r=0.001). The null hypothesis, therefore, is rejected.

The study found a strong correlation between effective change control processes and mega project completion on time. The findings correlate with the exposition of Mark and Ellis (2013) who reveal in their study that excessive changes and ineffective change-control processes are major factors contributing to the slippages in agricultural projects undertaken in Guyana. A further study undertaken by Norouzi et al. (2015) found a relationship between ineffective change controls with negative impacts on schedules and performance for large, complicated projects. Hence, the findings in Transnet Capital Projects correlate with previous studies.

Null Hypothesis 3: There is no relationship between correct skill sets in mega projects and mega project completion on time

The study found a positive relationship between the statements "correct skill sets in mega projects" and "mega projects are completed on time" (r=0.411, p<0.01). Therefore, the null hypothesis is rejected in this aspect.

The analysis of data demonstrates that there is a relationship between correct skill sets in Transnet Capital Projects and mega-project completion on time. This relationship is important and pertinent as established by Muller and Jugdev (2012), supporting the view that the appropriate level of resources must be maintained on mega-projects to effectively manage and control successful outcomes, or else the

Table 3. Correlation the correct skill sets in mega projects and mega project completion on time

Correlations				
			Correct Skill Sets in Mega Projects	**Mega Projects Are Completed on Time**
Spearman's rho	Correct skill sets in mega projects	Correlation Coefficient	1.000	.411**
		Sig. (2-tailed)	.	.000
		N	191	191
	Mega projects are completed on time	Correlation Coefficient	.411**	1.000
		Sig. (2-tailed)	.000	.
		N	191	191

project may face challenging outcomes. This notion is further aligned with Roe's (2014) view that, for organizations to deliver successful large projects, competent and experienced personnel must be used on the project teams.

Null Hypothesis 4: There is no relationship between rewarding good contractor performance and mega project completion on time

No significant relationships were found between rewarding good contractor performance and mega-project completion on time (r=0.111, p=0.125). Therefore, the null hypothesis is accepted.

Table 4. Correlation between rewarding contractor performance and mega project completion on time

Correlations				
			Good Contractor Performance Is Rewarded	**Mega Projects Are Completed on Time**
Spearman's rho	Good contractor performance is rewarded	Correlation Coefficient	1.000	.111
		Sig. (2-tailed)		.125
		N	191	191
	Mega projects are completed on time	Correlation Coefficient	.111	1.000
		Sig. (2-tailed)	.125	
		N	191	191

The outcome of the data processing in this study reveals that there is no relationship between the reward of contractor performance and mega-project completion on time. The findings are contrary to Apooja, Herrala, Pekuri, and Haappasalo (2013) and Bogus, Migliaccio, and Jin (2013) who concluded that when contractors were incentivized for performance, there were generally positive outcomes and project completion targets were met. The results from the survey appear to indicate that contractors appointed on mega-projects in Transnet are not motivated by performance rewards for project completion on time but by other factors. These factors may include regular payments to maintain cash flow, fair reimbursement for changes, and harmonious contracting relationships as illustrated by Amoatey, Ameyaw, Adaku, and Famiyeh (2015) in their study of large housing projects in Ghana. A further explanation of the results could be that public entities in South Africa such as Transnet do not typically offer incentives for early contract completion; therefore, in the public project regime, contractor schedules are not formulated with incentives in mind.

RECOMMENDATIONS

In order to address the challenge of design changes faced by mega project teams in Transnet Capital Projects, it is recommended that the project team spends sufficient time with its clients in the early stages of the mega project to understand, document, review and approve all design requirements and specifications prior to the detailed design phase and prior to the commencement of construction work. This approach will enhance the quality of client requirements, firm up the basis for designs and reduce the risk of changes in the project. Significant changes to the mega project scope should be avoided unless there are risks to the business case investment supporting a compelling motivation for change. In addition, when changes are unavoidable for technical reasons, any negative impacts on planned schedules must be proactively tackled and mitigations sought with the relevant parties to carefully adjust activities in an attempt to still meet planned schedules.

The mega-project team needs to set aside time upfront in the early stages of the project to develop robust project schedules through regular engagements with client bodies to develop schedule norms and common alignment for mega-project delivery. 'Lessons learned' on schedule delivery from previous projects are a useful intervention to be considered by Transnet Capital Projects. This intervention produces useful information on the duration of past activities that were successful and unsuccessful in its completed mega-projects. Useful learnings from the review of previous schedules will enhance the development of new mega-project schedules, provide guidance on evaluating contractor schedules, reduce schedule disputes, and increase the chances of mega-project delivery success. As an additional requirement, mega-project schedules should be peer-reviewed by independent experts who have previously undertaken similar work. Expert teams must interrogate and identify schedule risks and any impacts to targeted schedule delivery. Risks to the schedule must be rated and a 'Monte Carlo' type analysis undertaken to evaluate levels of confidence in achieving targeted activities and final project delivery. Finally, project activities need to be adjusted, realigned and robust mitigation plans developed where required.

The challenges related to the mobilization of inadequately skilled and inexperienced personnel to mega-project teams require an in-depth, focused investigation to understand at a granular level the mechanics of this matter. Based on the current diagnosis, the recommended short-term intervention would be the use of locally available, fixed-term contract workers or the use of expatriates. Experienced expatriates may be capable of immediately filling the short-term resources needs and they could additionally provide the transfer of skills to local team members. Another intervention for bridging the short-term skills gaps would be the use of 'turnkey' contracting strategies whereby the contractor is appointed to undertake all megaproject planning, design, and construction requirements. In the turnkey approach, it would be necessary for Transnet Capital Projects to make it a contractual requirement for inexperienced staff to be embedded within the Turnkey contract team with the requirement for the contracting team to guide, nurture and develop Transnet' personnel. An additional approach for the company is to adopt a joint venture approach with suitable organizations for project execution. The contracting strategy for this joint venture must cater to resource collaboration with a desired outcome in meaningful training, transfer of skills, and the development of appropriate attitudes and behaviours. Transnet Capital Projects personnel could further also be mobilized to international projects (mega rail, port, and pipeline infrastructure) for exposure, using exchange programs with experienced designers and construction contractors. An exchange program would create a win-win situation that benefits Transnet Capital Projects in developing skills whilst benefitting designers and contractors in achieving contract contribution targets.

LIMITATIONS OF THE STUDY

The study excluded respondents from the owner teams, consultants, and construction contractors; hence, it could be argued that these stakeholders' perspectives should be considered to provide an objective view of the overall situation.

CONCLUSION

The study provides valuable data and information for management considerations in continuously improving, refining, and stabilizing procedures and practices in Transnet Capital Projects. In actively adopting appropriate strategies, Transnet Capital Projects can demonstrate higher levels of confidence in delivering schedule commitments to its clients and stakeholders. Ultimately, Transnet Capital Projects will support Transnet in achieving its MDS goals of improved logistics and lowering the cost of doing business in South Africa.

The study of Transnet Capital Projects' mega-projects using empirical methods validates that there are several challenges in mega-projects impacting negatively on scheduled commitments. Respondents in the study agree that mega-projects are not completed as per committed planned schedules. Transnet Capital Projects respondents indicate that at the project planning stage, schedules are compressed to meet the business case commitments. Furthermore, these compressed schedules are unrealistic with high risks of not meeting completion dates. Another challenge contributing significantly to schedule slippages is the additional time requirements brought about by design changes during project execution. A further challenge hampering mega-project performance is the lack of skilled scheduling personnel mobilized onto mega-projects for the execution of the works.

FUTURE AREAS OF INTEREST

The area of infrastructure development in the African context is very limited and more research in the field in the African context is needed to assist the continent in its' quest for infrastructure development in mega-projects in this area. Research should also be extended to include owners' teams, consultants, and contractors to broaden and obtain a 360-degree view of mega-project challenges. It would be interesting to see further comparative studies in South Africa and the African continent on infrastructure and mega project scheduling challenges, as the author reflects that these could be beneficial in gaining new knowledge in the area that can assist in closing the scheduling gaps in megaprojects. Another perspective to be explored is a deep exploration of the competencies and skills requirements for mega projects as the authors advocate that such studies can reflect in adding much value in addressing the success of project execution.

REFERENCES

Adama, O. (2018). Urban imaginaries: Funding mega infrastructure projects in Lagos, Nigeria. *GeoJournal, 83*(1), 257–274. doi:10.100710708-016-9761-8

Amoatey, C., Ameyaw, Y., Adaku, E., & Famiyeh, S. (2015). Analysing delay causes and effects in Ghanaian state housing construction projects. *International Journal of Managing Projects in Business, 8*(1), 198–214. doi:10.1108/IJMPB-04-2014-0035

Andersen, B., Samset, K., & Welde, M. (2016). Low estimates – high stakes; underestimation of costs at the front-end of projects. *International Journal of Managing Projects in Business, 1*(1), 171–193. doi:10.1108/IJMPB-01-2015-0008

Andersen, B. S., Samset, K., & Welde, M. (2016). Low estimates – high stakes; underestimation of costs at the front-end of projects. *International Journal of Managing Projects in Business, 1*(1), 171–193. doi:10.1108/IJMPB-01-2015-0008

APM. (2016). *APM body of knowledge*. Retrieved from https://www.apm.org.uk/ Body of Knowledge

Apooja, A., Herrala, M., Pekuri, A., & Haappasalo, H. (2013). The characteristics of and cornerstones for creating integrated team. *International Journal of Managing Projects in Business, 6*(4), 695–713. doi:10.1108/IJMPB-09-2012-0056

Berg, M., & Karlsen, J. (2014). How project managers can encourage and develop positive emotions in project teams. *International Journal of Managing Projects in Business, 7*(3), 449–472. doi:10.1108/IJMPB-01-2013-0003

Bogus, S., Migliaccio, G., & Jin, R. (2013). Study of the relationship between procurement duration and project performance in design-build projects: Comparison between water/wastewater and transport sectors. *Journal of Management Engineering, 29*(4), 382–391. doi:10.1061/(ASCE)ME.1943-5479.0000165

Dalcher, D. (2012). The nature of project management. *International Journal of Managing Projects in Business, 5*(4), 643–660. doi:10.1108/17538371211268960

Department of Trade and Industry. (2011). *Strategy for broad-based black economic empowerment.* Retrieved from http://www.thedti.gov.za

Graham, R., & Englund, R. (2004). *Creating an environment for successful projects* (2nd ed.). Jhn Wiley and Sons.

Han, W., Yusof, A., Ismail, S., & Aun, N. (2012). Reviewing the notions of construction project success. *International Journal of Business and Management, 7*(1), 90–101.

Hazini, K., Dehghan, R., & Ruwanpura, J. (2014). A heuristic method to determine optimum degree of activity accelerating and overlapping in schedule compression. *Canadian Journal of Civil Engineering*, *41*(4), 382–392. doi:10.1139/cjce-2013-0194

He, Q., Wang, T., Chan, A. P. C., Li, H., & Chen, Y. (2019). Identifying the gaps in project success research: A mixed bibliographic and bibliometric analysis. *Engineering, Construction, and Architectural Management*, *26*(8), 1553–1573. doi:10.1108/ECAM-04-2018-0181

Ibrahim, C., Costello, S., & Wilkinson, S. (2015). Key indicators influencing the management of team integration in construction projects. *International Journal of Managing Projects in Business*, *1*(1), 300–323. doi:10.1108/IJMPB-04-2014-0028

Ibrahim, M., Ofori, G., Morcos, M., & Egbu, C. (2020). *A conceptual risk management framework in the construction of mega housing projects in Egypt.* Urban Regeneration, University of East London. https://openresearch.lsbu.ac.uk/item/8vz06

Ika, L., & Hodgson, D. (2014). Learning from international development projects: Blending critical project studies and critical development studies. *International Journal of Project Management*, *32*(7), 1182–1196. doi:10.1016/j.ijproman.2014.01.004

Joint Initiative on Priority Skills Acquisition (JIPSA). (2016). *Annual Report.* Retrieved from Available at www.pmg.org.xa

Kerzner, H. (2013). *Project management: A systems approach to planning, scheduling and controlling*. John Wiley & Sons.

Krejcie, R. V., & Morgan, D. W. (1970). Table for determining sample size from a given population. *Educational and Psychological Measurement*, *30*(1), 607–610. doi:10.1177/001316447003000308

Le Guern, S. (2013). *First fuel begins to flow through SA's new R23bn fuel pipeline.* Retrieved from www.engineeringnews.co.za

Marks, M., & Ellis, L. (2013). Delays in major agricultural infrastructure projects in Guyana: Causes and proposed solutions. *The West Indian Journal of Engineering*, *36*(1), 225–235.

McKinsey. (2016). *Bridging global infrastructure gaps.* Retrieved from https://www.mckinsey.com/industries/capital-projects-and-inf rastructure/our-insights/management

Merrow, E. (2011). *Industrial mega-projects; Concepts, strategies, and practices for success*. Wiley and Sons.

Merrow, E. (2012). Oil and gas industry mega-projects: Our recent track record. *Oil and Gas Facilities*, *1*(2), 38–42. doi:10.2118/153695-PA

Muller, R., & Jugdev, K. (2012). Critical success factors in projects. *International Journal of Managing Projects in Business*, *5*(4), 757–775. doi:10.1108/17538371211269040

Narbaev, T., & De Marco, A. (2013). Combination of growth model and earned schedule to forecast project cost at completion. *Journal of Construction Engineering and Management*, *1*, 130–138.

Nesheim, T., & Smith, J. (2015). Knowledge sharing in projects: Does employment arrangement matter? *Personnel Review*, *44*(2), 255–269. doi:10.1108/PR-11-2013-0203

Norouzi, G., Heydari, M., Noori, S., & Bagherpour, M. (2015). Mathematical modeling for scheduling and determining success probability of research projects considering complex-fuzzy networks. *Journal of Applied Mathematics*, 1–2. doi:10.1155/2015/809216

Parvaneh, F., & El-Sayegh, S. (2016). Project selection using the combined approach of AHP and LP. *Journal of Financial Management of Property and Construction*, *21*(1), 39–53. doi:10.1108/JFMPC-09-2015-0034

Project Management Institute. (2013). *A guide to project management body of knowledge*. PMI.

Roe, P. (2014). *Factors which contribute to successful projects*. Retrieved from www.apm.org.uk

Sawyer, M. (2012). *Vico software integrating construction*. Retrieved from www.vicosoftware.com

Sekaran, U., & Bougie, R. (2019). *Research methods for business: A skill buildding approach*. John Wiley and Sons.

The Standish Group. (2014). *CHAOS*. The Standish Group. Retrieved from https://www.projectsmart.co.uk/white-papers/chaos-report.pdf

TILOS. (2012). *TILOS linear project*. Retrieved from www.tilos.org

Transnet. (2014). *Market demand strategy*. Retrieved from www.Transnet.net

Transnet. (2015). *Sustainability Report*. Retrieved from www.transnet.net

Transnet. (2017). *Transnet sustainability report 2017*. Retrieved from www.transnet net

Varajao, J., Dominguez, C., Ribeiro, P., & Paiva, A. (2014). Critical success aspects in project management: similarities and differences between the construction and software industry. *Technical Gazette*, 586-587.

Wells, H. (2012). How effective are project management methodologies: An explorative evaluation of their benefits in practice. *Project Management Journal*, *43*(2), 43–58. doi:10.1002/pmj.21302

World Bank. (2015). *Capacity building in Africa*. World Bank.

Xaba, M. (2011). *Root cause analysis of major capital projects at Transnet freight rail*. UNISA.

Zhang, L., & Fan, W. (2013). Improving performance of construction projects: A project manager's emotional intelligence approach. *Engineering, Construction, and Architectural Management*, *20*(2), 195–207. doi:10.1108/09699981311303044

KEY TERMS AND DEFINITIONS

Infrastructure: In a broad context infrastructure relates to the systems and structures that surround a city. Town or area of a country, commonly known as roads, power supply, rail, airports or harbours to name but a few.

Megaprojects: Refers to complex large-scale multibillion-dollar developments in infrastructure like airports, harbours, motor ways, etc.

Project Failures: This is when a project that fails to meet or deliver the expected outcome to the relevant stakeholders, it could be a result of budget failure, scheduling failures, or deadline failures where the expected outcomes for that particular project do not occur as proposed by the project manager and his team.

Project Schedules: Within the context f project management, a schedule lists the project's key milestones, activities, and deliverables.

Project Success: This is when a project delivers within the budget, deadlines, and schedules.

South Africa: South Africa is a country in the African continent that is located on the southernmost tip of the African continent. It had a unique history of apartheid and is known for the legendary father of the South African nation Nelson Mandela, who was the first president sworn in when South Africa became a democratic state of the people.

Chapter 5
Application of Artificial Neural Networks for the Prediction of Cashflows in Public Road Works

Alexandros E. Grigoras
Aristotle University of Thessaloniki, Greece

Georgios N. Aretoulis
https://orcid.org/0000-0002-9248-3454
Aristotle University of Thessaloniki, Greece

Fani Antoniou
https://orcid.org/0000-0002-0773-5144
International Hellenic University, Greece

Stylianos Karatzas
University of Patras, Greece

ABSTRACT

An attempt was made to predict the cashflows of public road projects using artificial neural networks. In the context of the development of prediction models, an introduction to the financial flows, to the Greek legislation that defines them, and finally to artificial intelligence was made. Also, a literature review concerning the application of artificial intelligence in the construction industry was carried out. Neural networks were then applied based on 37 public road projects. The methodology highlighted three models for the prediction of cashflows for public road projects: a statistical exponential regression model, an artificial neural network model, and finally a hybrid model that combined the two previous ones. The hybrid model had

DOI: 10.4018/978-1-6684-7786-1.ch005

the lowest mean absolute prediction error, followed by the model using only artificial neural networks, and lastly the statistical regression model. Finally, the conclusions of the study, the limitations that existed, suggestions for the application of the model, and ideas for future research are presented.

1. INTRODUCTION

According to the Government Gazette (Law No. 4412/2016, 2016) the definition given for the project is the following: *"Project" is the result of a set of building or engineering works which is sufficient in itself to fulfil an economic or technical function"*.

The people who are assigned to manage a project are called project managers and work as leaders of the project team to meet the objectives set (PMI, 2017). The procedure for selecting the construction company that will undertake the completion of the project, that will be appointed as the project contractor, varies depending on the type of project. The most common form for contracting a public project is an auction, which can be divided into open (any contractor meeting the necessary criteria can participate) and closed (participants in the auction are invited by the developer to participate).

According to the first paragraph of Article 86 of Law 4412/2016 (Law No. 4412/2016, 2016), the criterion for the award of public contracts is the most economically advantageous tender. However, in order to avoid problems that may arise from this selection criterion, in the case of abnormally low tenders, a sufficiently detailed report must be made by the cost engineer to justify the discount submitted by him/ her and the way in which the work will be carried out at such a low cost and in line with the quality requirements set out in the original contract.

Key steps for the awarding authorities before the project is put out to tender include:

- Feasibility study
- Preliminary study
- Environmental Impact Assessment
- Final Studies and Expropriations

The first three phases are essentially preliminary steps of the final phases, where the final studies are carried out. Before a project reaches the tendering phase, it must be properly "matured" by the awarding authority that wishes to carry it out. *"The maturity phase of a project means the overall preconstruction period, covering the whole range of planning, studies, surveys, permits, etc."*

The following section analyzes briefly the concept of cashflow. Literature review is the next significant part of the chapter, aiming at recording all the relevant work. Then follows the case study analysis. The latter moves on to analyze the methodological approach and the creation of the appropriate models. The models have been analyzed, tested and assessed. Finally, Conclusions, limitations, future research and proposals are also presented within the chapter.

2. CASHFLOW

Cash flow can be defined as the schedule of payments to be made by the developer within a certain period of time in order to complete the project (Westney, 1997). Finding a way to finance a public project precedes the tendering phase, i.e. the resources must be secured in order for it to be able to be put out to tender and awarded to a contractor. Public projects are financed from various sources, the most common of which is the Public Investment Budget. The Public Investment Programme (PIP) is part of the General Budget of the State, which includes all actions and activities that are deemed to contribute to the development of the state and are therefore approved by the respective Minister and financed from the Public Investment Budget. Furthermore, the PIP is divided into two main sub-programmes:

- The national (financed exclusively from national resources)
- The co-financed financing with the assistance of national, European and international funds)

The National Strategic Reference Framework (NSRF) was formulated in consultation with the European Union, the corresponding ministries and the local and regional authorities in an effort to synthesize proposals and options for the development of the country's society and to serve the guidelines of the European Union through the optimal use of resources for the benefit of balanced regional development. For the financing of projects included in the NSRF, the main sources of funding are the European Union funds co-financed with public expenditure of the Public Investment Programme (PIP), the State Budget, Public Enterprises and Organisations (PBOs) and the national participation of the country in the corresponding programming period (National Strategic Reference Framework 2007-2013, 2007).

If deemed necessary by the study, in accordance with the decision of the Council of State, in order to facilitate the progress of the works and the timely completion of the project, an advance payment of up to 15% of the total value of the contract may be made in an escrow account, for conditional use in the supply of materials and machinery. The contractor shall prepare segmental accounts which detail the work (visible and invisible) for which he requests to be paid after it has been approved by the department through the relevant segmental measurements. If the measurements are correct and approved by the awarding authority, the invoice is subsequently prepared by the contractor. The approval of the invoice is also referred to as certification of the execution of the works. On the basis of the certification of the work carried out within the timeframe requested, the contractor is paid in instalments. For the supervision of public works, a supervisor or supervising engineers are appointed, with the appropriate specialization for the project at hand. Supervision of the project is carried out at regular intervals by the supervisor with on-site assessment to verify the correct implementation of the actions specified by the design for the contractor regarding time, quantities, construction and quality characteristics required.

3. LITERATURE REVIEW

Civil engineering projects include uncertainties and risks that originate from the special characteristics of the construction industry. A project in which the efforts of all participants, Planners, Engineers, Sub-contractors, and Suppliers are efficiently integrated, facilitate the application of successful construction know-how. Therefore, Construction Management, or more descriptively, Project Management, is a set of professional management activities which must be carried out in order to minimize the risks of time and cost uncertainties and to enhance the probability of successfully completing the Project (Aretoulis et al., 2006). It is necessary to estimate correctly the development and the final outcome of these parameters (Aretoulis et al., 2006). This section summarizes several articles published in reputable scientific journals that show the large-scale application of artificial intelligence and specifically artificial neural networks in the construction sector. The applications presented relate to various sectors of the construction industry where artificial neural networks seem to have a great contribution due to their prediction accuracy, their adaptability and their margin of improvement with new data provided over time. Construction projects are critical for the economic development of a country. More specifically in the case of Greece, technical projects implementation could have a positive effect on the national economy and development (Aretoulis, 2018). In this context, it is true that people in construction are the key for project success. Construction projects are dynamic and changes during project implementation are often occurring. The major stakeholders in the above procedure are the owner, the design consultant, the construction contractor and the project manager (Antoniou et al., 2013; Aretoulis et al., 2019). The decisions that need to be made by the technical world when faced with the need to construct and operate major infrastructure are numerous and highly complicated (Antoniou et al., 2018a). During this process, project managers are often called to make quick decisions that influence the project outcome and success. A lot of tools have been proposed to facilitate all the processes, that are based on expert systems and more specifically on artificial intelligence.

India (second country in terms of road network size worldwide) is planning to further develop its road network. A huge problem of the projects being undertaken is the delivery of the projects at a time or cost greater than the planned cost, which results in disputes among the project stakeholders. It is therefore necessary to anticipate these events. In the current article entitled "Development of prediction models for claim cause analyses in highway projects" (Dhaval et al., 2019), the causes of conflicts are grouped by the principle component analysis (PCA) method. To solve the problem, a conflict occurrence index was developed by analytical hierarchy process (AHP) decision analysis to investigate the probability of occurrence of conflicts. Finally, prediction models for additional time and cost of project completion were developed using linear regression and neural networks to understand and predict the cause-effect relationship.

In addition, one of the most important tools that a project manager needs would be a tool to accurately estimate the construction time of a project at an early stage, for successful project planning and good relationship between stakeholders. In their research (Petrusheva et al., 2019) five different hybrid models for estimating the completion time of an early stage project were developed. From the study, the model that proved to be the most accurate was the one that combined Bromilow's (Bromilow & Pawsey, 1987) time-cost as a process model and a regression neural network as a data model. It was noteworthy that this model using only the neural network had a significant reduction in accuracy.

Another problem is the optimization of cash flows of a project, due to the complexity of the problem and the multiple factors affecting it, the application of conventional cash flow optimization techniques are quite time consuming and require highly demanding calculations. It is therefore necessary to apply a technique that takes into account all those variables that affect this problem. Neural networks have demonstrated their potential in recent years, solving complex optimisation problems with great accuracy and efficiency. The neural network developed, has the ability to optimize cash flows depending on the scenario chosen by the project manager in order to either avoid risk or vice versa. The model was applied to ten projects in Hong Kong by a large construction company. The results demonstrated the dynamic nature of the methodology and that the final decision of the form of cash flow depends on the risk policy chosen by the project sponsor (Lam et al., 2001).

As mentioned previously in a similar article, a hybrid model was developed that combines empirical systems and neural networks to design the optimal layout of construction sites depending on the conditions being studied. The current model was used with great success in the construction of a building in Beijing, where the site structures and the distances between them were designed by the model and it was finally evaluated that the proposed solution was indeed the most functional (Zhang et al., 2002).

Antoniou et al. (2023) addresses the gap regarding construction cost estimates for the construction of underground metro stations. It facilitates preliminary cost estimation models using linear regression for use by the Greek underground metro public transport authority. The paper introduces material quantity prediction models and presents a two-stage preliminary cost estimation model for the construction of civil engineering works of underground metro stations. All models provide estimates within 25% discrepancies. Titirla et al. (2021) highlights estimation methods to predict the actual project duration of Greek highway projects. Focus is on the selection of the appropriate parameters that correlate with the actual project duration. Then the study presents a comparison of the performances of the main two methods, the linear regression (LR) with the neural network models (NN). This comparison is established on data available at the bidding stage. Various models have been proposed based on the examined method. The performance and the comparison of linear regression and neural network models to estimate the actual duration of Greek highway projects is also discussed in detail. In a similar context, Titirla and Aretoulis (2019) investigated selected similar Greek highway projects. The goal was to produce artificial neural network-based models in order to forecast their actual construction duration based on data available at the bidding phase. WEKA and Fast Artificial Neural Network (FANN) Tool were used to implement the proposed methodology.

The prediction of actual cost was the goal of the following study by Aretoulis (2019). A number of models were proposed. These incorporated specific and selected variables. The latter were chosen based on correlation analysis and WEKA. The identified variables were used as input neurons for neural network models. FANN Tool was used to construct neural network models. The optimum neural network model was based on budgeted cost, lowest awarding bid, technical work cost and electromechanical work cost.

Gkovedarou and Aretoulis (2017) have focused on data for twelve public projects of urban renewal originating from the municipality of Thessaloniki. A number of mathematical models have been created for cost and time prediction based on regression analysis. Moreover, the Fast Artificial Neural Network (FANN Tool) was implemented, to forecast the duration and the final cost of the projects. A number of parameters were considered. Among these variables volume of earthwork was included, as input in the artificial neural network. One of the interesting findings is that neural networks perform better than regression analysis' models, in the case of urban renewal projects. Pewdum et al. (2009) focused their studies on the recording of highway construction project data and subsequent processing to identify factors affecting project final budget and duration before producing the forecasting models. Their effort was based on Artificial Neural Network (ANN).

Antoniou et al. (2018b) proposed a model for cost pre-estimating and material quantities formulation is proposed for overpass bridges based on the processing of data from fifty seven existing bridges in order to assist project stakeholders in the bridge construction industry when selecting the most cost effective design solution in order to reduce the risk of failure and loss of funding.

Waziri et al. (2014) created models based on regression analysis to predict highway construction duration. The produced models incorporated relevant predictor variables, with statistically significant correlation with highway completion time. Jiang and Wu (2007), analyzed 1,818 projects. The projects originated from the area of Indiana and specifically from Indiana Department of Transportation. The analysis identified factors that influence directly the duration and the cost of each project. These parameters included: the type of the project, the production rates of the construction firm, the location of the project and the weather condition. Furthermore, Hola and Schabowicz (2010) created a neural network based model to forecast productivity for chosen sets of machines and to calculate the task execution time and cost.

Obianyo (2023) implemented soft-computing techniques to predict construction schedule and control of project activities in order to achieve optimal performance in execution of building projects. Artificial neural network and neuro-fuzzy models were produced based on data originating from a residential two-storey reinforced concrete framed-structure construction schedule and project execution documents. Jia et al. (2023) researched the Graph Neural Network (GNN). Their research was based on literature review. The findings of this paper offer new insights to the existing body of knowledge by highlighting the current state of GNNs in the construction industry. The paper offers significant recommendations to overcome challenges in real-world practice.

Chua et al. (1997) worked with neural network models based on field data aiming to identify potential factors of construction project success. The study identified eight key project management factors. These included: number of organizational levels between the project manager and craft workers, amount of detailed design completed at the start of construction, number of control meetings during the construction phase, number of budget updates, implementation of a constructability program, team turnover, amount of money expended on controlling the project, the project manager's technical experience. The produced model could also be used as a predictive tool to forecast budget performance of a construction project.

Alsugair et al. (2023) developed a model to predict final construction contract duration. The model is based on data in the early stages and shared for any contract (contract cost, contract duration, and sector). The study produced an Artificial Neural

Network (ANN) model. This model is based on 135 Saudi construction project data. Nguyen (2023) the current paper, used quantitative data collected directly from measuring equipment and onsite activities. Then artificial neural networks were used to model the productivity of two main construction tasks and identify influencing factors. The neural networks proved their ability to predict the behaviors of labor productivity of the formwork and rebar tasks in a test case of a high-rise building.

From the literature review, it is observed that research in the field of cost, time and other variables forecasting in the construction sector in recent years has made it necessary to incorporate neural networks into the toolbox of methods for dealing with the problems that arise. The complexity of the problems addressed and the constant use of new variables and information in the system under study requires revolutionary solutions that can combine all those variables that are proven to affect the system to some extent. Although neural networks are an excellent case for solving such problems, it is observed that research in recent years has tended to use a combination of multiple neural networks (as they are or with modifications to their architecture) and statistical methods to optimize the efficiency and accuracy of the final result. One solution that has been found is the development of hybrid models composed of two or more methods, the choice of which is determined by the nature of the problem being studied each time.

Current research facilitates the prediction of time and cost overruns. Unfortunately, overruns still influence the construction industry. Models were created based on artificial neural network (ANN). The research analyzed 191 construction projects completed in the Hashemite Kingdom of Jordan between 2011 and 2021. The neural network with tabular search optimization was a practical tool to implement during the early design phase, when there is typically a sparse or insufficient data (Al mnaseer et al., 2023).

In the same context the specific research highlights that cost and time overruns are currently creating a worldwide challenge in the implementation of construction projects. The aim of the current approach is to produce a model capable of predicting project cost and time overruns using an appropriate data analysis approach and cost overrun elements as predictors. Risk indicators were identified for building projects. Moreover, a case study was conducted to validate the model using an actual data set consisting of completed projects (Arabiat et al., 2023).

Research is focusing on solving the problem of defining the professional adaptive capabilities of construction management staff using artificial intelligence systems. An approach has been implemented for the training process of a machine learning model, specifically an artificial intelligence system that allows it to “learn” from training data. The findings of this research could optimize the knowledge and skills necessary for successful professional realization (Honcharenko et al., 2023).

The integration of the different models that are finally selected and that create a single set (hybrid model), is based on different techniques each time to combine these individual models. The ways identified in the literature include:

- Solving the problem with each model separately and applying the average to the individual results to identify the final
- The use of non-dynamical models (such as those of classical statistics) for the initial solution of the problem and the introduction of this solution as input to the final neural network.

5. CASE STUDY

5.1 Data Collection and Processing

The data used in the paper came from the Regional Development Fund of Thessaly. The collection of the project data has taken place with particular emphasis on completeness and on the existence of common characteristics between them. More specifically, all the projects that were finally selected were road projects with similar typical cross-sections, dimensions and traffic loads. The initial number of available projects was 90, which after a first screening was reduced to 37 due to the quality of the data. The following table (Table 1) shows the number of projects per year, that remained as a sample to be processed.

Table 1. Table of the year of inclusion of projects in the NSRF and the number of projects in the statistical sample

Year of Inclusion of Projects in the NSRF	Number of Selected Projects
2009	4
2010	5
2011	7
2012	8
2013	7
2014	6
Total	37

For each of the 37 projects, the payments made during the course of construction were extracted, the amount and date of execution for each entry was recorded and the existence or otherwise of an advance payment was also noted. In the end, a file of .xls type was created for use in the Microsoft Excel spreadsheet software of the Microsoft Office suite for each project with the key data to be processed being the cumulative construction time percentage and the cumulative payment amount percentage as well. The following table (Table 2) presents the projects sorted by their monetary size.

Table 2. Projects sorted by their monetary size and existence of advance payment

Total Number of Projects	Projects With Advance Payment	< €200k	≥ €200k and < 500k €	≥ €500k and < 1 Million €	≥ €1 Million and < €5 Million	≥ €5 Million
37	19	4	13	3	8	9

From the above Table 2 it can be observed that projects with advance payment constitute 51% of the total, i.e. about half of them which is positive for the equal distribution of the sample. It is also observed that within the database, there are project entries with a wide range in terms of construction costs. In particular, the project with the smallest size had a total cost of 30,149.84€ while the one with the largest size had a total cost of 15,334,220€.

5.2 Methodological Approach

A methodology is proposed to find the most accurate prediction model for the problem of forecasting cash flows in a road project for which only two characteristics are known:

- The total cost of the project, which is the result of the final study and is indicated in the call for tender
- The existence or not of an advance payment to facilitate the progress of the work

Based on these two basic characteristics and having as reference points previous projects, the following present the way of developing three models and the final comparison between them to find the best one. First, the data collection process is carried out, which is presented in detail in the corresponding section "Data

Collection" and the data is pre-processed in Microsoft Excel software. Practically each row of the final file is an account credit to a project at a specific time, while each column relates to the characteristics of this credit and the project to which it relates. This file is then split into 2 separate files, which will be used for different purposes, namely "Training" and "Testing". The first file is the "Training File", which is used to train the model under development at a time. And the second file is the file for testing "Testing File" the developed models, through which the final comparison of the three models is made, which is discussed in a following section.

In the next step, the first file is imported into the statistical analysis software "IBM SPSS Statistics 25". From there, the development of the models that are of concern to the paper are developed and analysed in greater depth below. In summary, three prediction models are created:

- Exponential regression model
- Neural network model
- Hybrid neural network and regression model

Figure 1. Flowchart of the modelling methodology and final comparison of the models

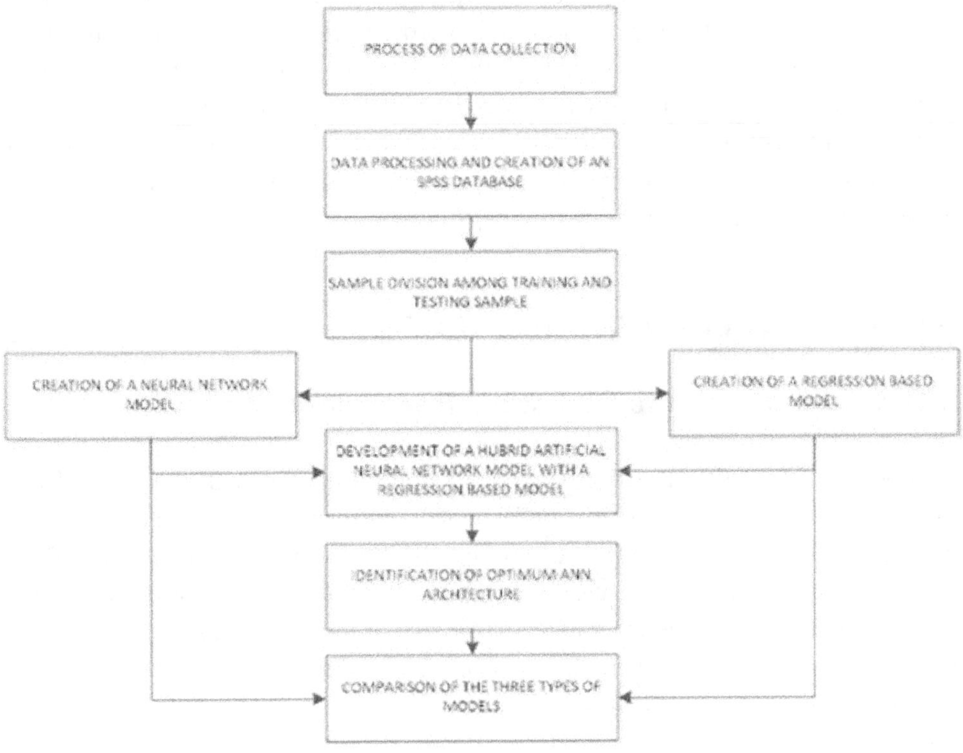

Table 3. Typical model errors of the statistical models obtained from the "Curve Estimation" procedure

Statistical Regression Model	Typical Model Errors
Linear (Linear)	16,261
Logarithmic (Logarithmic)	19,408
Inverse (Inverse)	26,762
Square (Quadratic)	16,141
Cubic (Cubic)	16,154
Combination (Compound)	0,522
Power (Power)	0,524
S curve	0,790
Growth (Growth)	0,522
Exponential (Exponential)	0,522
Accounting (Logistic)	0,522

For these three models the analytical way of their development is given, with more emphasis on the hybrid model, which combines the methods of the first two and for this reason its structure is modified in order to find the optimal architecture for the existing data. These three models are extracted by the software as .xml files (except for the statistical model which is extracted as a simple equation) and tested in the second file (Testing) prepared at the beginning and the test results are given in the corresponding section below. The flowchart of the previously described methodology is presented in the following Figure 1.

6. MODEL DEVELOPMENT AND TESTING

6.1 Development of the Statistical Regression Model

The process of selecting the first statistical model initiates with the help of the analytical procedure "Curve Estimation" where the software analyses each regression model selected by the user in the corresponding SPSS window. The statistical method that will be combined in the neural network to obtain the final hybrid model will be the one with the smallest error (Standard Error of the Estimate). Below is Table 3 with the regression methods and the errors obtained in the training dataset from the "Curve Estimation" procedure.

Figure 2. "Curvefit" diagram created in the output file by the "Curve Estimation" procedure

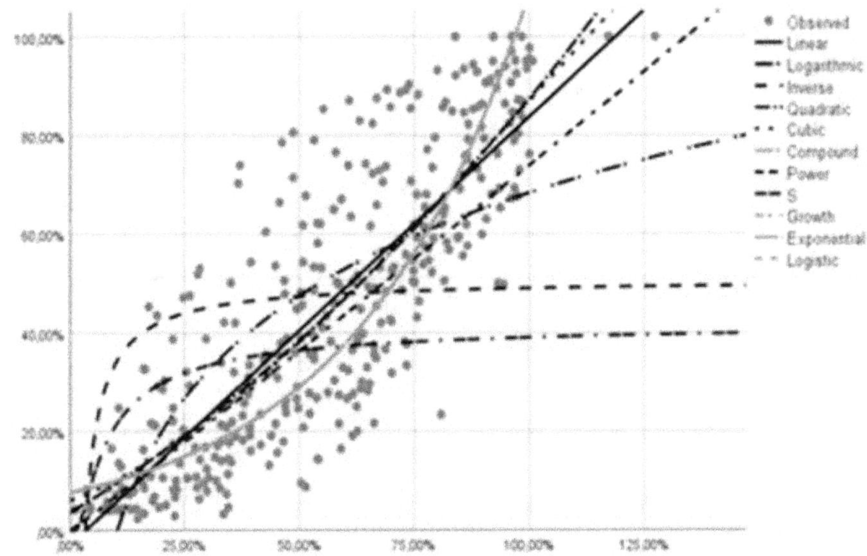

As it can be seen, the models with the lowest error are the Compound, Growth, Exponential and Logistic models with exactly the same Standard Error of the Estimate of 0.522. It is obvious from the Figure 2 illustrating the model curves below, the curves of these models mentioned above are identical to each other (shown in red in the figure) and are therefore determined by equations that give the same result. The horizontal axis presents the percentage of project time and the vertical axis presents the percentage of payments.

The equation of the Exponential model is obtained from the diagram which is as follows:

$$Payment\ Percentage = 7{,}738823857882883 * e^{(0.026440798504495173 * Time\ Percentage}$$

where PAYMENT RATE and PERIOD RATE are the percentage values

6.2 Development of Artificial Neural Network Models

6.2.1 Multilayer Perceptron (MLP)

First, a Multilayer Perceptron (MLP) neural network model is created to compare with the hybrid model, using only the initial available data. The development process will be done automatically by the software, with the instruction to experiment within the range of 1-50 neurons for each layer, to select the training algorithms and

Figure 3. Variance plot (y-axis) - forecasts (x-axis)

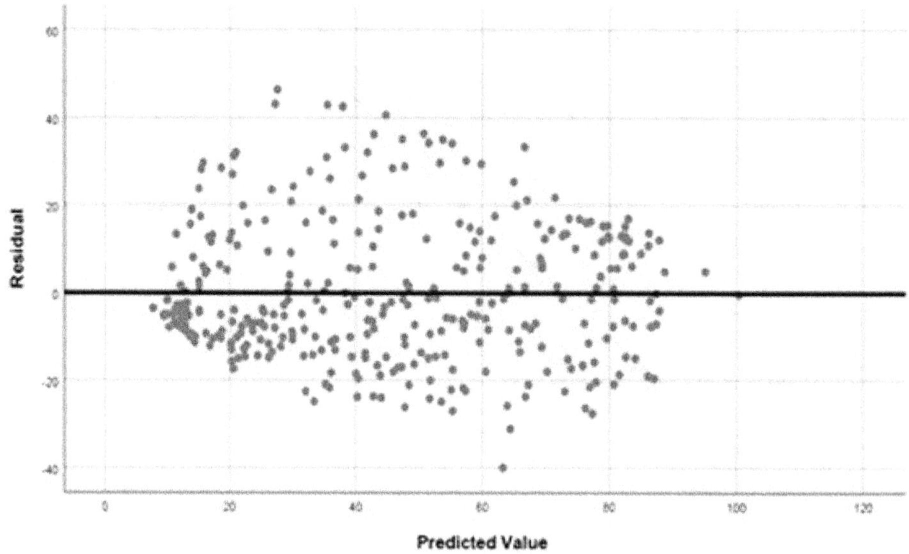

architecture that the software deems optimal. The result of this process is a neural network of a single hidden layer of 2 neurons. The independent variables include: Existence of Initial Payment, Time Percentage and Project Cost. The dependent variable is the Percentage Payment.

To investigate the capabilities of the software, two additional AI models were created with the restriction that the first time the network will have only one hidden layer, while the second time it will have two hidden layers. Thus, the three automatic options for MLP-type ANNs from the IBM software will be compared. Below are these two models as well as the variance plot (Figure 3) of the first model, which were identical in the other two models.

In Table 4, the relative training errors of the three models developed are summarized.

Table 4. Summary table of MLP-type models with their relative training stage errors

Model	Neurons at the First Hidden Level	Neurons at the Second Hidden Level	Related Error
mlp_1	2	-	0,305
mlp_2	3	-	0,297
mlp_3	3	2	0,293

Table 5. Summary table of RBF-type models with their relative training stage errors

Model	Hidden Level Neurons	Related Error
rbf_1	5	0,365
rbf_2	5	0,365
rbf_3	3	0,726
rbf_4	6	0,347
rbf_5	7	0,359
rbf_6	8	0,370

6.2.2 Radial Basis Function (RBF)

Subsequently, in the context of neural networks models, a series of Radial Basis Function (RBF) type ANN models are developed in order to find the optimal network architectural structure for this problem. In particular, a total of six models of this type were developed, each with a defined rationale in its creation. Initially, a model was developed utilizing the software's capabilities to automatically estimate the optimal settings for the RBF network under development. Knowing the fact that the RBF type models are of limited customization by the user in the software and only one hidden layer is allowed, the only variation in their structure can be done by changing the number of neurons of the hidden layer while maintaining the settings initially set in terms of the activation function which will maintain the "Normalized Radial Basis Function" due to the absence of complexity in the network as suggested by IBM (IBM, 2017) as well as overlapping iterations in automatic calculation by the software.

In the first model, on the basis of which an estimate of the number of neurons was made, the settings were all left to automatic. Having obtained from the first model that the number of neurons in the hidden layer is 5, a procedure can be followed to find the optimal number of neurons. The software was set to explore the neuron range with a minimum of 5 and a maximum of 20 neurons and the result was the second model with exactly the same neurons as the previous model. Therefore, the software judged that the network should remain as it was. Then, to explore all possibilities, the optimal structure in the range between one and four neurons will be sought, with the extracted network being that of the third model with 3 neurons in the hidden layer.

The optimal choice in the range between six and twenty neurons is then sought. The number 5 within the options is deliberately avoided, as it is known that the software considers 5 neurons as the optimal solution and therefore the same result

Figure 4. Variation in forecast values of the 1st RBF model

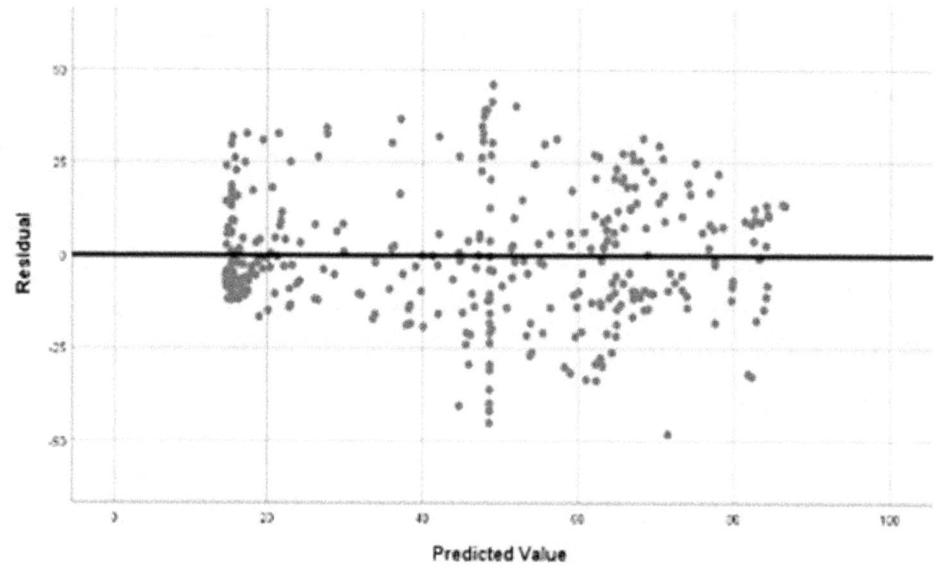

will be output all the time, which does not help the exploration. Therefore, fourth model, has as optimal number 6 neurons.

Figure 5. Variation of RBF Model 2 forecast values

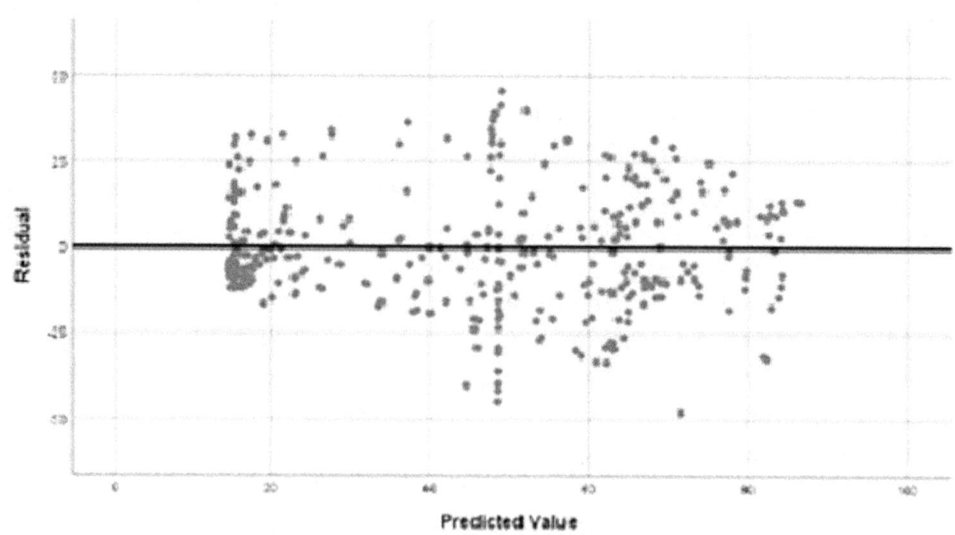

Figure 6. Variation of forecast values of the 3rd RBF model

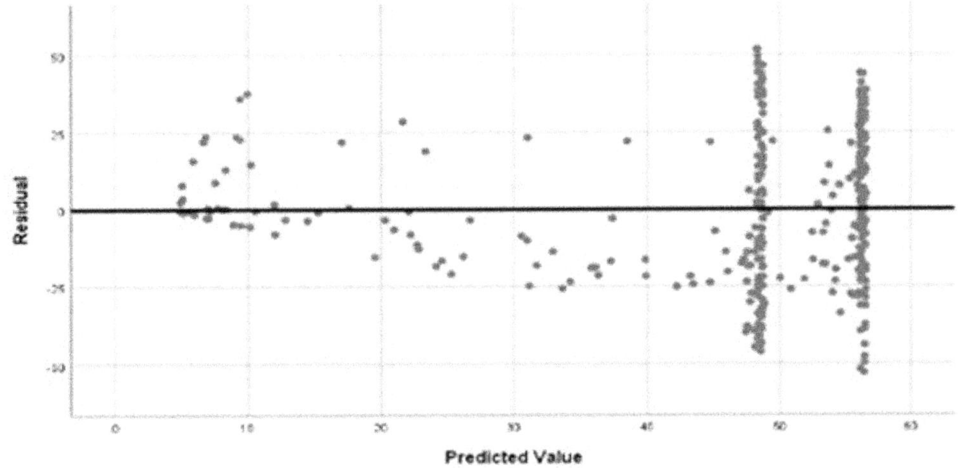

So it is observed that the tendency from the program to consider the closest to 5 again as the optimal solution. Finally, to confirm this conjecture, 2 more models are derived, with 7 and 8 neurons in the hidden layer respectively. For each of the 6 resulting models, statistical data were extracted at the end of their training in order to evaluate the process by the user. The following table (Table 5) lists the relative errors for each model from their training process.

In all the figures that follow the dependent variable is payment percentage:

Figure 7. Variation in forecast values of the 4th RBF model

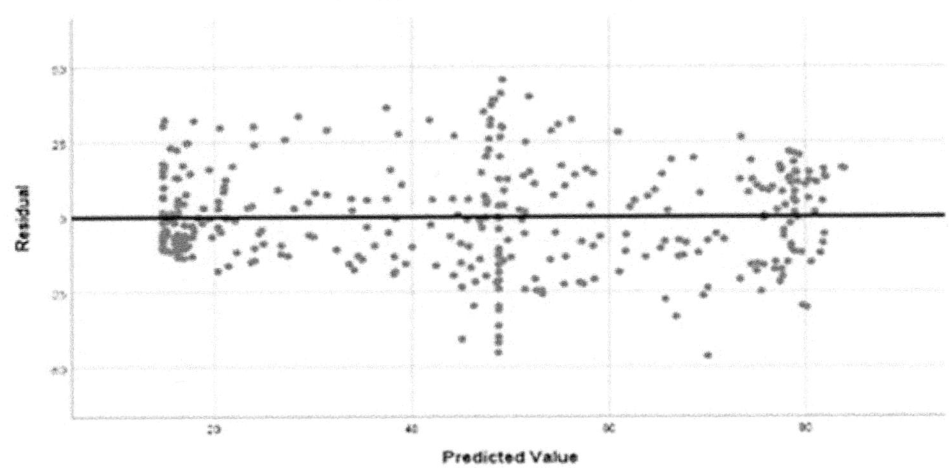

Figure 8. Variation in forecast values of the 5th RBF model

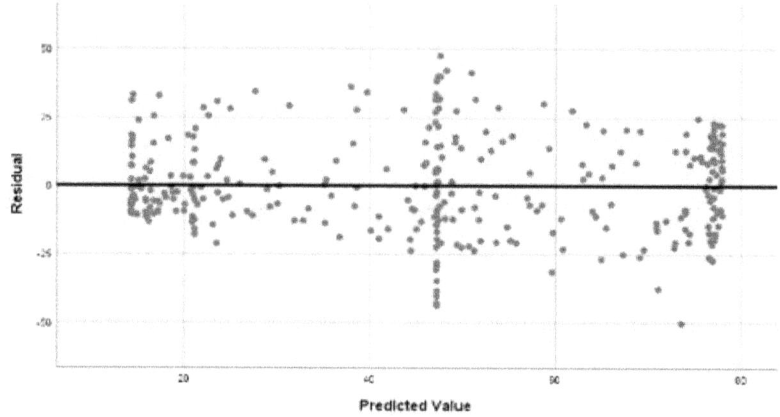

In the 3rd model as shown in Figure 6, the dispersion of the prediction values, i.e. the cumulative payoff rate, is concentrated at 49% and 56%, which indicates poor architectural structure in the network logically due to its overly simplified form due to the small number of neurons in the hidden layer. In the other models the scatter diagram shows a similar distribution with the notable fact that in models 4-6 in Figures 7-9, where there is an increase in the number of neurons by one at a time, the values seem to be more concentrated at the two edges and the centre of the graph, i.e. at the values of 10%, 50% and 77%.

Figure 9. Variation of forecast values of the 6th RBF model

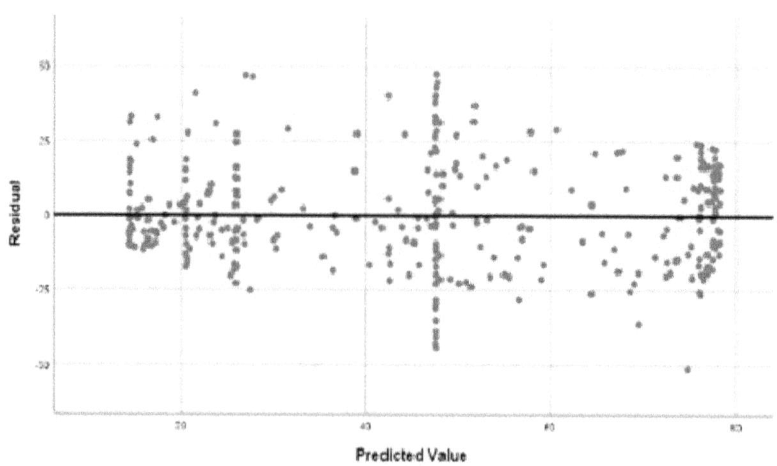

6.3 Development of a Hybrid Model Using Artificial Neural Networks and the Statistical Method

The next step is to develop the hybrid model through the final neural network. Its development process will be the Multilayer Perceptron to provide more freedom to modify it. After testing, the optimal network architecture ended up being a model with two hidden layers. The input variables included: Existence of Initial Payment, Time Percentage, Total Project Cost and the Exponential Prediction. The dependent variable was the Payment Percentage. The following pages describe the process by which this neural network was formed.

The network consists of 5 input neurons (and 1 Bias), 2 hidden layers with 6 neurons in each layer and 1 output neuron. The input variables included the prediction from the exponential model. The activation variable for the hidden layers was hyperbolic tangent, and for the output layer was Identity, with "None" selected for the Rescaling method.

The "Batch" method was used to train the network as it was judged that the "training dataset" file used to train the network was small in size and the optimization algorithm chosen was "Scaled conjugate gradient", as suggested by the software user manual when using the "Batch" method (IBM, 2017).

The procedure had the philosophy of the trial and error method, with 138 iterations, and the options considered in this procedure were the number of neurons in the two hidden layers, the activation functions, the parameters of the optimization algorithm, the minimum number of training iterations without reducing the error, and the options for stopping training based on the relative change in error. The test

Figure 10. Variance plot (y-axis) - forecasts (x-axis)

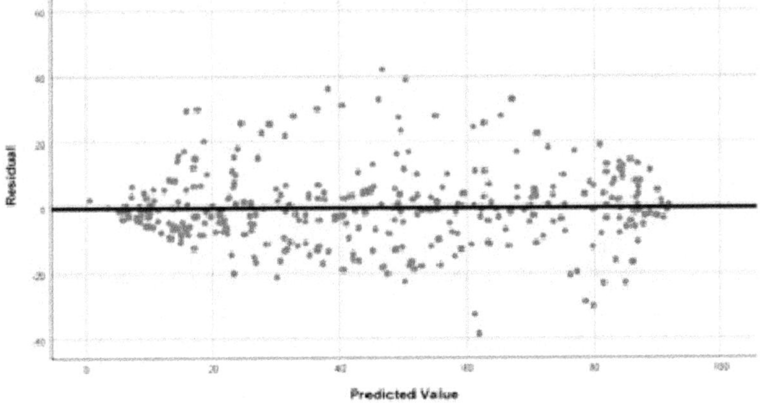

evaluation criterion was the relative error automatically calculated by the software when extracting "Output" results with the database given to the neural network for its training. It should be noted here that the relative error automatically provided by the software is not considered to be the most appropriate method of assessing the efficiency of the neural network as its calculation formula emphasizes the magnitude of the error relative to the value of each prediction. The variance of the model is presented in Figure 10.

6.4 Testing of the Models

As the main measure for comparing the effectiveness of the three forecasting models, the Mean Absolute Error is chosen. The formula by which this is calculated is as follows:

$$MAE = \frac{\sum_{i=1}^{n} |Ai - Bi|}{n}$$

Where:
Ai: Model prediction for the i entry of the testing dataset
Bi: Actual value
n: Total number of entries in the testing dataset

The reason for choosing the mean absolute error as a benchmark is that it evaluates the error of each case examined in the same way, which is desirable in this analysis as there is equal interest in the error of each prediction of the testing dataset. A fairly widespread way of comparing models is the Root Mean Square Error method, which gives more weight to larger errors and less weight to smaller errors, so MSE is more appropriate in this case. The same procedure will be used to derive the optimal TND model from those developed for the MLP (3 models,

Table 6. Minimum, maximum and average absolute error for each MLP neural network model

Model	Minimum Absolute Error (%)	Maximum Absolute Error (%)	Mean Absolute Error (%)	Std. Deviation (%)
mlp_1	,89	39,88	13,9056	9,36142
mlp_2	,31	40,54	14,3324	9,53299
mlp_3	,64	42,64	14,2216	9,80743

Table 7. Minimum, maximum, and average absolute error for each RBF neural network model

Model	Minimum Absolute Error (%)	Maximum Absolute Error (%)	Mean Absolute Error (%)	Std. Deviation (%)
RBF_1	,38	48,09	14,5097	11,34461
RBF_2	,38	48,09	14,5097	11,34461
RBF_3	,19	51,70	19,7870	14,08261
RBF_4	,21	46,56	13,7154	10,56116
RBF_5	,07	50,16	14,0263	10,90425
RBF_6	,03	51,36	15,0933	11,20214

Table 6) and RBF (6 models, Table 7). The models are subjected to the same test to determine the best of them with the mean absolute error as a benchmark.

The three models showed errors of the same order of magnitude, with the optimal one being the first one automatically generated by the "mlp_1" software, which may indicate that automatic selection may be optimal for this problem. It is worth noting that the relative errors from the training process performed in the previous stage ranked these three models in a different order than during testing.

As observed, the model with the lowest "Mean Absolute Error" is the fourth model "RBF_4" with 13.72% and 6 neurons in the hidden layer, as opposed to the optimal solution proposed by the software, namely the 1° model with 14.51%. Also, an observation that can be made is that the classification of models based on relative error done previously is consistent with the classification of the average absolute error, therefore for this problem it could indeed be used as a primary means of comparison between models for the purpose of model pre-estimation and screening at the training stage. Therefore, for the models with exclusive use of ANN, the best of both MLP and RBF methods are selected, as presented in Table 8 below.

Thus, the best model of these two methods turns out to be the RBF model with an average absolute error of 13.72%. The following Table 9 summarizes the

Table 8. The optimal model of each method (MLP and RBF) compared

	N (Cases)	Minimum Absolute Error (%)	Maximum Absolute Error (%)	Mean Absolute Error (%)	Std. Deviation (%)
MLP	75	,89	39,88	13,9056	9,36142
RBF	75	,21	46,56	13,7154	10,56116

Table 9. Summary of the minimum, maximum, and mean absolute error performance of each model and their corresponding deviation

Model	N (Cases)	Minimum Absolute Error (%)	Maximum Absolute Error (%)	Mean Absolute Error (%)	Std. Deviation (%)
Exponential	75	,94	44,18	14,3530	10,97603
Neural Network	75	,21	46,56	13,7154	10,56116
Hybrid	75	,11	45,82	13,5019	11,48611

performance of the three final models through their absolute error in the predictions each made on the testing dataset.

The above table shows that the model with the lowest mean absolute error is the hybrid model with 13.50%, followed by the RBF model with 13.72% and finally the exponential model with 14.35%. Also noteworthy is the fact that the hybrid model, which ultimately had the best average absolute error performance, also had both the smallest and 2nd largest error in its overall predictions.

Then, three projects (with relatively smooth cash flows) were selected from the model test database, with the main criterion being that there should be enough certifications so that the cumulative payments-time graph is "dense". Furthermore, these projects have increasing total costs. The first project selected, is with advance payment (Figure 11), the second without advance payment (Figure 12), and then the third higher-budget project is selected, again with advance payment (Figure 13). The

Figure 11. Graph of the cumulative payments - time percentage, applying the 3 best forecasting models for a project with a budget of 485.412,05€ with advance payment

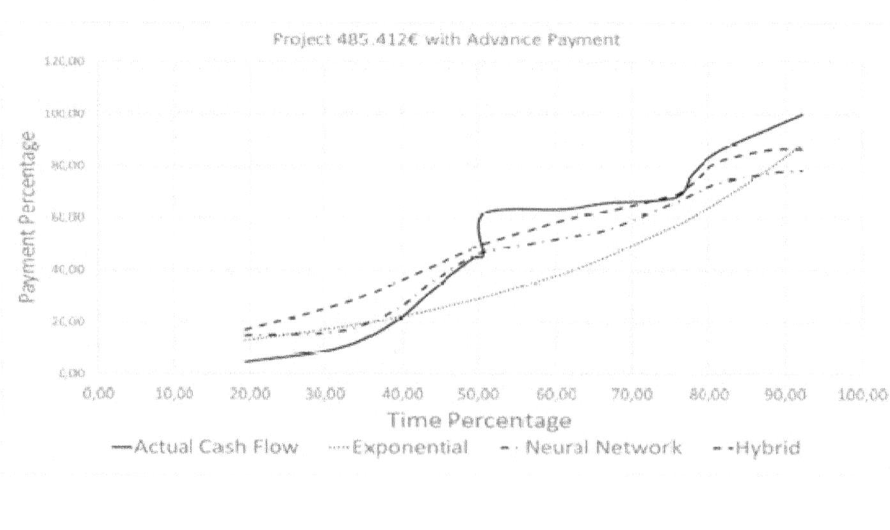

Figure 12. Graph of cumulative payments - time percentage, applying the 3 best forecasting models for a project with a budget of 2847598,28 € without advance payment

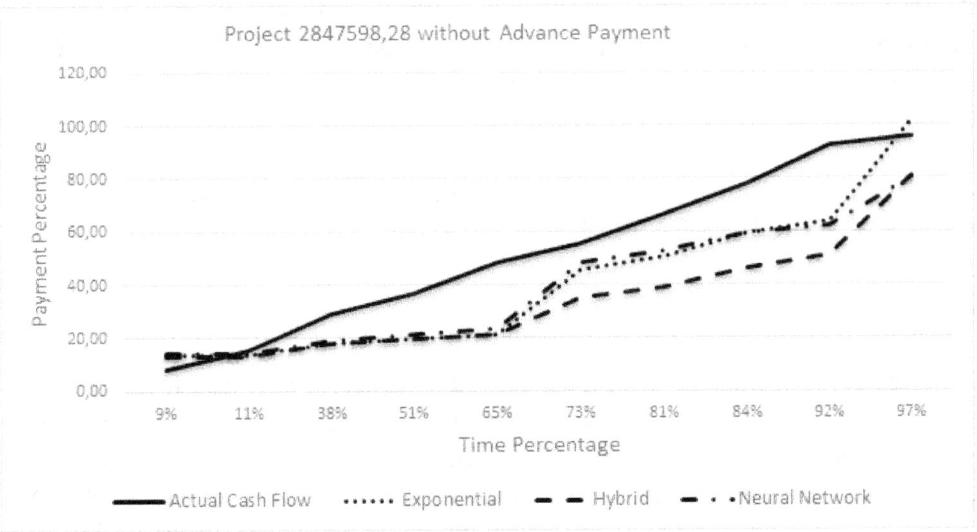

Figure 13. Graph of cumulative payments - time percentage, applying the 3 best forecasting models for a project with a budget of 5.830.674,28€ with advance payment

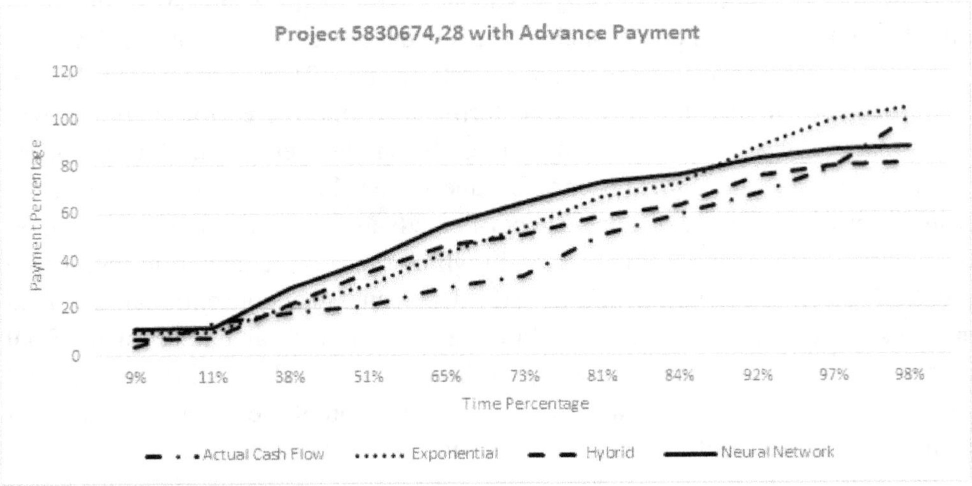

account certifications are placed as points on the cumulative payments - time graph. The solid line represents the actual cash flow of the project. Next, the predictions of the three best resulting models are placed, thus representing the estimated cash flows of the models in practice for visual valuation. The Exponential model, the Neural Network model and finally the Hybrid model along with the Actual Cash Flow are represented with different lines.

7. CONCLUSIONS, LIMITATIONS, RECOMMENDATIONS AND FUTURE RESEARCH

7.1 Conclusion

All three types of models developed showed satisfactory accuracy for the amount of data provided and their estimates had errors of the same order of magnitude. The most accurate of the final three models proved to be the hybrid model combining the exponential regression method with neural networks and showed an average absolute error of 13.50%, followed by the artificial neural network model with 13.72% and lastly the statistical regression model with 14.35%. It is also considered quite important that the hybrid model seemed to be quite influenced by the variables advance and total cost in the sensitivity analysis performed, in contrast to the exclusively artificial neural network models where these two variables seemed to have little contribution to the network prediction. This fact is particularly encouraging, as these variables in this case are essentially the only way to categorize the projects, otherwise the result would have been a fixed curve, such as the one developed in the statistical model.

The best neural network models are MLP (mlp_1), RBF (rbf_4) and the Hybrid. Regarding each model developed and starting with the regression model, it was found that the exponential function yielded the smallest error and did not follow the S-curve schematically. This may be due to the difference in the size of the projects introduced, the existence or not of an advance payment and various other characteristics such as the time period in which their implementation took place and the difficulties encountered. This is the disadvantage of conventional statistical methods, as they do not include multiple variables in the calculation of the final model they extract. Neural networks, on the contrary, include all these data and with the right amount of data and the right observation of the variables that affect it, they can yield a result adapted to the particularities of each case.

For neural network models, it was observed that the RBF method yielded better results compared to MLP for automatic model development procedures and is therefore preferred over the latter. On the contrary, the second method was also used to create the hybrid model (Hybrid) due to the multitude of options that can be parameterized and ultimately showed the best accuracy among all the models.

7.2 Limitations

A key limitation that was presented was the freedom of user choice in the "IBM SPSS Statistics 25" software. Although using the "Multilayer Perceptron" (MLP) method the options were considerably more than using the "Radial Basis Function" (RFF) method, it is noted that some choices would have been legitimate to provide more alternatives for the user. In particular, up to a maximum of two hidden layers, selection of specific activation functions and optimization algorithms were possible from the software. Also, the network architecture was clearly defined with simple feed-forward exclusively and learning was supervised. These limitations arose from the nature of the software and limited the range of experimentation to identifying the optimal neural network architecture.

Moreover, an important problem during the development of the artificial neural network models was the evaluation of the accuracy of the model by the software having as a criterion during training the relative error, which decisively influenced the choices made both by the software automatically and by the user, since as already mentioned the relative error formula was not the best possible in the evaluation of the models, since large deviations in smaller percentages had a greater impact on the error.

7.3 Proposals

A forecasting model, such as the ones developed in this paper, can be used by a project manager as a powerful strategic tool to estimate the cash flows of a project at any time before the start or during its implementation (even before the tendering process), simply by specifying in the model the existence or not of an advance, the total cost of the project and the times when the user wants to know the cumulative payment rate. The curve resulting from the model is placed on the cumulative time - cumulative payment graph and the results can be used in a variety of applications such as:

- Developing an appropriate strategy for the optimal management of the project before its launch
- Better management of the resources available to the manager and therefore better scheduling and management
- Estimation of payment delays by the developer and corresponding actions to address the problem

- Estimation of the final delivery date of the project and associated risks that may arise
- Securing construction machines and building materials at the best cost and timely arrangement to be available when they are needed, since the point in time when they will be required is known at an earlier stage
- Assessment of whether it is worthwhile for the technical company concerned to participate in the tendering of the project
- Preparation and submission of the best possible financial offer since there is more information available for the contractor
- Management and adjustment of the financial situation, possible borrowing at specific periods of time

7.4 Future Research

The result of combining statistical regression model and artificial intelligence with neural networks proved to be quite promising, which confirms the assessment of the latest research of the literature review conducted in the paper. The main issue that should be addressed in the next stage is the application of the model to more recent data of public road projects, since the data used concerned projects from 2009 to 2014, in order to evaluate both the effectiveness of the model over time and the difference in the financial flows of the projects. Also, the wider project environment should be taken into account, as in these time periods there was an economic recession in the country and general economic problems were being faced.

Another interesting approach to the problem would be to take more data as the project progresses, so that more information about each entry in the neural network can be provided, and therefore better categorization of the data can be done by the neural network. For example, such variables could be various economic indicators for the projects, for the project owner and for the contractor. Of course, since the complexity of the network and the neurons at the input level will increase, care should be taken to gather a sufficiently larger database for project training, otherwise problems of incomplete learning in the network could occur.

A different consideration for future research is the problem of initially estimating the values of the synapse weights of the neurons in the neural network. In the software used, this process was done automatically. Something that could perhaps contribute to the accuracy of the predictions is to assign initial values to the weights through some method of estimating the significance of each input such as the hierarchical decision analysis method or the decision tree method.

A different neural network architecture with more hidden layers could also be considered, but this would have to be done outside the software and perhaps in a programming environment, as SPSS allows the use of a maximum of two hidden layers, which limits to some extent the user's experimentation. Additionally, to change the structure, a feedback network could be tested, which again makes the structure more complex and perhaps more efficient when trained appropriately.

Finally, it would be legitimate to follow the same methodological approach to investigate the accuracy of predictions in projects of different types and compare them with each other in order to see if the model structure and the use of specific options are better suited to a particular category of construction projects.

REFERENCES

Al mnaseer, R., Al-Smadi, S., & Al-Bdour, H. (2023). Machine learning-aided time and cost overrun prediction in construction projects: application of artificial neural network. *Asian Journal of Civil Engineering, 24*(7), 2583–2593. doi:10.1007/s42107-023-00665-7

Alsugair, A. M., Al-Gahtani, K. S., Alsanabani, N. M., Alabduljabbar, A. A., & Almohsen, A. S. (2023). Artificial Neural Network Model to Predict Final Construction Contract Duration. *Applied Sciences (Basel, Switzerland), 13*(14), 8078. Advance online publication. doi:10.3390/app13148078

Antoniou, F., Aretoulis, G., Giannoulakis, D., & Konstantinidis, D. (2023). Cost and Material Quantities Prediction Models for the Construction of Underground Metro Stations. *Buildings, 13*(2), 382. doi:10.3390/buildings13020382

Antoniou, F., Aretoulis, G. N., Konstantinidis, D. K., & Kalfakakou, G. P. (2013). An empirical study of researchers' and practitioners' views on compensating major highway project contractors. *International Journal of Management and Decision Making, 12*(4), 351–375. doi:10.1504/IJMDM.2013.056883

Antoniou, F., Konstantinidis, D., Aretoulis, G., & Xenidis, Y. (2018a). Preliminary construction cost estimates for motorway underpass bridges. *International Journal of Construction Management, 18*(4), 321–330. doi:10.1080/15623599.2017.1358076

Antoniou, F., Konstantinidis, D., Aretoulis, G., & Xenidis, Y. (2018b). Preliminary construction cost estimates for motorway underpass bridges. *International Journal of Construction Management, 18*(4), 321–330. doi:10.1080/15623599.2017.1358076

Arabiat, A., Al-Bdour, H., & Bisharah, M. (2023). Predicting the construction projects time and cost overruns using K-nearest neighbor and artificial neural network: A case study from Jordan. *Asian Journal of Civil Engineering, 24*(7), 2405–2414. doi:10.100742107-023-00649-7

Aretoulis, G. N. (2018). Gender Based Perception of Successful Construction of Project Managers' Attributes. *Social Sciences (Basel, Switzerland)*, *7*(7), 112. doi:10.3390ocsci7070112

Aretoulis, G. N. (2019). Neural network models for actual cost prediction in Greek public highway projects. *International Journal of Project Organisation and Management*, *11*(1), 41–64. doi:10.1504/IJPOM.2019.098712

Aretoulis, G. N., Angelides, D. C., Kalfakakou, G. P., Fotiadis, G. S., & Anastasiadis, K. I. (2006). A prototype system for the prediction of final cost in construction projects. *Operations Research*, *6*(3), 323–332. doi:10.1007/BF02941260

Aretoulis, G. N., Papathanasiou, J., & Antoniou, F. (2019). PROMETHEE-based ranking of project managers based on the five personality traits. *Kybernetes*, *49*(4), 1083–1102. doi:10.1108/K-10-2018-0551

Bromilow, F. J., & Pawsey, M. R. (1987). Life cycle cost of university buildings. *Construction Management and Economics*, *5*(4), S3–S22. doi:10.1080/01446193.1987.10462089

Chua, D. K. H., Loh, P. K., Kog, Y. C., & Jaselskis, E. J. (1997). Neural networks for construction project success. *3rd Singapore International Conference on Intelligent Systems (SPICIS 97),* 317–328. 10.1016/S0957-4174(97)00046-8

Dhaval, P. (2019). Development of Prediction Models for Claim Cause Analyses in Highway Projects. *Journal of Legal Affairs and Dispute Resolution in Engineering and Construction*, *11*(4), 4519018. doi:10.1061/(ASCE)LA.1943-4170.0000303

Gkovedarou, M., & Aretoulis, G. N. (2017). Neural Networks and Statistical Analysis for Time and Cost Prediction Models of Urban Redevelopment Projects. *International Journal of Information Systems and Social Change*, *8*(4), 37–52. doi:10.4018/IJISSC.2017100103

Hola, B., & Schabowicz, K. (2010). Estimation of earthworks execution time cost by means of artificial neural networks. *Automation in Construction*, *19*(5), 570–579. doi:10.1016/j.autcon.2010.02.004

Honcharenko, T., Akselrod, R., Shpakov, A., & Khomenko, O. (2023). Information system based on multi-value classification of fully connected neural network for construction management. *IAES International Journal of Artificial Intelligence*, *12*(2), 593–601. doi:10.11591/ijai.v12.i2.pp593-601

Jia, Y. L., Wang, J., Shou, W. C., Hosseini, M. R., & Bai, Y. (2023). Graph neural networks for construction applications. *Automation in Construction, 154*, 104984. Advance online publication. doi:10.1016/j.autcon.2023.104984

Jiang, Y., & Wu, H. (2007). A method for highway agency to estimate highway construction durations and set contract times. *International Journal of Construction Education and Research, 3*(3), 199–216. doi:10.1080/15578770701715052

Lam, K. C., Hu, T., Cheung, S. O., Yuen, R. K. K., & Deng, Z. M. (2001). Multi-project cash flow optimization: Non-inferior solution through neuro-multiobjective algorithm. *Engineering, Construction, and Architectural Management, 8*(2), 130–144. doi:10.1108/eb021176

Law, No. 4412/2016, Pub. L. No. A 147 / 08.08.2016, 692 (2016). https://europam.eu/data/mechanisms/PP/PP Laws/Greece/1.LawNo.4412of2016_ENG,consolidated, last amended in 2020.pdf

National Strategic Reference Framework 2007-2013. (2007). Retrieved August 28, 2020, from https://www. certh. gr/dat/7190CCE2/file. pdf

NguyenD. A.TranD. Q.NguyenT. N.TranH. H. (2023). Modeling labor productivity in high-rise building construction projects using neural networks. *Archives of Civil Engineering, 69*(1), 675–692. https://doi.org/ doi:10.24425/ace.2023.144195

Obianyo, J. I., Udeala, R. C., & Alaneme, G. U. (2023). Application of neural networks and neuro-fuzzy models in construction scheduling. *Scientific Reports, 13*(1), 8199. Advance online publication. doi:10.103841598-023-35445-5 PMID:37211564

Petrusheva, S., Car-Pušić, D., & Zileska-Pancovska, V. (2019). Support Vector Machine Based Hybrid Model for Prediction of Road Structures Construction Costs. *IOP Conference Series. Earth and Environmental Science, 222*, 012010. doi:10.1088/1755-1315/222/1/012010

Pewdum, W., Rujirayanyong, T., & Sooksatra, V. (2009). Forecasting final budget and duration of highway construction projects. *Engineering, Construction, and Architectural Management, 16*(6), 544–557. doi:10.1108/09699980911002566

PMI. (2017). *A guide to the Project Management Body of Knowledge (PMBOK guide)* (P. M. Institute, Ed.; 6th ed.). Project Management Institute Newton Square.

Titirla, M., & Aretoulis, G. (2019). Neural network models for actual duration of Greek highway projects. *Journal of Engineering. Design and Technology, 17*(6), 1323–1339. doi:10.1108/JEDT-01-2019-0027

Titirla, M., Larbi, W., & Aretoulis, G. (2021). Prediction methods for the actual duration of greek highway projects. *WSEAS Transactions on Business and Economics*, *18*, 1389–1396. doi:10.37394/23207.2021.18.128

Waziri, B. S., Jibrin, A. T., & Kadai, B. (2014). Functional duration models for highway construction projects in Nigeria. *Arid Zone Journal of Engineering, Technology and Environment*, *10*, 13–23.

Westney, R. E. (1997). *The Engineer's cost handbook: tools for managing project costs*. CRC Press. doi:10.1201/9780203910016

Zhang, J. P., Liu, L. H., & Coble, R. J. (2002). Hybrid intelligence utilization for construction site layout. *Automation in Construction*, *11*(5), 511–519. doi:10.1016/S0926-5805(01)00071-1

Chapter 6
Investigating the Risks of Time and Cost Overruns in Infrastructure Projects

Kleopatra Petroutsatou
https://orcid.org/0000-0003-4477-8693
Aristotle University of Thessaloniki, Greece

Theodora Vagdatli
Aristotle University of Thessaloniki, Greece

Marina Chronaki
Hellenic Open University, Greece

Panagiota Samouilidou
Hellenic Open University, Greece

ABSTRACT

The purpose of this chapter is to investigate and quantify through real case studies the risks involved in time and cost overruns of infrastructure projects from the procurement to the delivery stage. Although the literature is very rich with a variety of analyses of the factors causing cost and time overruns, there is a gap in investigating the risks in the procurement phase to delivery of such projects. A holistic approach of risks identified in the procurement and construction phase of such projects is presented by using probabilistic analyses of time and cost overruns compared to contractual agreements. Three real case studies are presented with and without the risks identified, results are discussed, and conclusions are derived. This approach could enhance public authorities' processes for successful procurement and delivery. Furthermore, the quantification of these risks in terms of time and cost could pave the way for a more sustainable organization of the authorities in order to deliver successful projects within their time constraints and budget.
DOI: 10.4018/978-1-6684-7786-1.ch006

ANALYSING THE RISKS OF TIME AND COST OVERRUNS IN INFRASTRUCTURE PROJECTS FROM THE PROCUREMENT TO THE DELIVERY PHASE

The construction sector accounts of a large share of gross domestic product (GDP) and employs many people in all developed countries. According to (Mckinsey, 2017) construction-related spending accounts for 13% of the world's GDP. The industry's size suggest that its efficiency is important to the overall performance of the economy. Thus, both public authorities and contractors should work to reduce wasteful practices and adopt sustainable approaches. In fact, the construction industry has been plagued by time delays and cost overruns reaching further than what was set out initially (Adam et al., 2017; Agyekum-Mensah & Knight, 2017; Antoniou, 2021; Baudrit et al., 2019; Çevikbaş & Işık, 2021; Derbe et al., 2020; Ghaleh et al., 2021; Koulinas et al., 2020; Welde & Dahl, 2021).

The industry lacks a systematic activity based risk factor list and the impacts of risks factors are rarely considered when allocating operational risk factors (Rasheed, Shahzad, Khalfan, & Rotimi, 2022; Jiang, Yang, Jiang, Martek, & Gao, 2022). However, beyond demonstrating poor cost and time performance, many of the studies are not investigating in activity level large and complex projects and the studies approaches the risks based on the macroeconomic environment. Furthermore, there was not found in the literature any research on investigating holistically the risks that could exist throughout the procurement and construction phase of infrastructure projects and conclude to time and cost overruns. The analyses made so far focused mainly on the construction period leaving out the lifecycle span which starts with the conception of the project and ends with the demolition or change of use.

This chapter presents a holistic approach of identified risks for the procurement and construction phase of infrastructure projects by using probabilistic analyses regarding time and cost overruns that are quantified in relation with the contractual schedule and budget of the project. Three real case studies are presented, namely a building, a redevelopment and a road infrastructure project with and without the risks identified and results are discussed and conclusions are derived. Also, a sensitivity approach is performed and through Tornado diagrams the impact of the most important risks are determined and discussed.

A Description of the Discrete Phases of a Public Works Contract

The main processes of each phase are:

1. Planning Phase: this phase includes the conceptualization of the project and the cost-benefit analysis. Also, the stage of any permits required must be finalized now such as expropriations, archaeological permits etc. The acquired financing must be ensured now with the inclusion of the project in a funding program.
2. Procurement Phase: this phase incorporates the procurement process with all the required steps according the European and National Directives (2014/24/EU, Law 4782/2021)
3. Construction Phase: This phase comprises all the processes (i.e., work packages) that are incorporated in the contract for the successful completion of the project.

For all the three phases, potential risks are identified as described in the following chapters and a risk registry was developed. This registry was used in order to qualify and quantify risks encountered though the lifecycle of a Public Works Contract that ends with the successful delivery of the project to its Owner.

PERFORMING RISK ANALYSIS IN ENGINEERING PROJECTS

Achieving construction cost, time and quality are the primary objectives for successfully delivering engineering projects. Due to their long-term nature and complexity, public construction projects typically pose significant financial risks deriving from various uncertainty factors that may affect the smooth completion of the project. Particularly, time and cost overruns can occur in any construction project, with their magnitude differing among project types (Naderpour, Sardroud, Mo, & Xenidis, 2019). Previous studies reveal the shortage of risk assessment and management approaches in the construction industry for developed and developing countries worldwide (Le, Chileshe, Kirytopoulos, & Rameezdeen, 2020). To overcome this problem, project risk evaluation seems inevitable.

Project risk management is one of the most challenging processes for delivering projects according to schedule, budget, and proposed quality (Koulinas, Demesouka, Sidas, & Koulouriotis, 2021). Among others, the project management body of knowledge (PMBOK) guide is regarded as one of the most valuable risk management models (Ghaleh et al., 2021). According to (PMI, 2021), project risk management includes identifying, analyzing and responding to project risks in order to both maximize the results of positive events and minimize the volume of adverse events.

After the crucial stage of risk identification, the risk analysis stage follows, divided into two successive main categories, qualitative and quantitative risk analysis. The former is applied to the list of upcoming risks for providing the risk managers with the most influential (positive or adverse) risks establishing their relative priority, whilst the latter deals only with the risks highlighted as high priority and might either threaten or enhance the project's objectives (PMI, 2019).

Qualitative Risk Analysis in Project Management

Qualitative Risk Analysis is considered a cost-effective way for the priority establishment of risk response and foundation setting for Quantitative Risk Analysis (Gupta & Thakkar, 2018). Hence, after the specification of the possible risks for each project operation category, the two-dimensional "Risk Matrix" approach was used to assign the two relative attributes in each risk, namely the Probability and Impact factors, for identifying the risk's significance level according to the probability-impact matrix of Table 1 by multiplying the Probability percentage by the Impact percentage (PMI, 2019). For scaling the two risk attributes, both Impact values (assigned on the X-axis) and Probability values (assigned on the Y-axis) of the Risk Matrix range from 1 to 5 ("very low" to "very high" level). The ranges of these five linguistic variables were scaled according to (PMI, 2021) (Table 2) and used in the questionnaires for the subsequent analysis. High-risk factors are located in the red area, medium-risk are found in the yellow area, while the green region reflects low-risk factors.

Table 1. Probability and impact matrix (PMI, 2019)

Probability	Very High (VH)	0.045	0.09	0.18	0.36	0.72
	High (H)	0.035	0.07	0.14	0.28	0.56
	Medium (M)	0.025	0.05	0.10	0.20	0.40
	Low (L)	0.015	0.03	0.06	0.12	0.24
	Very Low (VL)	0.005	0.01	0.02	0.04	0.08

Table 2. Classification ranges of the probability and impact scales

	Probability (%)	Impact on Duration & Cost
Very Low (VL)	1-10	0-5
Low (VL)	11-30	6-10
Medium (M)	31-50	11-20
High (H)	51-70	21-40
Very High (VH)	>70	>40

Quantitative Risk Analysis in Project Management

Quantitative Risk Analysis utilizes a model for mathematically analyzing and evaluating the combined effects of individual risks on overall project objectives. In Quantitative Risk Analysis, only the risks identified as of high priority in Qualitative Risk Analysis are considered (PMI, 2008). One of the most common techniques for performing Quantitative Risk Analysis is the Monte-Carlo simulation (MCS) to assess the project's risks in probabilistic terms. Generally, the MCS is a repetitive process using a set of random input values for extracting a probability distribution function for the project as a whole, providing more comprehensive information about the project's risk profile (European Commission, 2014). In this study, the project's cost and schedule overruns were examined as output variables via the MCS process, eventually resulting in a distribution of possible total project cost and completion dates, respectively.

Assigning Probability Distributions and Certain Ranges

Modelling the variability of projects' costs and times results in the possible outcomes extraction for the total cost and time into value ranges presented with a probability distribution form. The selection of the probability distribution type for the input variables in the MCS is considered crucial for obtaining more accurate results from the simulation run.

Thus, a distinction between actual data fit and experts' judgement seems vital. This separation is known as the "level of knowledge (LoK)" on the uncertain variables, suggesting that parametric distributions (e.g., Normal, Gamma or Beta) should be assigned when uncertain variables are well defined in the literature or by actual data (high LoK). Otherwise, non-parametric distributions (such as Beta-PERT, triangular or uniform) should be used for uncertain variables relied on experts' judgements (Vose, 2008). According to the extant body of the literature, the most frequently used distributions types for both the cost and time estimations are triangular, normal, lognormal and Beta (Chou et al., 2009; Moghayedi & Windapo, 2022; Moret & Einstein, 2016; Vagdatli & Petroutsatou, 2021). Additionally, Weibull and Gamma distributions seem to be used for cost variability (Chou et al., 2009; Salling & Leleur, 2011).

In order to proceed with the Quantitative Risk Analysis in the present study, some necessary assumptions regarding the type and range of the selected probability distributions for the input variables to the MCS were made. Given that there was no historical dataset available regarding the activities' costs and durations, the probability distribution types were derived from literature and experts' judgments. From the above available distribution types, specifically, the triangular distribution is a suitable option for capturing continuous uncertainty when not much historical information is available, since it only needs the determination of three parameters, namely the most likely value estimation, frequently corresponding to the base case scenario, and a minimum and maximum value as lower and upper bounds, respectively (Koulinas et al., 2020). Hence, the triangular distribution was assigned to the cost and time overruns variables. The variation range of the most likely value of the triangular distribution stemmed from the questionnaire's responses for each risk affecting the project's activities according to real fluctuations in projects in Greece. Thus, the three parameters of triangular distribution, namely the minimum, the most likely and the maximum values could be specified. Moreover, the selected distribution type for the occurrence probability was the Bernoulli as more suitable since it was considered that each risk would appear once.

APPLICATION OF RISK ANALYSIS IN THREE DIFFERENT CONSTRUCTION PROJECTS IN GREECE

In the present study, the proposed approach was applied to analyze the duration and cost overruns in three different real projects in Greece, namely a building, a redevelopment and a road infrastructure project, in order to derive conclusions regarding the risk function in these project types. Initially, the structural analysis of the projects was carried out where all the activities required from maturation to their implementation were classified into three successive work categories, namely the Public Project's "Planning", "Procurement" and "Construction" Phases (Table 3).

Specifically, the first project concerns the construction of a school building of 3,550,000 € (with VAT) with a total duration timeline from its maturation to its implementation of approximately 93 months. The second project concerns the urban redevelopment in the center area of the city of Katerini with a budget of 4,900,000 € (with VAT), while the third project concerns the improvement of an agricultural road in the municipality of Katerini with a budget of 935,290 € (with VAT). The total duration from maturation to implementation for the last two projects is about 147 months.

Data Collection

For conducting the qualitative and quantitative risk analyses, first, the risks that may affect the examined activities were identified through relative literature review and interviews with experts. There was not found in the literature any reference on specific activities and their related risks as it is attempted in this research. The study was conducted via questionnaires distributed to 88 employees of Municipalities and

Figure 1. Rates of respondents based on (a) education level, (b) years of experience, (c) occupation

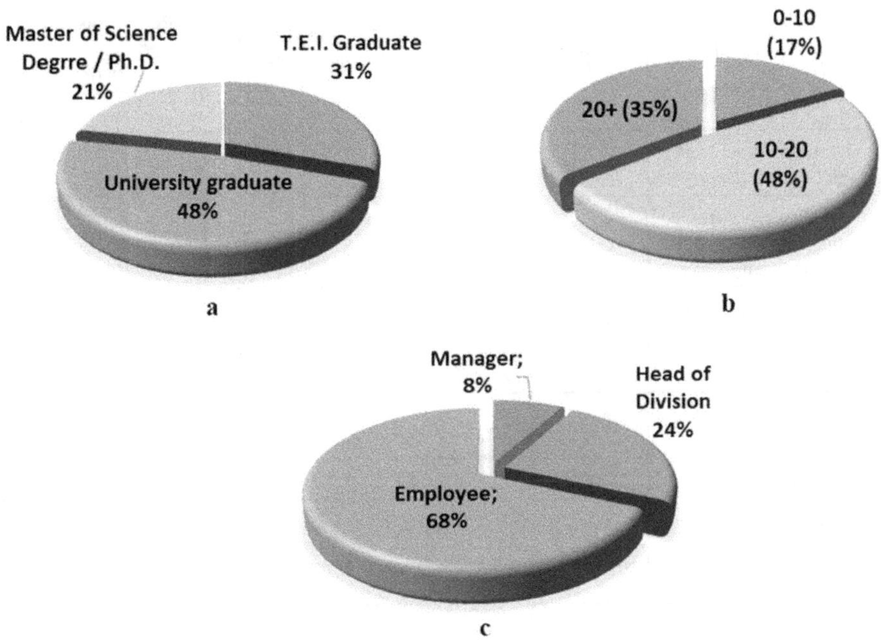

Regional Units in Greece. The profile of the questionnaire respondents is displayed in Figure 1.

For each project type, the necessary information, derived from the collected data and will be used as inputs for proceeding into the following steps of the risk analysis, are:

i. the projects' initial schedule and costs,
ii. the most severe risks that may occur during the different phases of the project life-cycle,
iii. the Impact of possible risks on the duration and cost of each project's activity as a percentage increase of activities' duration and cost respectively,
iv. the Probability of occurrence for all possible risks.

Notably, the individual activities are briefly presented in Tables 3-4 along with their durations and costs for each project type and Table 5 displays the risk inventory of the most severe risks that will be analyzed for facilitating the understanding of the practitioners' perceptions of risk factors. It is noted that possible overlaps among projects' activities were neglected in the present research, hence the examined

Table 3. Duration of the projects' main activities

ID	Activity	Duration (%)		Duration in Months	
		Building PROJECT	**Redevelopment & Road Infrastructure Projects**	**Building Project**	**Redevelopment & Road Infrastructure Projects**
Planning Phase					
A1.1	Maturation process by the operator agency	6.47%	8.18%	6	12
A1.2	Evaluation of the proposal by the funding authority	1.08%	0.68%	1	1
A1.3	Project Declaration Procedure	0.54%	0.34%	0.50	0.50
Procurement Phase					
A2.1	Project Design in ESIDIS*	0.22%	0.14%	0.2	0.20
A2.2	Opening of bids	1.08%	0.68%	1	1
A2.3	Contract Signature procedure	3.24%	2.04%	3	3
Construction Phase					
A3.1	Administration of contract - performing tasks	29.13%	26.58%	27	39
A3.2	Contractor's performance	12.94%	16.36%	12	24
A3.3	Payments	25.89%	24.54%	24	36
A3.4	Management Authority findings	19.42%	20.45%	18	30
Total		**100%**	**100%**	**92.7**	**146.7**

*An electronic platform for the public procurement processes

risks were assumed to be independent without taking into account the covariance perspective of them. In this way, the worst scenario was considered for being on the safe side for the exported estimations,

Results of Qualitative Risk Analysis

After collecting the data from the questionnaires, their statistical analysis triggered the performance of the Qualitative Risk Analysis for constructing the risk matrix and yielding fruitful results regarding risk level. Particularly, Table 6 depicts the interviewees' responses regarding the Probability (P) and Impact (I) of the studied

Table 4. Costs of the projects' main activities

ID	Activity	Cost (%)			Cost of the Studied Case-Studies (€)		
		Building Project	Redevelopment Project	Road Infrastructure Project	Building Project	Redevelopment Project	Road Infrastructure Project
Planning Phase							
A1.1	Maturation process by the operator agency	15%	20%	20%	532,500	980,000	187,058
A1.2	Evaluation of the proposal by the funding authority	10%	10%	10%	355,000	490,000	93,529
A1.3	Project Declaration Procedure	5%	5%	5%	177,500	245,000	46,764.50
Procurement Phase							
A2.1	Project Design in ESIDIS	5%	5%	5%	177,500	245,000	46,764.50
A2.2	Opening of bids	5%	5%	5%	177,500	245,000	46,764.50
A2.3	Contract Signature procedure	5%	5%	5%	177,500	245,000	46,764.50
Construction Phase							
A3.1	Administration of contract - performing tasks	15%	20%	20%	532,500	980,000	187,058
A3.2	Contractor's performance	20%	20%	20%	710,000	980,000	187,058
A3.3	Payments	10%	5%	5%	355,000	245,000	46,764.50
A3.4	Management Authority findings	10%	5%	5%	355,000	245,000	46,764.50
Total		**100%**	**100%**	**100%**	**3,550,000**	**4,900,000**	**935,290**

risks (rows) on every activity (columns). Specifically, the displayed linguistic values derived from the classification of the questionaries' numerical results into their corresponding linguistic category according to Table 2.

It is worth mentioning that a given potential risk may have a different occurrence probability and impact on the various studied activities. The results of such differentiation are apparent in the significance level (SL) of each risk resulting as a product of the multiplication of Probability by Impact (Table 6) and used for classifying each risk into one of the three areas of the risk matrix. Specifically, the bold records for risks' SL of Table 6 belong to the orange or red areas of the risk matrix and pass to the Quantitative Risk Analysis. Totally, eighteen and thirteen risks seemed to affect the most the project's schedule andcost, respectively. Contrarily,

Table 5. Identified risks in the procurement and delivery phase

Risk ID	Description	Risk ID	Description
R1	Insufficient maturity of the operation to be financed during its integration phase	R11	The amendments to the contract were not made in accordance with its provisions and the legislation on the execution of Public Works
R2	Failure to comply with the institutional framework	R12	Insufficient staffing of the Contractor
R3	Non-use of the tender standard documents	R13	Non-timely payment of the Contractor
R4	Failure to comply with the rules of publicity and transparency during the Competition	R14	Occurrence of unforeseen events that led to schedule violations & demand for contractual time extension
R5	Incorrect completion of the ESIDIS platform fields during the design phase	R15	Occurrence of problems during the implementation of the contract between the Contractor and the Contracting Authority
R6	Failure to properly follow the required steps during the unsealing process	R16	The implementation of the Physical Object does not agree with the inclusion decision and the legal commitment of the sub-project
R7	Failure to properly follow the steps during the contract signing process	R17	The procedure of pre-approval or notification of the Administrative Authority for any modifications of the legal commitment was not followed
R8	Non-existence of even an electronic signature with the right to an exact copy	R18	Violation of the project's schedule
R9	Failure of the Contracting Authority to respond to communication and obligations towards the Contractor (timely approvals - communication - information - cooperation, etc.)	R19	The conditions laid down in the funding letter were not met
R10	Non-observance of the procedures and deadlines stipulated by the Law on the part of the Contracting Authority during the execution of the Contract	R20	The Beneficiary did not comply with the recommendations of the on-site verifications / audits of the Administrative Authority & other audit bodies

the remaining risks falling into the green area were eliminated because they are regarded as accepted since they do not affect the project's objectives and will be only monitored for a possible alteration of their impact or probability occurrence.

Table 6. Probability and Impact ranking for individual risks according to PMI scaling and resulting significance level

Risks	Project Objective	Activities																										
		A1.1			A1.2			A1.3			A2.1			A2.2			A2.3			A3.1			A3.2			A3.3 & A3.4		
		P	I	SL	P	I	SL	P	I	SL	P	I	SL	P	I	SL	P	I	SL	P	I	SL	P	I	SL	P	I	SL
R1	Time	L	L	0.03	L	VH	**0.24**		-			-			-			-			-			-			-	
	Cost	L	H	**0.12**	L	VH	**0.24**		-			-			-			-			-			-			-	
R2	Time	L	VH	**0.24**	L	VH	**0.24**		-			-			-			-			-			-			-	
	Cost	L	VH	**0.24**	L	VH	**0.24**		-			-			-			-			-			-			-	
R3	Time		-		VL	M	0.02	VL	M	0.02		-			-			-			-			-			-	
	Cost		-		VL	M	0.02	VL	M	0.02		-			-			-			-			-			-	
R4	Time		-			-		VL	VH	**0.08**		-			-			-			-			-			-	
	Cost		-			-		VL	H	0.04		-			-			-			-			-			-	
R5	Time		-			-			-		VL	VH	**0.08**		-			-			-			-			-	
	Cost		-			-			-		VL	M	0.02		-			-			-			-			-	
R6	Time		-			-			-			-		VL	VH	**0.08**		-			-			-			-	
	Cost		-			-			-			-		VL	M	0.02		-			-			-			-	
R7	Time		-			-			-			-			-		VL	VH	**0.08**		-			-			-	
	Cost		-			-			-			-			-		VL	M	0.02		-			-			-	
R8	Time		-			-			-		VL	M	0.02	VL	M	0.02	VL	M	0.02		-			-			-	
	Cost		-			-			-		VL	M	0.02	VL	M	0.02	VL	M	0.02		-			-			-	
R9	Time		-			-			-			-			-			-		VL	H	0.04		-			-	
	Cost		-			-			-			-			-			-		VL	M	0.02		-			-	
R10	Time		-			-			-			-			-			-		VL	H	0.04		-			-	
	Cost		-			-			-			-			-			-		VL	M	0.02		-			-	
R11	Time		-			-			-			-			-			-		VL	H	0.04		-			-	
	Cost		-			-			-			-			-			-		VL	M	0.02		-			-	
R12	Time		-			-			-			-			-			-		L	H	**0.12**	L	H	**0.12**		-	
	Cost		-			-			-			-			-			-		L	M	0.06	L	H	**0.12**		-	

Monte-Carlo Simulation Results and Discussion

MCS Results for Projects' Percentage Duration and Cost Overruns

The Quantitative Risk Analysis for assessing the most significant risks was performed via the @Risk software using the MCS as an add-in in the Excel spreadsheets. Suitable distribution functions were used to demonstrate the particular features of the given risks and quantify their probability of occurrence and impact on both the duration and cost of the project's activities. Particularly, as described above, the Bernoulli

Table 6. (Continue) Probability and Impact ranking for individual risks according to PMI scaling and resulting significance level

		Project Objective	Activities																	
			A1.1	A1.2	A1.3	A2.1	A2.2	A2.3	A3.1			A3.2			A3.3			A3.4		
			P	I	SL	P	I	SL	P	I	SL	P	I	SL	P	I	SL	P	I	SL
Risks	R13	Time	-	-	-	-	-	-	L	H	**0.12**	L	H	**0.12**	L	H	**0.12**		-	
		Cost	-	-	-	-	-	-	L	M	0.06	L	H	**0.12**	L	H	**0.12**		-	
	R14	Time	-	-	-	-	-	-	H	H	**0.28**	H	H	**0.28**	H	H	**0.28**		-	
		Cost	-	-	-	-	-	-	H	H	**0.28**	H	H	**0.28**	H	M	**0.14**		-	
	R15	Time	-	-	-	-	-	-	L	H	**0.12**	L	H	**0.12**	L	H	**0.12**		-	
		Cost	-	-	-	-	-	-	L	H	**0.12**	L	H	**0.12**	L	H	**0.12**		-	
	R16	Time	-	-	-	-	-	-	VL	L	0.01		-		VL	L	0.01	VL	L	0.01
		Cost	-	-	-	-	-	-	VL	M	0.02		-		VL	L	0.01	VL	L	0.01
	R17	Time	-	-	-	-	-	-	VL	L	0.01		-		VL	L	0.01	VL	L	0.01
		Cost	-	-	-	-	-	-	VL	L	0.01		-		VL	L	0.01	VL	L	0.01
	R18	Time	-	-	-	-	-	-	VL	VL	0.005		-			-		VL	VL	0.005
		Cost	-	-	-	-	-	-	VL	VL	0.005		-			-		VL	VL	0.005
	R19	Time	-	-	-	-	-	-	VL	VL	0.005		-		VL	VL	0.005	VL	VL	0.005
		Cost	-	-	-	-	-	-	VL	L	0.01		-		VL	L	0.01	VL	L	0.01
	R20	Time	-	-	-	-	-	-		-			-			-		VL	VL	0.005
		Cost	-	-	-	-	-	-		-			-			-		VL	L	0.01

distribution was used for the risks' probability of occurrence since it was regarded that each risk may occur only once, while the triangular distribution was used for the impact's probabilistic determination. The two risk attributes, i.e., the probability of occurrence and impact on the project's duration and cost, were inserted as input variables into the probabilistic analysis. The total number of risk occurrences, duration and cost overruns were considered as output variables for each project type. The output variables were connected with the input ones with sum equations as linkage forms. During the MCS run, 10,000 iterations were executed, resulting in the formulation of the probability density functions (PDFs) and cumulative density functions (CDFs) of the percentage overruns of duration and cost (Figures 2-3) and the total number of risk occurrences (Figures 4-5) for the three studied project types. The descriptive results of all probabilistic output variables exported from the MCS process can be seen in Tables 7-8.

The analysis of the probabilistic model for building projects yielded that the variations ranged from 7.9% to 43% and 5.6% to 34.8% within a two-sided confidence

Figure 2. Probability and cumulative density functions of (a) duration overruns (%), (b) costs overruns (%) of building projects

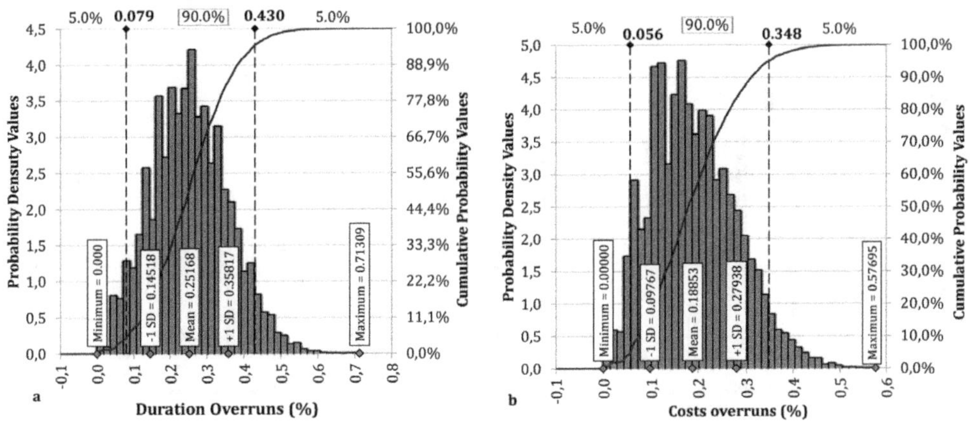

Figure 3. Probability and cumulative density functions of (a) duration overruns (%), (b) costs overruns (%) of redevelopment and road infrastructure projects

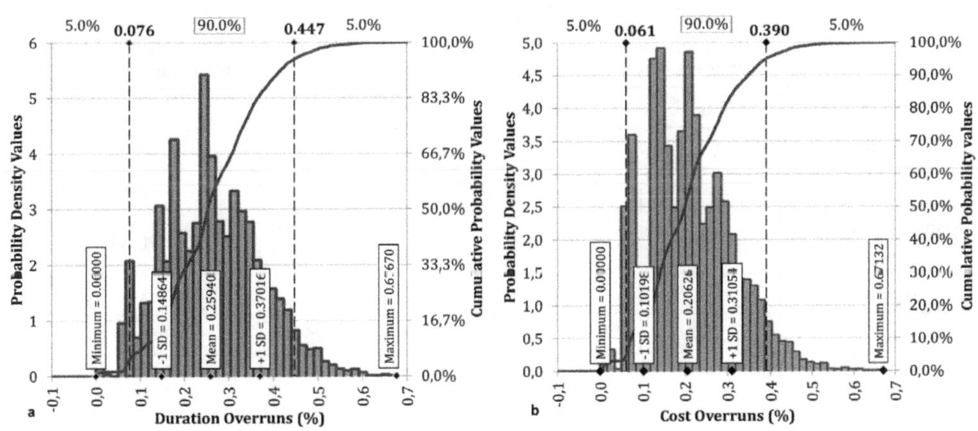

interval of 90% for the duration and cost overruns, respectively (Figure 2). As might be expected, the MCS revealed that the redevelopment and road infrastructure projects had the same probabilistic ranges regarding their percentage duration and cost overruns, with the range for the duration being between 7.6% and 44.7% while the cost variations fluctuate between 6.1% and 39% (Figure 3). Given the selected distributions for the input variables, Figures 4-5 reveal that the mean value of the risks that could be appeared simultaneously was set to four for both time and cost investigation in any project type. The minimum and maximum values in the range

Figure 4. Probability and cumulative density functions of the total number of risk occurrences of MCS for (a) time, (b) cost for building projects

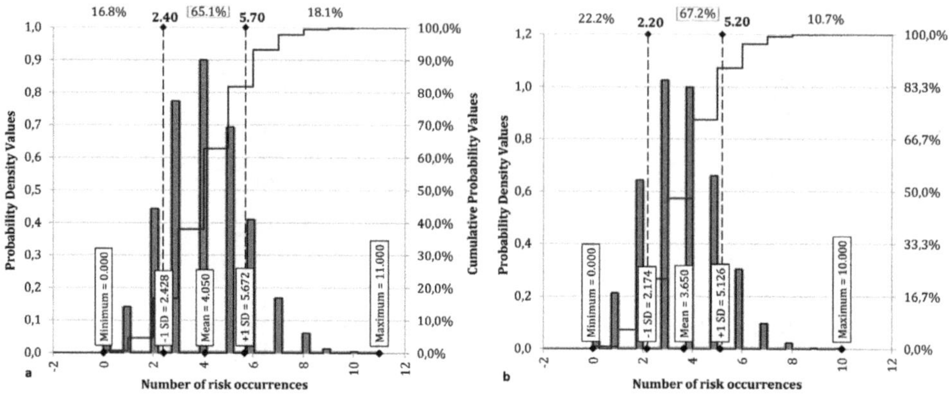

Table 7. Descriptive statistics of the Monte-Carlo simulation outputs for percentage overruns of duration and cost

	Duration Overruns (%)		Cost Overruns (%)	
	Building Project	**Redevelopment & Road Infrastructure Projects**	**Building Project**	**Redevelopment & Road Infrastructure Projects**
Minimum (%)	0.00	0.00	0.00	0.00
Maximum (%)	71.31	67.67	57.69	67.13
Mean (%)	25.17	25.94	18.85	20.63
Standard Deviation (%)	10.65	11.08	9.09	10.43
Skewness	0.17	0.20	0.43	0.45
Kurtosis	2.89	2.91	2.96	2.99

of $\pm 1\sigma$ (standard deviation) were roughly 2 and 5 risks, with the probability within the range of $\pm 1\sigma$ to be around 65%.

These outcomes are precious during the decision-making process of similar projects for both the duration and cost overruns of the projects since they can be used for informing the stakeholders of the possible quantified range of cost and duration overruns in projects of the same type. Particularly, the duration and the budget of any given project can be multiplied by the corresponding exported percentage overruns (Figures 2-3) to formulate an opinion for the overrun quantities of the specific project. Furthermore, the majority of probabilities (i.e., 65%) for simultaneous risks to occur are limited to the range of 2 to 5 risks which is far away

Figure 5. Probability and cumulative density functions of the total number of risk occurrences of MCS for (a) time, (b) cost for redevelopment and road infrastructure projects

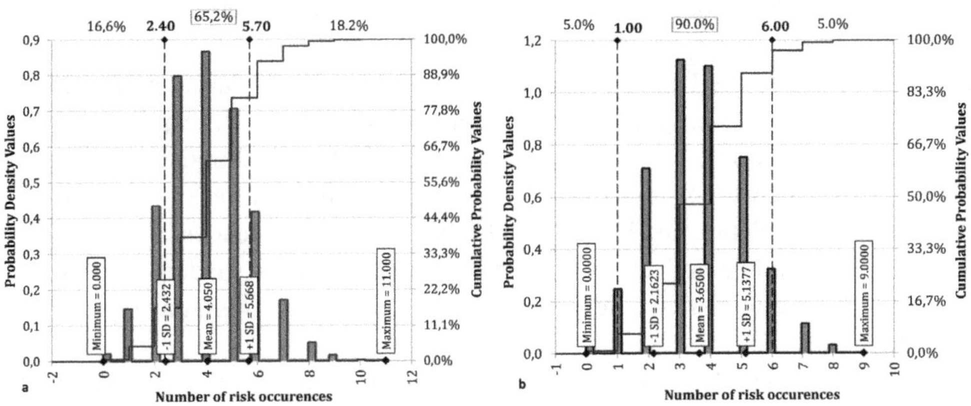

Table 8. Descriptive statistics for the total number of risk occurrences for duration and cost MCS runs

Total Number of Risks Occurrences				
	MCS for "Duration" Objective		MCS for "Cost" Objective	
	Building Project	Redevelopment & Road Infrastructure Projects	Building Project	Redevelopment & Road Infrastructure Projects
Minimum	0.00	0.00	0.00	0.00
Maximum	11	11	10	9
Mean	4.05	4.05	3.65	3.65
Median	4	4	4	4
Standard Deviation	1.62	1.62	1.48	1.49
Skewness	0.25	0.25	0.25	0.25
Kurtosis	3.08	2.96	2.99	2.96

from the initial eighteen and thirteen risks inserted into the MCS for time and cost examination. This fact demonstrates the importance of risk analysis on how severe the risks might be for the project's seamless operation. Overall, the risk managers will be qualified to decide whether the total risk is acceptable or not in advance and provide alternative actions if necessary.

MCS Results for Projects' Quantities of Duration and Cost Overruns

To make it more explicit, three illustrative examples were conducted using specific quantities of Tables 3 and 4 for the three distinct projects of building, redevelopment and road infrastructure type. The PDFs and CDFs of the quantities of duration and cost overruns from the 10,000 iterations of MCS runs are displayed in Figures 6-8 for the building, redevelopment and road infrastructure project, respectively. The corresponding descriptive statistics are depicted in Table 9. Additionally, the shaded diagrams of Figures 7-9 illustrate the probabilistic distribution of the expected final project completion and budget due to the duration and cost escalations given the risks. It should be noticed that the minimum value of the shaded distributions refers to the deterministic value of the initial project's duration and cost without considering the risks.

Indicatively, in probabilistic quantifying terms, the duration overruns in building projects could reach 66.103 months, with the final project's duration leaning between 92.70 and 158.803 months, depending on the nature of the emerged risks (Figure 6a). Accordingly, the cost overruns for the building project would not exceed 2,048,172.5 € and the final project's cost could vary from 3,550,000 € to 5,598,172.5 € (Figure 6b).

Redevelopment and Road Infrastructure projects have the same variation in duration overruns, ranging from 0.00 to 99.27 months (Figure 7a & Figure 8a) since they have the identical initial duration, namely 146.70 months and the same percentage increase (as derived from the first step of MCS for the percentage overruns - Figure 3a). By applying the same percentage of cost overruns (Figure 3b) to the different initial costs for redevelopment and road infrastructure projects,

Figure 6. Probability and cumulative density functions of (a) duration overruns and final project's duration (in mths), (b) cost overruns and final project's cost (in €) of the studied building project

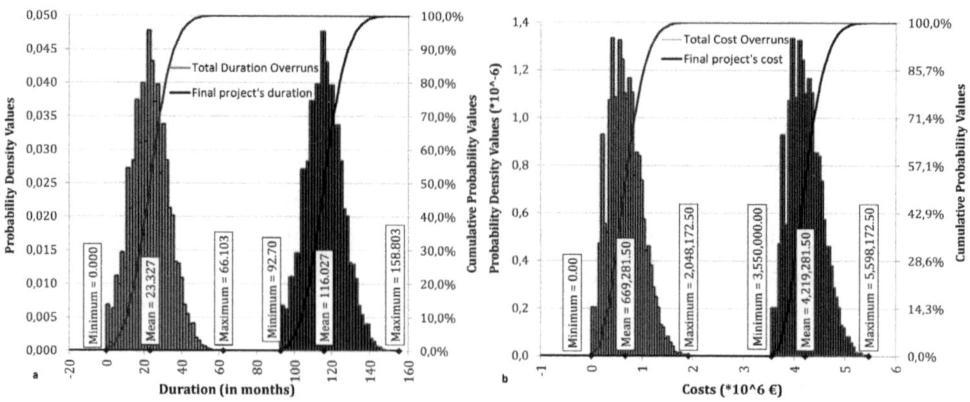

Figure 7. Probability and cumulative density functions of (a) duration overruns and final project's duration (in mths), (b) cost overruns and final project's cost (in €) of the studied redevelopment project

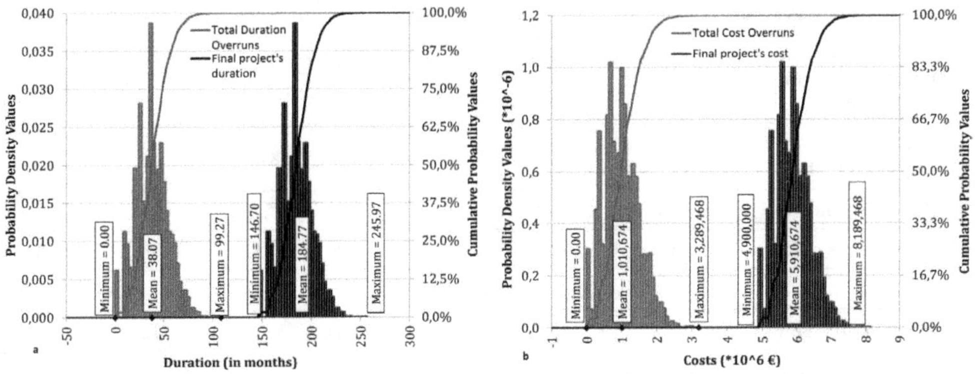

Figure 8. Probability and cumulative density functions of (a) duration overruns and final project's duration (in mths), (b) cost overruns and final project's cost (in €) of the studied road infrastructure project

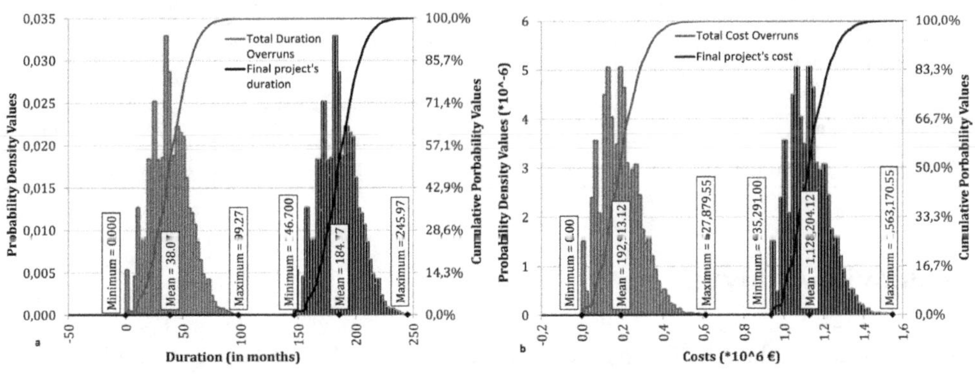

the probability distributions of Figure 7b & Figure 8b are stemmed. Concerning the redevelopment project, the final costs ranged from 4,900,000 € to 8,189,468 € considering a peak of 3,289,468 € in cost overruns. A relatively lower cost amount appeared in the road project where the final project's costs ranged from 935,291 € to 1,563,170.55 €.

Table 9. Summary descriptive statistics of Monte-Carlo simulation outputs for duration and cost quantities

	Minimum	Maximum	Mean	Standard Deviation	Skewness	Kurtosis
Building Project						
Duration Overruns (mths)	0.00	66.103	23.33	9.87	0.17	2.86
Total project's duration (mths)	92.70	158.803	116.03	9.87	0.17	2.86
Cost Overruns (€)	0.00	2,048,172.5	669,281.5	322,553	0.43	2.98
Total project's cost (€)	3,550,000	5,598,172.5	4,219,281.5	322,553	0.43	2.98
Redevelopment Project						
Duration Overruns (mths)	0.00	99.27	38.07	16.25	0.23	2.93
Total project's duration (mths)	146.70	245.97	184.77	16.25	0.23	2.93
Cost Overruns (€)	0.00	3,289,468	1,010,674	510,972	0.43	2.96
Total project's cost (€)	4,900,000	8,189,468	5,910,674	510,972	0.43	2.96
Road Infrastructure Project						
Duration Overruns (mths)	0.00	99.27	38.07	16.25	0.24	2.96
Total project's duration (mths)	146.70	245.97	184.77	16.25	0.24	2.96
Cost Overruns (€)	0.00	627,879.55	192,913.12	97,532	0.48	3.06
Total project's cost (€)	935,291	1,563,170.55	1,128,204.12	97,532	0.48	3.06

Sensitivity Analysis

After conducting the MCS, sensitivity analysis was performed using tornado charts. In this way, the projects' sensitivity to the duration and cost deviations is examined by analyzing the degree to which individual risks affect them. Hence, the most influential risks to which the projects are exposed are ranked in descending order.

This process yielded the tornado charts for all project types of Figure 9-10, in which each bar shows the range of minimum-maximum project percentage deviation from its mean value in both duration and time overruns caused by a specific risk range each time. Specifically, risks that appeared in the "Construction" phase (namely R12-R15) seem to affect more the project's schedule (Figure 9a & Figure 10a), whilst risks from both the "Planning" and "Construction" phases have a great influence on the project's cost, regardless of project's type (Figure 9b & Figure 10b). The

Figure 9. Tornado chart with the 10 most influencing risks for (a) the duration overruns (%), (b) the cost overruns (%) of building projects

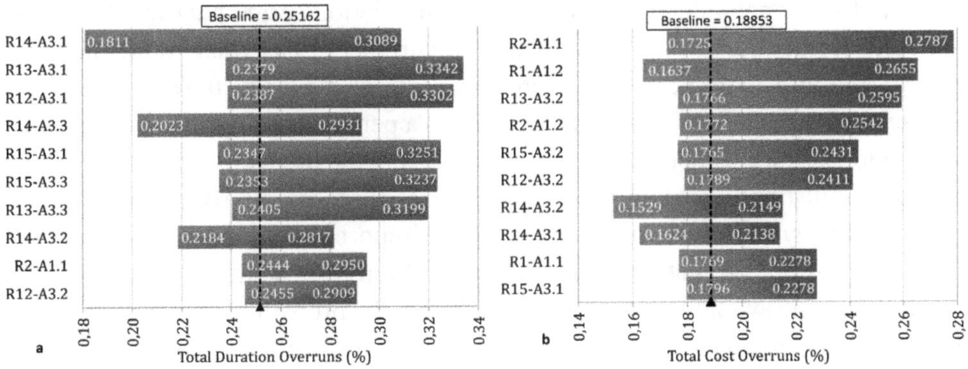

Figure 10. Tornado chart with the 10 most influencing risks for (a) the duration overruns (%), (b) the cost overruns (%) of redevelopment and road infrastructure projects

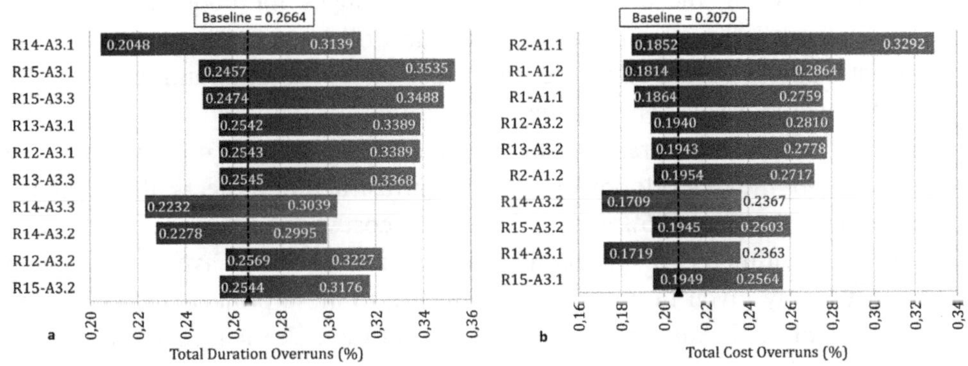

risks that emerged in the "Procurement" phase do not seem to affect the project's objectives considerably, since they do not belong to the top ten involving risks.

These practical conclusions are beneficial for gaining more insight into the causality between the given risks and final duration and costs and the determination of the risks as tolerable or not. This leads to better prioritization of the most appropriate response to each individual risk or group of risks during the implementation of mitigation measures according to available financial resources and the manager's risk appetite each time.

CONCLUSION

Project risks are encountered not only in the construction period but even before the sign of a contract i.e. in the Planning and Procurement Phase that could endanger project's viability. In the academia, there is no research regarding the risks identified in these phases, let alone their quantification as a percentage of project's budget. In this chapter, a first attempt is presented of analyzing the lifecycle of a Public Works Contract by distinguishing in its discrete phases the possible risks that could be found. The analysis showed that these risks are important in terms of cost and time and can jeopardize project's financial viability. Moreover, in the early stage of the project, when the available information is limited, the probabilistic approach seems to be imperative to predict the project's final duration and costs to take into account the inherent uncertainty in such projects. In the present attempt, two probabilistic models are proposed for predicting the duration and cost overruns of the projects given the possible risks that may occur and, ultimately, their final duration and costs.

Three real case studies were investigated for representing three main categories of construction projects, i.e., the building, the redevelopment and road infrastructure projects. Considering the distribution type and ranges for both "Impact" and "Probability" attributes of all possible risks according to the literature and the respondents' answers, the MCS yielded the percentages of duration and cost overruns into confidence intervals. The results revealed that for the building projects, the duration and cost overruns ranged approximately from 7.9% to 43% and 5.6% to 34.8%, while for the redevelopment and road infrastructure projects, the range for the duration was between 7.6% and 44.7% and the cost variations fluctuate between 6.1% and 39% within a two-sided confidence interval of 90%. Given the schedule and budget of any given future project belonging to these project categories, the percentage analysis results can be used to consult the risk managers with proper estimates regarding the project's potential overruns. Furthermore, the results of the sensitivity analysis inform the risk managers about the risks that are not acceptable and affect the project's objectives in order to better comprehend in which project phase to perform risk mitigation actions.

The limitation of the present study could be that it investigates the worse scenario in terms of time and cost overruns since it does not take into consideration that more risks could happen simultaneously in an activity and the delay or cost overrun incurred could be not necessarily the amount that was studied for every risk analyzed independently.

Overall, the proposed probabilistic models can provide prediction results according to the extent of risk tolerance of the stakeholder and can support the decision-making procedure by incorporating the uncertainty in the preliminary stages of construction projects. The prediction performance of the models is expected to be improved whether adding a variety of cases in the database when generating the parameters of the used distribution types. Finally, in the future the analysis could distinguish the risks according their initial sources and thus quantify costs and time overruns in accordance with their source of origin i.e. the Public Authority or the Contractor.

REFERENCES

Adam, A., Josephson, P. E. B., & Lindahl, G. (2017). Aggregation of factors causing cost overruns and time delays in large public construction projects: Trends and implications. *Engineering, Construction, and Architectural Management*, *24*(3), 393–406. doi:10.1108/ECAM-09-2015-0135

Agyekum-Mensah, G., & Knight, A. D. (2017). The professionals' perspective on the causes of project delay in the construction industry. *Engineering, Construction, and Architectural Management*, *24*(5), 828–841. doi:10.1108/ECAM-03-2016-0085

Antoniou, F. (2021). Delay risk assessment models for road projects. *Systems*, *9*(3), 1–17. doi:10.3390ystems9030070

Baudrit, C., Taillandier, F., Tran, T. T. P., & Breysse, D. (2019). Uncertainty Processing and Risk Monitoring in Construction Projects Using Hierarchical Probabilistic Relational Models. *Computer-Aided Civil and Infrastructure Engineering*, *34*(2), 97–115. doi:10.1111/mice.12391

Çevikbaş, M., & Işık, Z. (2021). An overarching review on delay analyses in construction projects. *Buildings*, *11*(3), 109. Advance online publication. doi:10.3390/buildings11030109

Chou, J. S., Yang, I. T., & Chong, W. K. (2009). Probabilistic simulation for developing likelihood distribution of engineering project cost. *Automation in Construction*, *18*(5), 570–577. Advance online publication. doi:10.1016/j.autcon.2008.12.001

Derbe, G., Li, Y., Wu, D., & Zhao, Q. (2020). Scientometric review of construction project schedule studies: Trends, gaps and potential research areas. *Journal of Civil Engineering and Management*, *26*(4), 343–363. doi:10.3846/jcem.2020.12317

European Commission. (2014). Guide to Cost-benefit Analysis of Investment Projects: Economic appraisal tool for Cohesion Policy 2014-2020. Publications Office of the European Union. https://doi.org/ doi:10.2776/97516

Ghaleh, R. M. B., Pourrostam, T., Sharifloo, N. M., Sardroud, J. M., & Safa, E. (2021). Delays in the road construction projects from risk management perspective. *Infrastructures*, *6*(9), 135. Advance online publication. doi:10.3390/infrastructures6090135

Gupta, V. K., & Thakkar, J. J. (2018). A quantitative risk assessment methodology for construction project. *Sadhana - Academy Proceedings in Engineering Sciences*, *43*(7), 1–16. doi:10.1007/s12046-018-0846-6

Jiang, W., Yang, Q., Jiang, J., Martek, I., & Gao, F. (2022). Operational Risk Management of Public–Private Partnership Infrastructure Projects: A Bibliometric Literature Review. *Buildings*, *12*(11), 1905. Advance online publication. doi:10.3390/buildings12111905

Koulinas, G. K., Demesouka, O. E., Sidas, K. A., & Koulouriotis, D. E. (2021). A TOPSIS — Risk Matrix and Monte Carlo Expert System for Risk Assessment in Engineering Projects. *Sustainability*, *13*(2), 1–14. doi:10.3390u132011277 PMID:34123411

Koulinas, G. K., Xanthopoulos, A. S., Tsilipiras, T. T., & Koulouriotis, D. E. (2020). Schedule delay risk analysis in construction projects with a simulation-based expert system. *Buildings*, *10*(8), 134. Advance online publication. doi:10.3390/buildings10080134

Le, P. T., Chileshe, N., Kirytopoulos, K., & Rameezdeen, R. (2020). Investigating the significance of risks in BOT transportation projects in Vietnam. *Engineering, Construction, and Architectural Management*, *27*(6), 1401–1425. Advance online publication. doi:10.1108/ECAM-08-2019-0439

McKinsey. (2017). *Reinventing Construction: A Route to Higher Productivity*. Author.

Moghayedi, A., & Windapo, A. (2022). Modelling the uncertainty of cost and time in highway projects. *Infrastructure Asset Management*, *9*(2), 73–88. doi:10.1680/jinam.21.00004

Moret, Y., & Einstein, H. H. (2016). Construction Cost and Duration Uncertainty Model: Application to High-Speed Rail Line Project. *Journal of Construction Engineering and Management*, *142*(10), 05016010. doi:10.1061/(ASCE)CO.1943-7862.0001161

Naderpour, A., Sardroud, J. M., Mo, M., & Xenidis, Y. (2019). *Uncertainty management in time estimation of construction projects : A systematic literature review and new model development.* doi:10.24200/sci.2017.4605

PMI. (2008). A guide to the project management body of knowledge (PMBOK Guide) (4th ed.). Project Management Institute.

PMI. (2019). *The Standard for Risk Management in Portfolios, Programs and Projects*. Project Management Institute.

PMI. (2021). *A Guide to the Project Management Body of Knowledge (PMBOK® Guide)* (7th ed.). Project Management Institute.

Rasheed, N., Shahzad, W., Khalfan, M., & Rotimi, J. O. B. (2022). Risk Identification, Assessment, and Allocation in PPP Projects: A Systematic Review. *Buildings*, *12*(8), 1109. Advance online publication. doi:10.3390/buildings12081109

Salling, K. B., & Leleur, S. (2011). Transport appraisal and Monte Carlo simulation by use of the CBA-DK model. *Transport Policy*, *18*(1), 236–245. doi:10.1016/j.tranpol.2010.08.007

Vagdatli, T., & Petroutsatou, K. (2021). CBA and probabilistic risk analysis tool for non-revenue generating infrastructure projects. The case of Greece. *Case Studies on Transport Policy*, *9*(1), 103–124. doi:10.1016/j.cstp.2020.10.004

Vose, D. (2008). Risk Analysis – A Quantitative Guide (3rd ed.). John Wiley and Sons.

Welde, M., & Dahl, R. E. (2021). Cost escalation in road construction contracts. *Transportation Research Record: Journal of the Transportation Research Board*, *2675*(9), 1006–1015. doi:10.1177/03611981211005462

KEY TERMS AND DEFINITIONS

Cost Overruns: Cost overrun is the financial amount by which the actual cost of a project exceeds the estimated cost and can be measured either in absolute or in relative terms.

Probabilistic Model: A probabilistic model is a model that involves stochastic estimation techniques for incorporating the uncertainty of the examined parameters, thus yielding results into confidence intervals.

Probability Distribution: A probability distribution, or probability density function, is the appropriate statistical function formed from an infinitely large set of values that gives the probabilities of occurrence of different possible outcomes for a given variable.

Project: A project is an undertaken investment action, with a specific starting point and a specific ending point, incorporating a sequence of activities and assignments towards the accomplishment of a comprehensive task (product or service) which has specific economic and technical nature as well as predefined objectives.

Project Management: Project management is the suitable application and integration of knowledge, skills, techniques and tools to project functions in order to meet project requirements efficiently.

Project Risk Management: Project Risk Management is a set of successive processes, including risk management planning, identification, analysis, response planning and implementation and monitoring, with the ultimate objective of increasing the probability and/or impact of positive risks and diminishing the probability and/or impact of negative risks so as to optimize the odds of project success.

Sensitivity Analysis: Sensitivity analysis is an analytical technique which assesses the robustness of the project's results to possible changes in key project variables. The analysis is carried out by varying one variable at a time and determining the effect of that change on the final outcome.

Chapter 7
Attributes of an Effective Project Manager:
The Case of European Operational Programs in the Public Sector

Dimitra Korakaki
Technical University of Crete, Greece

Stratos Kartsonakis
Technical University of Crete, Greece

Evangelos Grigoroudis
https://orcid.org/0000-0001-8613-9350
Technical University of Crete, Greece

Constantin Zopounidis
Technical University of Crete, Greece

ABSTRACT

It is widely accepted that every project aiming at specific outcomes is unique, since it is not a routine operation. In this context it is important to identify and study certain common characteristics of an effective project manager. The aim of this research is to examine the importance of the attributes of an effective project manager by analyzing how satisfied his/her collaborators are. The study focuses on the project management of EU Operational Programs in the public sector. Based on the literature, the effective project manager should be able to understand and influence the key parameters of any project (physical, technical, scientific, etc.), such as the duration, the financial resources, the human resources, the legislation, and the operation. To analyze the degree of satisfaction and the importance of project manager characteristics, the MUSA method has been applied, which is a multiple-criteria decision-analysis approach in the field of preference disaggregation.
DOI: 10.4018/978-1-6684-7786-1.ch007

INTRODUCTION

Project management is a set of activities aiming to implement a series of actions with the ultimate goal of achieving a final result or a change. To achieve this, a team is created that follows a timetable and has a budget at its disposal. The team simultaneously considers technical limitations until the project is fully implemented (Munns & Bjeirmi, 1996). Fundamentally, project management is just a part of the overall business process that carries out the implementation of the project.

The process (of project management) is a set of functions such as design, development, and production of a project. Each process involves actions, changes, and operations that lead to a result when there is an appropriate budget and timetable (MD137675, 2018). When all the necessary elements are present, the strategic planning of a project is essentially carried out.

However, what is the definition of a project? According to JMD126829 (2015), it could be all the energy that is consumed in order to implement a final product or service that is unique in its kind. A natural characteristic of the project is its beginning and end (life cycle), while its result, which is the product/service, is always similar but never identical from a different perspective. The types of projects can be discriminate into three main categories according to the Project Management Institute (2013):

a. Implementation of a new product or service.
b. Influence on the structure or staffing of a service.
c. Creation of modern software for optimal performance.

Also, the following should be noted:

- The start of the project has a clear date.
- The end of a project is determined by a date or the final outcome.
- A project has a clearly defined objective.
- The final outcome (product) is unique.
- There are usually important restrictions on the basic necessary resources.

The main phases of any project overall with the project life cycle, but they can help to understand the sequence of necessary operations. These phases are typical and can be roughly considered as follows (Horine, 2009):

- *1st phase – Project initiation*: It includes project definition and other key elements, such as the purpose, the benefits, the risks, the stakeholders of the project, etc. All these are usually defined in a Project Initiation Document (PID).

- *2nd phase - Project definition and planning*: This stage refers to the assessment of the goals and the project scope. It also includes the development of a project plan and work breakdown schedule.
- *3rd phase – Project launch and implementation*: In this stage the project is put into action, by carrying out all the necessary tasks and activities. Particular attention is given to the required deliverables.
- *4th phase – Project monitoring and control*: It focuses on measuring project progression and performance. Usually monitoring and control often overlap with execution.
- *5th phase – Completion and delivery of the project*: This stage refers to the project closure, which however does not always imply success (e.g., project cancellation). In several cases, a post-implementation project review is performed.

Overall, project management can be a valuable tool for organizations, but it is important to be aware of its potential challenges and drawbacks. Some of the positive and negative elements of project management are presented in Table 1 (Richman, 2011; Brown, 2007).

Having established the basic concepts of project and project management, the main purpose of this study is threefold. First to quantify the characteristics of an effective project manager for EU Operational Programs employed in the public sector, as well as their importance. Second, to measure the satisfaction of coworkers in each characteristic/attribute of an effective project manager with the aforementioned profile. This collaboration takes place the submission or the evaluation of a proposal or the implementation of a project. Third, to perform a SWOT analysis of the characteristics of an effective project manager, identifying the strengths, weaknesses, opportunities, threats regarding the project management of EU Operational Programs in the public sector.

Hence the rest of the chapter is organized as follows: Section 2 presents an extended overview on the profile of project management and a brief presentation of the nature and scope of EU Operational Programs. Section 3 gives the description of methodological framework of this paper, including an overview of the MUSA (Multicriteria Satisfaction Analysis) method, while section 4 is devoted to the detailed presentation of the obtained results. Finally, section 5 summarizes the main findings of this research and discusses potential future research.

Table 1. Advantages and disadvantages of project management

Advantages	Disadvantages
• The flexibility it offers to the project allows for readiness in terms of possible changes, and therefore provides a more competitive result. • It operates within an environment of concentration and communication characteristics that increase the effectiveness of the organization that manages the project. • It allows for easier shifting between external and internal relocation. • Economic losses are reduced as it allows for entire steps of the project to be cancelled earlier than predicted in the project lifecycle. • The relationships between clients and project workers are more direct, contributing to the development of the project. • Control is more comprehensive and immediate. • There is a plethora of information that makes it easier to extract results.	• There is often a lack of respect and adherence to operating principles by the higher-ups in the organization. • Poor communication can lead to misunderstandings, delays, and increased costs. • Some projects may require too much management, which can be a burden on the organization. • Implementation may require specialized training, which may add costs to the project. • Organizational complexity often arises.

PROJECT MANAGER AND EU OPERATIONAL PROGRAMS

Project Manager

Project managers are professionals who deal with management (Bowenkamp & Kleiner, 1987). They are responsible for the planning, acquisition, organization, execution, and completion of a project regardless of its nature. They need to be experienced and disciplined to be able to achieve their goals for the best possible outcome. It should be noted once again that they have the responsibility and authority to complete the assigned task till the end. However, what is impressive is that the project manager may need to work for a shorter duration of time than the project itself.

There are several characteristics that shape an effective project manager (Sommerville et. al., 2010). Firstly, certification is required to become a project manager. Specifically, project managers need leadership and process oversight skills. They need to be fully committed and trained to respond to and manage various problems of all kinds, people, and situations with the ultimate goal of completing the project in a specific way and in a specific time frame.

Another key characteristic of the project manager (Burke, 2013) is communication. A project manager needs to be able to effectively communicate with the clients, the stakeholders, and the team partners he collaborates with as it can have a high impact during the execution of a project. Additionally, the project manager needs to be a leader, motivational, and inspiring.

Besides communication, a project manager needs to be productive. They need quality and wisdom in managing and organizing the projects they have undertaken. Moreover, they need to manage their timetable properly and organize their tasks, resources, and supplies. It is understood that technical knowledge is essential for various professional fields. Finally, risk management is a key attribute, as the project manager needs to be vigilant to identify and reduce possible dangers without changing the duration and quality of the project.

A project manager is responsible for a project from start to finish. Therefore, during a project, he/she needs to take on various roles. Figure 1 summarizes a project manager's key roles:

Figure 1. Project manager's roles and responsibilities

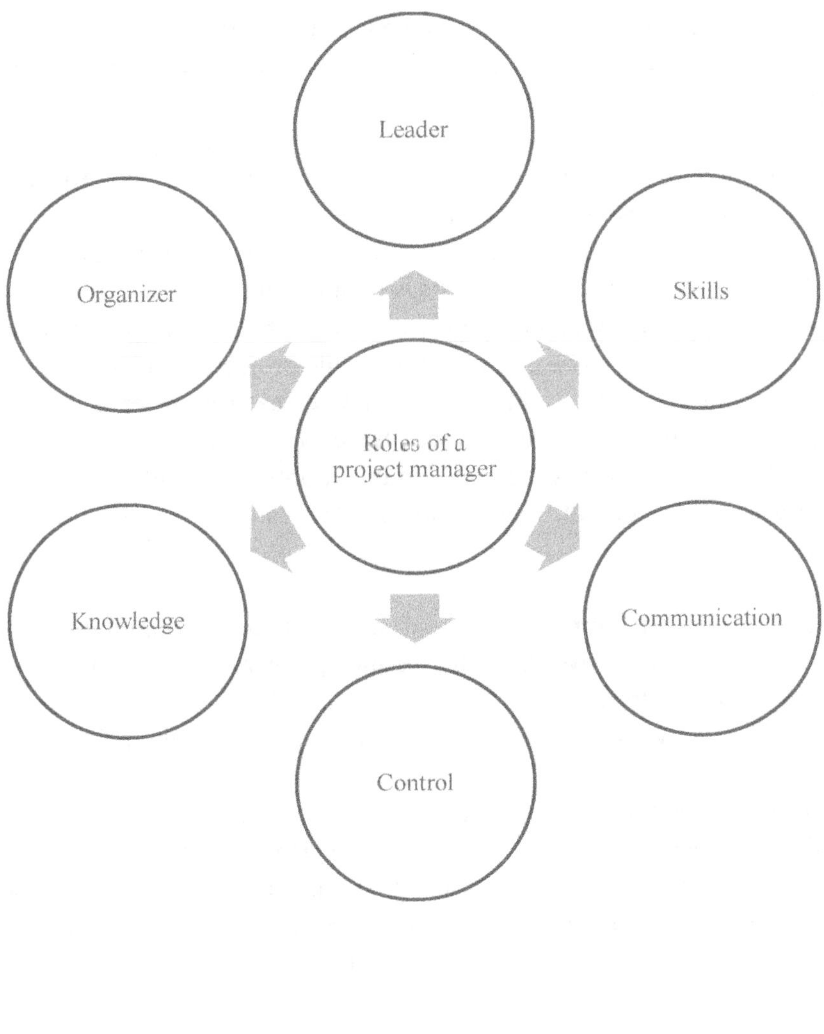

- *Organizer*: The manager of a project needs to initially collaborate with both the project team and management personnel responsible for defining the purposes, goals, quality, and cost to complete the project (Brown, 1998).
- *Skills*: He/she needs to collaborate with the project team to determine the purpose and vision, the determination of materials and their cost. Once all of these are determined, the manager establishes the plan and schedule, as well as the needs for tasks and personnel based on their skills (Globerson & Zwikael, 2002).
- *Control*: The project manager oversees the project and his/her team, examines how resources are progressing, and if necessary, makes necessary changes. Furthermore, he/she checks for potential problems and risks and, depending on his knowledge, communication skills, and collaboration with other participants, tries to correct these problems and risks (Alvarenga, 2019).
- *Communication*: Uses diplomacy, active listening, courtesy, understanding and empathy, relevance, appropriate behavior and attitude, and collaboration in all internal and external communications that occur during the project (Alvarenga et al., 2020).
- *Knowledge*: Knows how to manage incoming or outgoing information, has knowledge of scientific project management methods, as well as tools such as computer programs for project management.
- *Leader*: He/She sets an example to follow and is always responsible for what he does. He has organizational skills and knows how to make decisions under pressure. By communicating with his/her team, he/she assigns each member the appropriate role to be executed within the project, while maintaining the proper hierarchy of tasks. He/She encourages each member of his team to improve, inspires confidence, respect, honesty, and integrity. He rewards his team daily and finds ways to solve complex problems while also having the ability to assign and attribute responsibilities fairly (Podgórska & Pichlak, 2019).

Additional skills and competencies, particularly in a new digital environment, are also discussed in recent works (se for example, Holzmann et al., 2022; Wang et al., 2023; Wu, 2022; Omer et al., 2022; Ghorbani, 2023).

At this point we would like to note that besides the main key roles of a project manager, emphasis should be also placed on the associated behaviors of a manager. According to Fisher (2010) an effective project manager, in addition to his/her leadership skills, needs to understand and adopt various behavioral characteristics in order to deal with people in different situations and circumstances. Moreover he/she needs to be influential to the team members and show genuine concern for others. Finally, a project manager should be able to effectively resolve conflicts on work issues and display awareness and understanding of cultural differences among team members.

However, every project is unique, and consequently risks and uncertainties are inherent to each project. Due to this fact, different strategies should be applied by project managers in order to overcome unexpected or possible obstacles. In this context, Carvalho and Rabechini Junior (2015) suggested that the hard skills of a project manager are able to cover only a part of a project uncertainties, and soft skills, such as the management of interpersonal relationships and the notion of project ecology, also need to be integrated. Furthermore, depending on the type of the project, the importance of the management skills and the knowledge expertise can vary as Hawng and Ng (2013) demonstrated in their study, where they compared the traditional management skills in traditional and green constructing projects.

EU Operational Programs

The Management and Control System (MCS) 2014-2020 for the Operational Programs of the European Regional Development Fund (ERDF), the European Social Fund (ESF), and the Cohesion Fund (CF) is the set of administrative authorities that are interdependent, have a specific structure and organizational framework with activities that aim at good financial management of resources (economy, effectiveness, and efficiency).

For the structures and processes of the MCS in Greece, the information provided to various authorities such as beneficiaries (municipalities, business services, private bodies) is of vital importance. The task of the beneficiaries is to implement Operational Programs for the period 2014-2020. Beneficiaries need to know who to address, as well as the rules and applicable procedures for co-financed actions:

- Eligibility rules,
- Issuing a call,
- Funding application,
- Selection process,
- Legality checks of public contracts,
- Verification and audits of the physical and financial object of the actions,
- Fraud prevention and combat measures, etc.

The new MCS was based on the corresponding program of the 2007-2013 period and included Regulation (EU) 1303/2013 for the period 2014-2020. In Greek legislation, it is referred to as Law 4314/2014 - Part I and includes:

- The Managing Authorities (MAs), which are responsible for managing the Operational Programs. There are 18 MAs for each OP. The 5 Sectoral OPs that include all MAs are special services and belong to the Ministry of Economy and Development. There are also 13 Regional OPs, each with their own MAs that are special services under the respective Region.
- The Certification Authority is responsible for exercising the certification powers and is common to all Operational Programs (18) and is also under the Ministry of Economy and Development.
- The Control Authority (CA) is responsible for the proper functioning of the MSC. Again, for all the 18 Operational Programs, it belongs to the Ministry of Finance, and is called "Committee of Public Financial Control" (EDPES).
- The Intermediate Bodies (IBs) manage part of an Operational Program.
- The National Coordination Authority (NCA), which connects and informs the European Commission, and it has the role of coordinator regarding the activities of other authorities and bodies and helps in the proper implementation of EU and national law. It consists of 6 Special Services and is also under the Ministry of Economy and Development.

The structure of the European Structural and Investment Funds (ESIF's) 2014 - 2020 in Greece consists of 7 Sectoral Operational Programs, considering the respective ones for Rural Development and Fisheries, which cover various sectors and are implemented throughout the country. These are as follows:

- Competitiveness, Entrepreneurship, and Innovation
- Transport Infrastructure, Environment and Sustainable Development
- Human Resources Development, Education and Lifelong Learning
- Reform of the Public Sector
- Technical Assistance Program
- Rural Development Program
- Fisheries and Maritime

Also 13 Regional Operational Programs (ROP) are included in the NSRF 2014-2020, one for each region of Greece, which are implemented with the respective Regional Governor responsible. The 13 ROPs are: ROP Eastern Macedonia and Thrace, ROP Central Macedonia, ROP Western Macedonia, ROP Epirus, ROP Thessaly, ROP Ionian Islands, ROP Western Greece, ROP Central Greece, ROP Attica, ROP Peloponnese, ROP North Aegean, ROP Southern Aegean, and ROP Crete (see also Figure 2 for a map of Greek regions).

Figure 2. Regions of Greece

Finally, there are also European Territorial Cooperation programs aiming at collaborations between EU countries, as well as third countries bordering the EU. The Interreg programs between EU member states are divided into cross-border, transnational, and interregional programs. They are further divided into bilateral and multilateral programs.

The bilateral / cross-border programs aim to address problems or general issues that concern bordering areas, to develop perspectives and to strengthen cooperation with the aim of strengthening the relationships between the European countries. These programs are:

- Cross-border Program Greece - Bulgaria 2014-2020

- Cross-border Program Greece - Italy 2014-2020
- Cross-border Program Greece - Cyprus 2014-2020
- Cross-border Program Greece - Republic of North Macedonia 2014-2020
- Cross-border Program Greece - Albania 2014-2020

In addition, Greece participates in the following multilateral programs through the following regions:

- Adriatic - Ionian (interstate)
- MED (interstate)
- MED ENI CBC (cross-border)
- Black Sea basin ENI CBC (cross-border)
- INTERREG EUROPE (interregional)
- Balkan Mediterranean (interstate)

The research focused on the Sectoral Operational Programs (SOP) and the Regional Operational Programs (ROP). The next section presents the methodological framework applied to evaluate the attributes of a project manager that handles EU Operational Programs.

MUSA METHOD

The MUlticriteria Satisfaction Analysis method (MUSA) is a multicriteria preference disaggregation technique and belongs to the family of the UTA methods (Siskos et al., 2016; Grigoroudis & Siskos, 2010). It aims to provide quantitative measures of customer satisfaction while taking into consideration the qualitative nature of customers' judgments. The method's main goal is to aggregate individual judgments into a collective value function, assuming that a customer's overall satisfaction is influenced by a set of criteria or variables that represent different dimensions of a product or service.

To gather the necessary information for the MUSA method, a questionnaire is administered to customers, requiring them to assess the product or service provided. The questionnaire asks customers to express their opinions on both their overall satisfaction and their satisfaction in a set of criteria using a predefined ordinal satisfaction scale, as shown in Figure 2 (The same satisfaction scale is adapted to this research).

The MUSA method estimates global and partial value (satisfaction) functions, denoted as Y^* and X_i^* respectively, based on customers' judgments Y and X_i. It

Figure 3. Example of an ordinal satisfaction scale

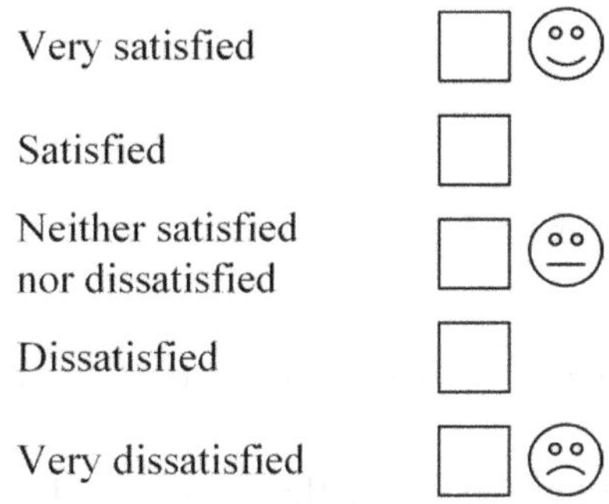

is worth noting that the method follows the principles of ordinal regression analysis, while utilizing linear programming techniques to impose constraints.

The main linear program (LP) of the MUSA method is the following:

$$\begin{cases} [\min] F = \sum_{j=1}^{M} \sigma_j^+ + \sigma_j^- \\ \text{subject to} \\ \sum_{i=1}^{n} \sum_{k=1}^{t_{ij}-1} w_{ik} - \sum_{m=1}^{t_j - 1} z_m - \sigma_j^+ + \sigma_j^- = 0 \quad \forall j \\ \sum_{m=1}^{\alpha - 1} z_m = 100 \\ \sum_{i=1}^{n} \sum_{k=1}^{\alpha_i - 1} w_{ik} = 100 \\ z_m, w_{ik}, \sigma_j^+, \sigma_j^- \geq 0 \quad \forall i, j, k, m \end{cases} \tag{1.1}$$

where σ_j^+ and σ_j^- are the overestimation and underestimation error for customer j, M is the number of customers (responses), z_m and w_{ik} are model variables for the estimation of Y^* and X_i^*, n is the number of satisfaction criteria, α and α_i are the number of global and partial satisfaction scales, respectively (ordinal scales), and x_j and x_i^j are the *j*-th levels on which variables Y and X_i are estimated (i.e., global and partial satisfaction judgments of the *j*-th customer).

As the MUSA method is based on linear programming modeling, a stability analysis is performed as a post-optimality problem, where n LPs are solved. Each LP maximizes the weight of a criterion and has the following form:

$$\begin{cases} [\max]F' = \sum_{k=1}^{\alpha_i - 1} w_{ik} \\ \text{subject to} \\ F \leq F^* + \varepsilon \\ \text{all the constraints of the main LP} \end{cases} \tag{1.2}$$

where F^* is the optimal value of the objective function of the main LP and ε is a small percentage of F^*.

The main results of the MUSA method include the global and partial value functions, the weights of the criteria, the average satisfaction indices, as well as the action and improvement diagrams.

The global and partial value functions are the most important outcome of the MUSA method, as they express the real value that the respondents assign to each level of the global or marginal ordinal satisfaction scale. The form of these functions determines the degree of demandingness of the respondents (Grigoroudis & Siskos, 2010):

- The case of a linear function refers to "neutral" respondents, that is, respondents who, as much as they declare they are satisfied, the greater the percentage of their expectations are fulfilled.
- The case of a convex function corresponds to "demanding" respondents, that is, respondents who are not satisfied unless they are offered the optimal level of services.
- In the case of a concave form respondents are called "non-demanding" because they declare they are satisfied even though a small percentage of their expectations are fulfilled.

The weights of the criteria are presented in a simple and understandable way (percentages) to show which of the criteria has the highest importance and which does not. On the other hand, the average satisfaction indices show the level of satisfaction for each criterion. They show the average satisfaction level for all respondents, either overall or for a specific evaluation criterion.

Action diagrams combine weights with average satisfaction indices and identify the strengths and weaknesses of the respondents, as well as where improvement efforts should be directed (Figure 4). Every action diagram is divided into quadrants based on performance (average satisfaction indicators) and the importance (weights) of the criteria.

In a similar context, the improvement diagrams can indicate the output or the extent of improvement efforts and assist in prioritizing these efforts. The improvement

Figure 4. Action diagram (Grigoroudis & Siskos, 2010)

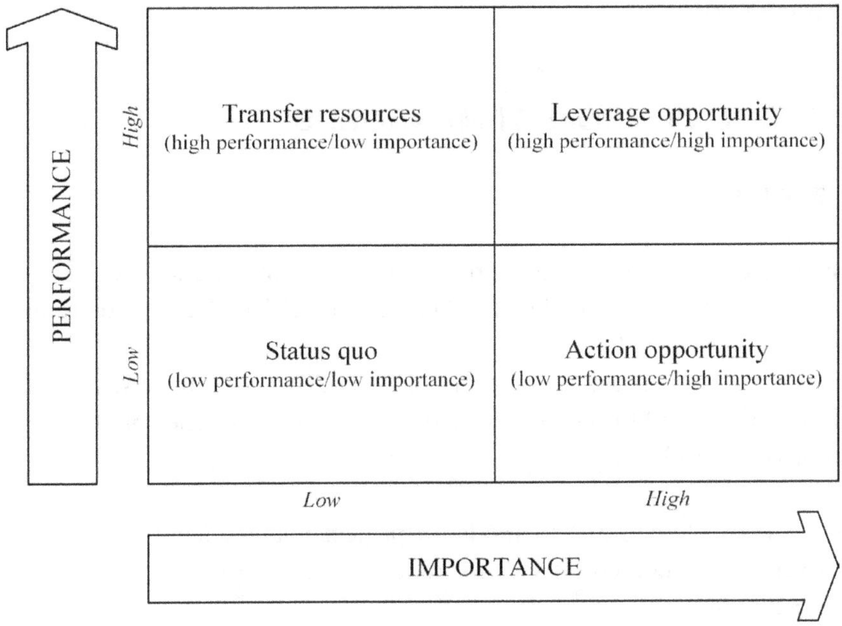

Figure 5. Improvement diagram (Grigoroudis & Siskos, 2010)

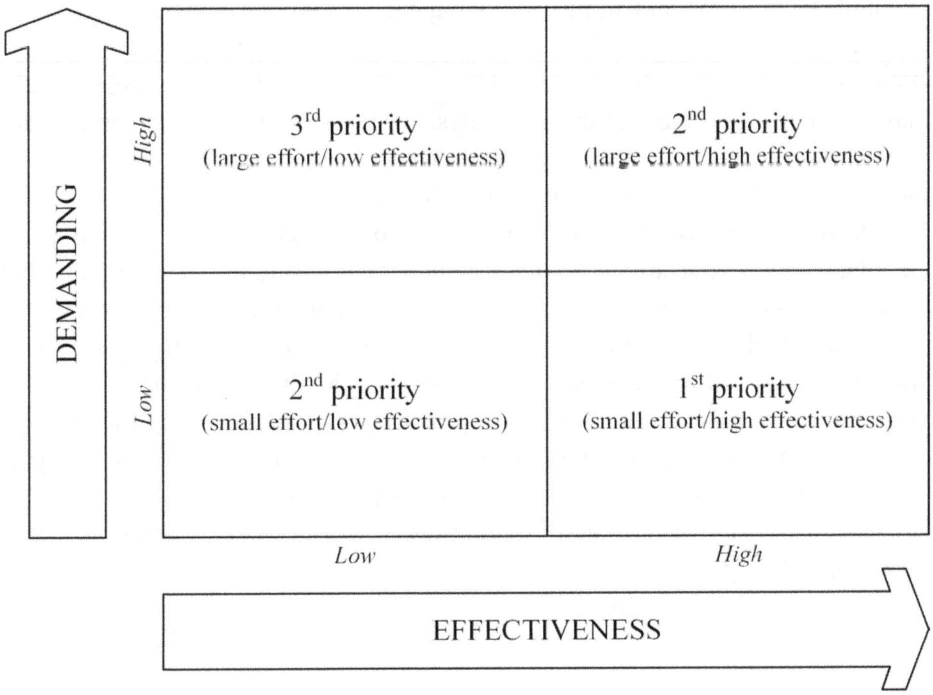

diagrams are separated into quadrants by combing the demanding and improvement indices (Figure 5).

EVALUATION OF PROJECT MANAGERS

Evaluation Criteria

Four major criteria are considered for the evaluation of project managers: knowledge, skills, communication, and leadership (Dimitriadis, 2019). A detailed discussion of these criteria is given below.

The knowledge of a project manager (Kokkosis, 2016; Dimitriadis, 2019; Zervaki, 2023) is an indicator of the achievement of their goals. The types of knowledge can be categorized as follows:

- Knowledge of scientific methods for project management: Good knowledge of scientific methods used to obtain valid information about project management.
- Knowledge of tools such as computer programs for project management: Good knowledge of many computer programs used to fulfill project management tasks. High level of education, preferably in the field of computer science or engineering for technical project managers.

Project managers should also have business skills, as well as a background in management, budget preparation, and analysis (Alvarenga et al., 2020). In addition, project Managers should have exceptional communication skills and be comfortable managing multiple tasks simultaneously (Alvarenga et al., 2020).

Leadership in project management focuses on the efficiency of a competent project manager. The factors that affect and shape this satisfaction level, and how they are categorized according to the demographic characteristics of the employee, are also examined. The ultimate goal is to study and evaluate through research the advantages and disadvantages of the manager from his/her perspective, as well as the perspective of his/her collaborators. By examining the abilities of the manager, it is possible to make improvement proposals, as the positive and negative aspects of the competent manager will be measured and quantified.

Based on the above four major dimensions, the detailed evaluation criteria include the following:

1. Knowledge
    - Scientific methods
    - Additional knowledge (e.g., project management software)
2. Skills
    - Effectiveness
    - Determination
    - Self-control
    - Negotiation
    - Problem-solving
    - Diligence
    - Predictability
    - Decision making
    - Practical thinking
3. Communication
    - Diplomacy
    - Active listening
    - Kindness
    - Comprehension
    - Clarity
    - Behavior
    - Cooperation
4. Leadership
    - Trust inspiration
    - Respect inspiration
    - Integrity
    - Complex problem-solving skills
    - Task prioritization
    - Delegation of responsibilities
    - Decision making under pressure
    - Organization skills
    - Example to other
    - Responsibility

Additional goals of this research are to record the employees' expectations and by extension the expectations that citizens (clients) have from the project manager.

Questionnaire and Survey

The survey was conducted in October 2021 among employees in Management Authorities of EU Operational Programs in Greece. It was distributed via their email addresses, a link to the corresponding Google form questionnaire, to which 199 employees of various specialties (e.g., engineers, computer scientists, economists, business administrators, accountants, lawyers, administrators, environmentalists, etc.) finally responded.

The questionnaires in this kind of research play a crucial role in order to extract valuable outcomes. In general, a questionnaire should have the following characteristics (Vavra, 1997):

- It should be simple and free of comprehension problems,
- It should include specific questions that do not cause confusion,
- It should be easily structured so that it is easy to complete.

Furthermore, according to Dutka (2005), Nauman & Giel (1995) and Woodruff & Gardial (1996) the questionnaire should include an introduction, demographic information, satisfaction questions, and behavior questions.

Research through a questionnaire is a process that consists of the following six steps (Fowler, 1993):

1. Determination of research goals
2. Determination of satisfaction dimensions
3. Determination of the satisfaction measurement process
4. Sample selection and determination of the research process
5. Development of the questionnaire
6. Questionnaire testing

The content and structure of a questionnaire is the most important factor for the success of a survey. When a company wants to distribute a questionnaire, it applies a two-way process through the questionnaire it distributes, in the following order (Dutka, 2005):

a. The company determines the desired information.
b. The desired information is encoded into a questionnaire.
c. The questionnaire is sent to customers.
d. Customers decode the questionnaire.
e. Customers mentally form an answer.
f. Customers select the best alternative answer.
g. Customers return the questionnaire to the company.
h. The company decodes the responses.

Figure 6. Satisfaction criteria and subcriteria

Knowledge	Skills	Communication	Leadership
• Scientific methods • Additional knowledge	• Effectiveness • Determination • Self-control • Negotiation • Problem-solving • Diligence • Predictability • Decision making • Practical thinking	• Diplomacy • Active listening • Kindness • Comprehension • Clarity • Behavior • Cooperation	• Trust inspiration • Respect inspiration • Integrity • Complex problem -solving skills • Task prioritization • Delegation of responsibilities • Decision making under pressure • Organization skills • Example to other • Responsibility

The questionnaire of the present survey is divided into two parts. The first part includes demographic questions, such as gender, age, education level, and occupation. In the second part, there are four evaluation categories, which are evaluated on a 5-point ordinal scale (dissatisfied, rather dissatisfied, neither dissatisfied/nor satisfied, rather satisfied, satisfied). Each major criterion is divided into a different number of subcriteria, as shown in Figure 6. These specific satisfaction criteria and subcriteria are the factors that determine an effective project manager.

Results

The first demographic question refers to the gender of the participants. The results are shown in Figure 7, according to which the participants were approximately 50% male and 50% female. The next demographic question concerns the age of the participants. The results are shown in Figure 5. According to this, the largest percentage belongs to individuals aged 51-60 years (44.60%), followed by individuals aged 41-50 with an equally high percentage. Participants aged 61 and above, 31-40, and finally those belonging to the age group 18-30 follow with a significant difference.

The next question refers to the educational level of the participants. The resulting graph is presented in Figure 9. The majority of participants by a significant margin have an MSc degree, followed by participants with university education. Next, we encounter participants with a PhD degree, those with technological education, and finally those with secondary education.

Figure 7. Participants by gender

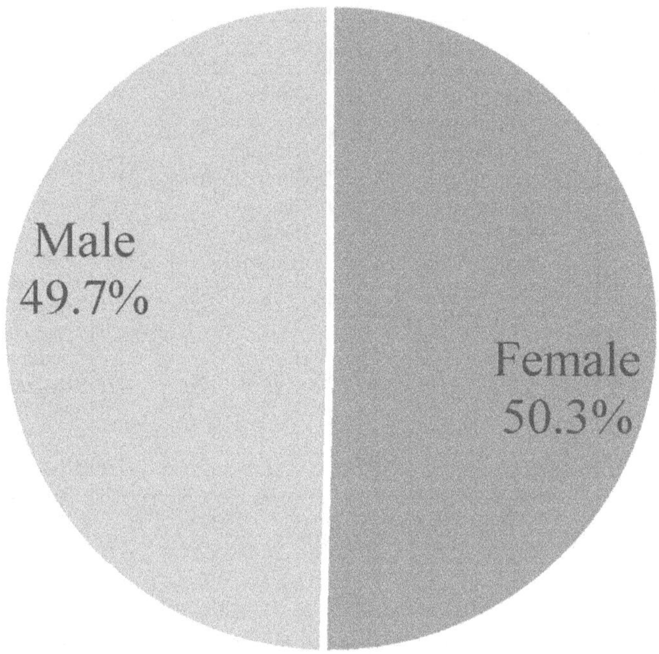

Figure 8. Participants by age

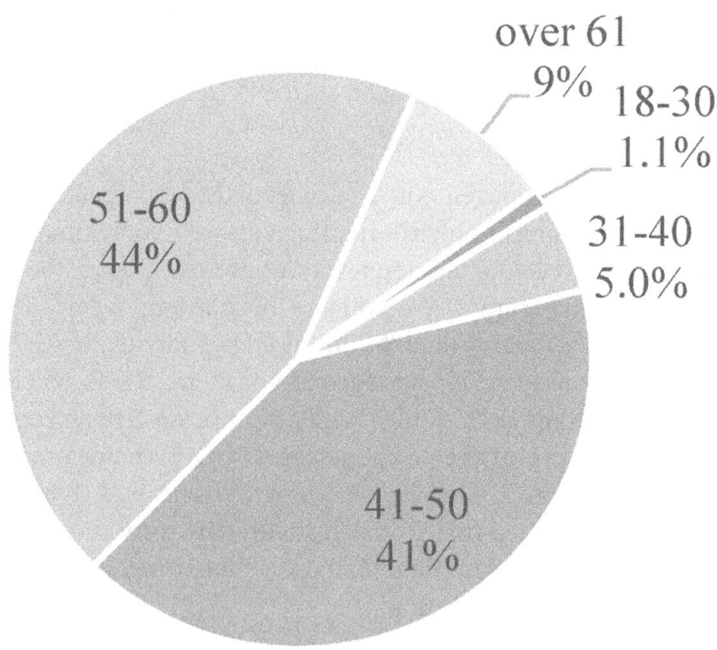

Figure 9. Participants by educational level

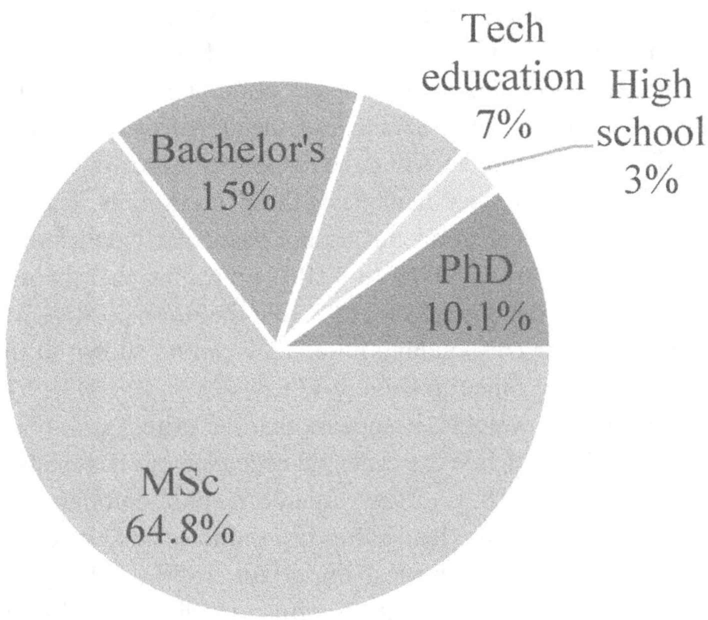

Figure 10. Participants by specialty

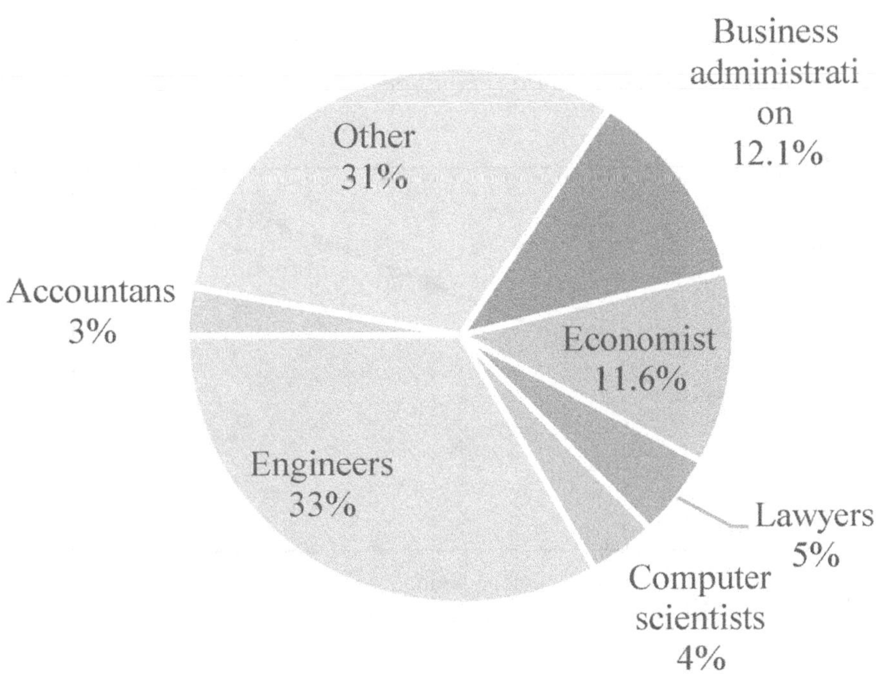

Finally, the last demographic question concerns the specialization of each participant, as presented in Figure 10. Most participants are engineers, followed by those with another specialty, and with a significant difference, those with specialties in business administration, economists, lawyers, computer science, and accountants.

Regarding the results of the MUSA method, the global average satisfaction index is estimated at 76%, which indicates that the respondents are not very satisfied with their cooperation with the project manager of the EU programs. The demand index is -40%, indicating that the respondents are not particularly demanding. Note that the demand index ranges from -100% to +100%, meaning that the more negative it is, the less demanding the customers are, while the more positive it is, the more demanding the customers (respondents) are. This can be shown in the estimated global value (satisfaction) function (Figure 11).

Regarding the criteria weights, it appears that the criterion of communication has the lowest importance, while the criterion of leadership has the highest (Table 2). At the same time, according to the research results, communication has the highest satisfaction index, while leadership has the lowest. This result shows that respondents are more satisfied with less important criteria and less satisfied with more important criteria. It appears that the demand indices for all four criteria are negative, which means that respondents are not demanding. At the same time, the criterion of leadership has the highest mean improvement index, which means it is the characteristic that contributes the most to the dissatisfaction of the respondents.

Figure 11. Global value (satisfaction) function

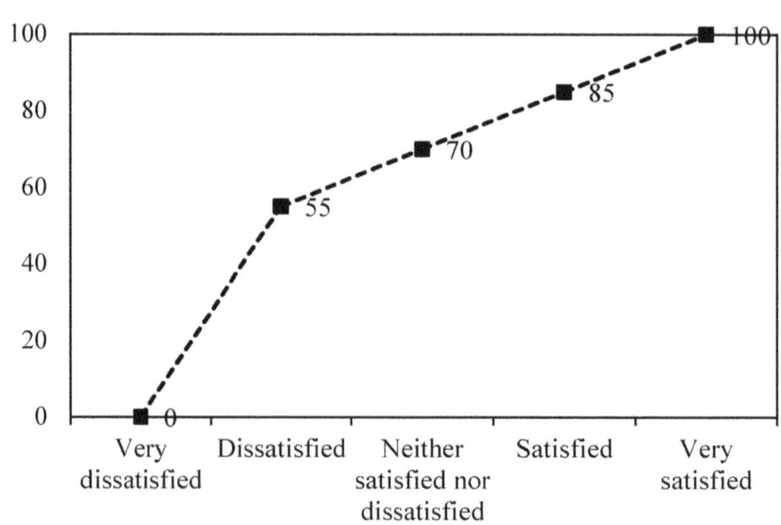

Table 2. Main MUSA results

Criteria	Weights	Average Satisfaction Index	Average Demanding Index	Average Improvement Index
Knowledge	24.10%	73.30%	-45.20%	6.40%
Skills	23.30%	77.60%	-52.30%	5.20%
Communication	22.10%	81.70%	-55.40%	4.10%
Leadership	30.40%	70.00%	-35.40%	9.10%
Global satisfaction	-	76.00%	-40.00%	-

Figure 12 shows the action diagram for the main criteria of the research. It appears that the criteria with the highest performance are communication and skills, but without high importance. On the other hand, the leadership criterion is the most important characteristic, but the respondents are less satisfied with it. The action diagram is similar to a SWOT analysis. Therefore, in conclusion, leadership is the characteristic that a special focus is needed to improve the effectiveness of project managers.

The improvement diagram (see also Figure 12) indicates that all main criteria have the same improvement priority. However, it seems that leadership and knowledge have the highest effectiveness, thus, potential improvements in these characteristics may have a greater impact on the overall assessment of project managers.

Having examined the main results, it is important to analyze the results for each criterion and their corresponding subcriteria.

Figure 12. Action and improvement diagrams (main criteria)

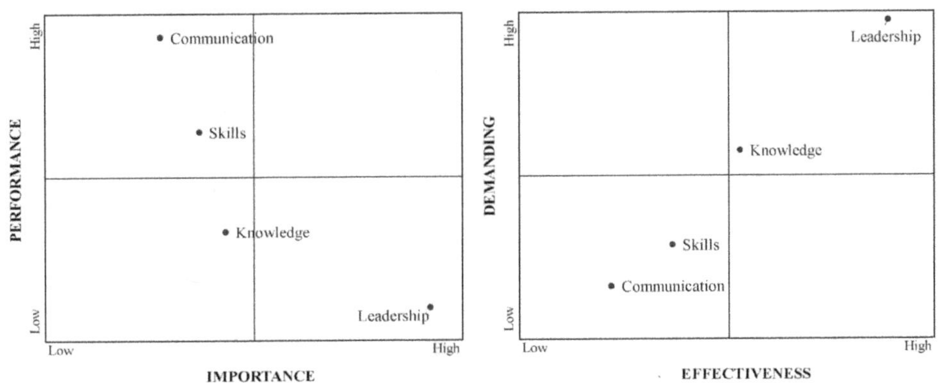

Knowledge

Table 3 shows that the most important subcriterion for knowledge is the second one, which is the additional knowledge of project managers (e.g., project management software). However, both subcriteria do not satisfy the respondents, as the corresponding percentages are very low (14.5% and 16.9%). Furthermore, the demanding indices have positive high values, with the index for scientific methods being higher, indicating that the respondents are particularly demanding. On the other hand, the improvement indices are lower, but not indifferent. In fact, it is observed that for the subcriterion of scientific methods, for which the respondents were more demanding, are less satisfied.

Table 3. MUSA results (knowledge)

Criteria	Weights	Average Satisfaction Index	Average Demanding Index	Average Improvement Index
Scientific methods	33.10%	14.50%	81.90%	28.30%
Additional knowledge	66.90%	16.80%	77.50%	55.60%

Figure 13 presents the action diagram of the knowledge subcriteria, where it is indicated that the additional knowledge is the strong point of project managers, while scientific methods, despite their low importance, are a potential future threat. Moreover, the improvement diagram of these specific subcriteria, hint that the subcriterion of additional knowledge is a factor that needs improvement, despite

Figure 13. Action and improvement diagrams (knowledge)

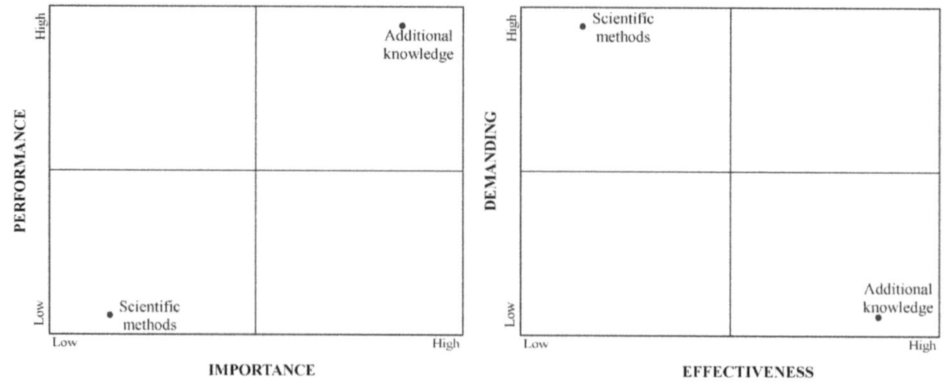

being high on effectiveness. It is observed that the additional knowledge is highly demanding and effective, which means that the respondents may be demanding, but improving this subcriterion can significantly enhance overall satisfaction.

Skills

Regarding the subcriteria of skills, the most important are the criteria of problem-solving skills and effectiveness and practical thinking (Table 4). Generally, the average satisfaction scores are relatively low. Higher satisfaction is observed in the subcriterion of effectiveness and the lowest in the subcriterion of problem-solving. Additionally, it is observed that the demanding indices of the subcriteria for the skills criterion are mainly positive. The only negative index is in the case of the subcriterion of effectiveness, which means that the respondents are not demanding for this subcriterion. On the contrary, the index of the subcriterion of problem-solving is quite high (80.50%). Similar to the subcriteria of knowledge, the average improvement index is lower in the subcriteria where the respondents are not demanding, while it is higher in the subcriterion of problem-solving, where the respondents are demanding.

Table 4. MUSA results (skills)

Criteria	Weights	Average Satisfaction Index	Average Demanding Index	Average Improvement Index
Effectiveness	10.60%	73.80%	-43.10%	2.80%
Determination	7.80%	42.00%	23.30%	4.50%
Self-control	7.80%	42.90%	23.33%	4.50%
Negotiation	7.30%	46.30%	18.30%	3.90%
Problem-solving	30.70%	16.30%	80.50%	25.70%
Diligence	8.30%	67.20%	-27.50%	2.70%
Predictability	7.30%	48.90%	4.10%	3.70%
Decision making	9.00%	36.70%	33.60%	5.70%
Practical thinking	11.10%	33.10%	46.00%	7.40%

Figure 14 demonstrates the action and improvement diagram of the subcriteria of skills criterion, where a gap is observed between what the respondents desire and what they receive. Specifically, problem-solving is considered a significant weakness of the skills criterion, as respondents are dissatisfied, even though they

Figure 14. Action and improvement diagrams (skills)

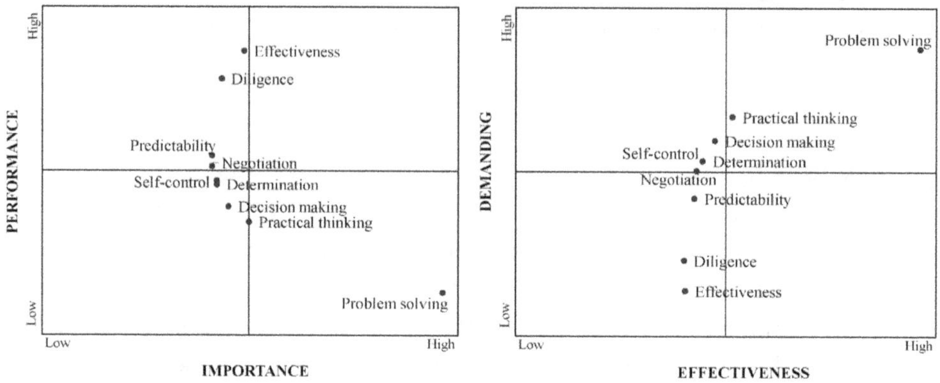

are placing great emphasis on this criterion. Problem-solving is also a priority for improvement, mainly due to the high effectiveness it exhibits (despite the high demands of the respondents). Also, improvement priorities should be considered the criteria of diligence and effectiveness, which with relatively little effort can lead to a small improvement in satisfaction.

Communication

As shown in Table 5, the most important criterion for communication is behavior, while respondents appear to be relatively satisfied with these criteria, except for the criteria of diplomacy and active listening, where satisfaction indices are particularly low. It should be noted that respondents are more satisfied with the most important subcriterion of behavior. In the criterion of communication, the demanding indices of most criteria are negative, meaning that respondents are not demanding. The only two subcriteria where the demanding indices are positive are diplomacy and active listening.

The communication action diagram (Figure 15) shows that the behavior of project managers has great importance while diplomacy and active listening are the possible threats of this criterion, and there is no subcriterion in the quadrant of weaknesses (high significance and low satisfaction).

In the improvement diagram (see also Figure 15), active listening and diplomacy are located in the area of high demanding but also high effectiveness. Also, the behavior criterion is on the vertical axis, but it is closer to the first improvement priority quadrant, indicating that possible improvement actions should focus there. Finally, all other subcriteria are located in the area of low demanding and low effectiveness.

Table 5. MUSA results (communication)

Criteria	Weights	Average Satisfaction Index	Average Demanding Index	Average Improvement Index
Diplomacy	7.70%	53.00%	58.00%	3.60%
Active listening	8.40%	43.00%	28.90%	4.80%
Kindness	8.40%	75.00%	-28.90%	2.10%
Comprehension	9.30%	72.00%	-35.20%	2.26%
Clarity	10.90%	73.90%	-44.80%	2.80%
Behavior	41.00%	92.50%	-85.40%	3.10%
Cooperation	14.30%	84.00%	-58.00%	2.30%

Figure 15. Action and improvement diagrams (communication)

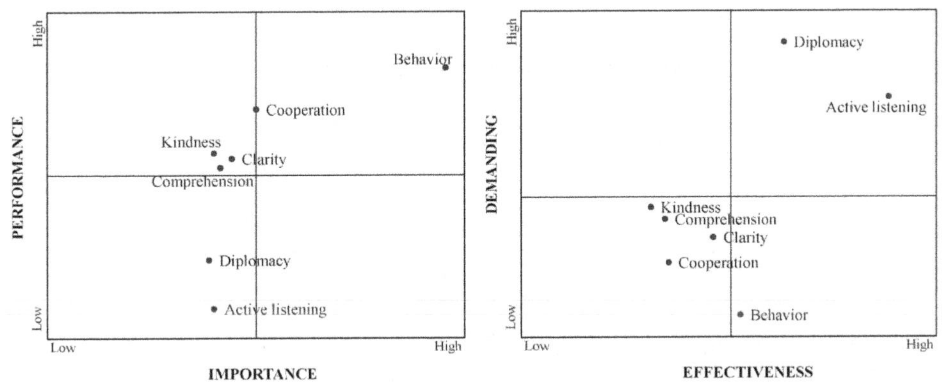

Leadership

As shown in Table 6 the most important subcriterion of leadership is respect inspiration. The level of satisfaction of the respondents varies depending on the criterion: trust and respect inspiration, integrity, task prioritization, and responsibility have the highest average satisfaction scores, while complex problem-solving, delegation of responsibilities, decision-making under pressure, organizational skills, and the example to others present low satisfaction scores. For leadership, the demanding criteria indicators are diverse. Some are positive, which means that respondents are demanding, and others are negative, with the respect inspiration lowest demanding index, which means that respondents are not demanding.

Table 6. MUSA results (leadership)

Criteria	Weights	Average Satisfaction Index	Average Demanding Index	Average Improvement Index
Trust inspiration	10.00%	72.00%	-40.00%	2.80%
Respect inspiration	18.50%	83.90%	-65.90%	3.00%
Integrity	7.90%	70.80%	-23.70%	2.30%
Complex problem-solving	7.90%	41.80%	23.70%	4.60%
Task prioritization	9.20%	69.20%	-34.80%	2.80%
Delegation of responsibilities	9.10%	35.80%	34.10%	5.80%
Decision making under pressure	8.30%	41.30%	28.00%	4.90%
Organization skills	10.00%	37.80%	34.90%	6.20%
Example to others	9.10%	35.10%	34.10%	5.90%
Responsibility	10.00%	75.00%	-40.00%	2.50%

Figure 16. Action and improvement diagrams (leadership)

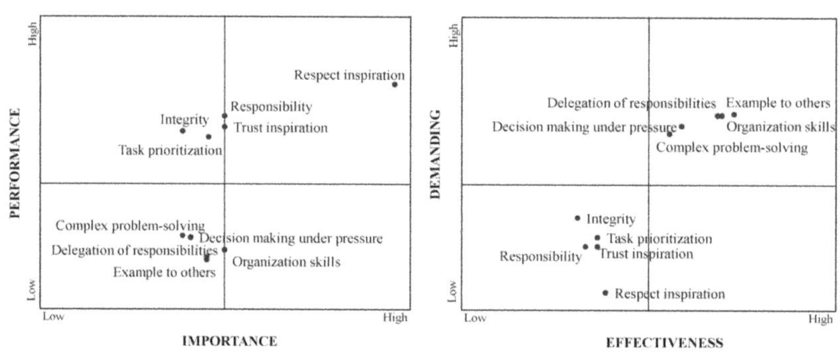

Figure 16 presents the action and improvement of the leadership subcriteria. Similar to the previous criterion, there is no significant gap between satisfaction and importance. Thus, the subcriterion of respect inspiration is presented as the strong point of this specific criterion. However, particular attention should be given to the subcriterion of organizational skills, as it is located between the quadrant of threats and weaknesses. Finally, the improvement diagram shows that all subcriteria have the same priority for improvement, although they are divided into two categories: the first concerns subcriteria with high demand and effectiveness, while the second with low demand and effectiveness. The final decision on selecting potential improvement actions should consider the available resources and the desired level of improvement.

In conclusion, the results of the MUSA method highlight the importance of leadership in project management. This is consistent with numerous previous studies that note that, although there are different forms of leadership (e.g., transformational, adaptive, transactional), this particular soft skill is necessary to run effective projects. It is important to note that leadership requires skills in both managing people and tasks. For this reason, an effective project manager needs leadership skills in order to assemble the team, devise the plan and manage resources to maintain the schedule and keep within budget.

CONCLUSION AND FUTURE RESEARCH

Effective project management is necessary in EU Operational Programs, given their wide range that covers different national sectors and/or regions. Some of these include a small number of highly focused large-scale projects (e.g., infrastructures) that are managed by project management organizations staffed with professionally qualified project managers. Given the scale of such projects, their appraisal, particularly regarding time and cost objectives, is based on tangible deliverables. However, EU Operational Programs also contain a number of small scale 'soft' projects in specific areas such as education and training, business innovation, culture etc. (Ipsilantis et al., 2008). In addition to the beneficiary population, a large number of different stakeholders may be found in EU Operational Programs (e.g., European and National Government Authorities, Programme Management Authorities, Project Organizations). All these justify the complexity of project management in EU Operational Programs and the need to study the attributes of an effective project manager.

This research explored the importance of several attributes that a project manager of EU Operational Programs should hold. It is initially noted that respondents are not demanding in terms of the criteria and subcriteria of the questionnaire. Additionally, in most of their answers, the respondents exhibit a moderate level of satisfaction, as they state that they are neither dissatisfied nor satisfied. The results in the four basic criteria (knowledge, skills, communication, leadership) do not indicate much differentiation in terms of importance. However, it appears that leadership is considered the most important characteristic and communication the least important among project managers.

Regarding the sample, there is a good dispersion in terms of gender (50% male - 50% female), while a similar dispersion is also observed in the specialty (same percentage of engineers and others). Furthermore, the respondents are 40 to 50 years old and mainly hold a master's degree.

The results of the multicriteria analysis show the following:

- The overall satisfaction index is estimated at 76%, indicating that respondents are not generally very satisfied with their cooperation with the project manager of European Operational Programs.
- Communication has the lowest significance, while leadership has the highest significance.
- Communication has the highest satisfaction index, while leadership has the lowest.
- The demanding indices for the basic criteria are negative, meaning that respondents are not demanding.
- Leadership has the highest mean effectiveness index, indicating that it is the characteristic that contributes the most to respondents' dissatisfaction.

The first improvement priority concerns the characteristics of leadership and knowledge (high effectiveness and low demandingness), while the second priority for improvement is the characteristics of communication and skills (low effectiveness and high demandingness).

All in all, a project manager in order to effectively implement EU Operational Programs should sharp its leadership capabilities with focus on his/her organizational skills but without neglecting the other factors that form an effective leader. Moreover, communication skills, especially his/her behavior, and attitude, should be carefully monitored. Also, the results indicate that an effective project manager should have great problem-solving skills which he/she should always enhance.

Additional analyses for the evaluation subcriteria can identify the strengths and weaknesses, as well as improvement priorities of EU project managers. Potential future directions of this specific research may involve expanding the sample, both quantitatively and qualitatively. For example, future research could include not only executives, but also regular employees of public bodies involved in EU projects. Additionally, the research could be expanded to address not only to a Greek audience. Such an extension of the sample would allow for additional comparative analyses aimed at identifying possible different preferences.

REFERENCES

Alvarenga, J. C., Branco, R. R., Guedes, A. L. A., Soares, C. A. P., & Silva, W. S. e. (2020). The project manager core competencies to project success. *International Journal of Managing Projects in Business*, *13*(2), 277–292. doi:10.1108/IJMPB-12-2018-0274

Bowenkamp, R. D., & Kleiner, B. H. (1987). How to be a successful project manager. *Industrial Management & Data Systems, 87*(3/4), 3–6. doi:10.1108/eb057468

Brown, M. (1998). *Successful project management* (2nd ed.). Hodder & Stoughton Ltd.

Brown, T. J. (2007). *The handbook of program management.* McGraw-Hill.

Burke, R. (2013). *Project management: Planning and control techniques* (5th ed.). Jon Wiley and Sons Ltd.

Carvalho, M. M. D., & Rabechini, R. Junior. (2015). Impact of risk management on project performance: The importance of soft skills. *International Journal of Production Research, 53*(2), 321–340. doi:10.1080/00207543.2014.919423

Dimitriadis, A. (2019). *Project management.* New Technologies Publications.

Dutka, A. (1995). *AMA handbook of customer satisfaction: A complete guide to research, planning and implementation.* NTC Business Books.

Fisher, E. (2011). What practitioners consider to be the skills and behaviours of an effective people project manager. *International Journal of Project Management, 29*(8), 994–1002. doi:10.1016/j.ijproman.2010.09.002

Fowler, F. J. (1993). *Survey research method.* SAGE Publications.

Ghorbani, A. (2023). A review of successful construction project managers' competencies and leadership profile. *Journal of Rehabilitation in Civil Engineering, 11*(1), 76–95. https://do.org/10.22075/jrce.2022.24638.1560

Globerson, S., & Zwikael, O. (2002). The impact of the project manager on project management planning processes. *Project Management Journal, 33*(3), 58–64. doi:10.1177/875697280203300308

Grigoroudis, E., & Siskos, Y. (2010). *Customer satisfaction evaluation methods for measuring and implementing service quality.* Springer. doi:10.1007/978-1-4419-1640-2

Holzmann, V., Zitter, D., & Peshkess, S. (2022). The expectations of project managers from artificial intelligence: A Delphi study. *Project Management Journal, 53*(5), 438–455. doi:10.1177/87569728211061779

Horine, M. (2017). *Absolute beginner's guide to project management* (4th ed.). Que Publishing.

Hwang, B. G., & Ng, W. J. (2013). Project management knowledge and skills for green construction: Overcoming challenges. *International Journal of Project Management, 31*(2), 272–284. doi:10.1016/j.ijproman.2012.05.004

JMD 126829. (2015). *Joint Ministerial Decision (JMD) 126829/EYΘY/1217/8.12.2015- System of fiscal corrections and procedures for the recovery of sums unduly or illegally paid from resources of the NSRF 2014-2020 state budget* (Official Gazette 2784/B/21.12.2015). Retrieved May 1, 2023, from https://www.espa.gr/el/Pages/eLibraryFS.aspx?item=2332

Kokkosis, A. I. (2016). *Management of projects*. Modern Publishing Publications. (in Greek)

MD 137675. (2018). *Ministerial Decision (MD) 137675/EYΘY/1016/19.12.2018- Replacement of MD 110427/EYΘY/1020/20.10.2016 (Official Gazette 3521/B/01.11.16) for the legality audits of NSRF public contracts 2014-2020.* Retrieved May 1, 2023, from https://www.espa.gr/el/Pages/eLibraryFS.aspx?item=2450

Munns, A. K., & Bjeirmi, B. F. (1996). The role of project management in achieving project success. *International Journal of Project Management, 14*(2), 81–87. doi:10.1016/0263-7863(95)00057-7

Naumann, E., & Giel, K. (1995). *Customer satisfaction measurement and management: Using the voice of the customer*. Thomson Executive Press.

Omer, M. M., Mohd-Ezazee, N. M. A., Lee, Y. S., Rajabi, M. S., & Rahman, R. A. (2022). Constructive and destructive leadership behaviors, skills, styles and traits in BIM-based construction projects. *Buildings, 12*(12), 2068. doi:10.3390/buildings12122068

Podgórska, M., & Pichlak, M. (2019). Analysis of project managers' leadership competencies: project success relation: What are the competencies of polish project leaders? *International Journal of Managing Projects in Business, 12*(4), 869–887. doi:10.1108/IJMPB-08-2018-0149

Project Management Institute. (2013). *Project management body of knowledge*. Project Management Institute.

Richman, L. (2011). *Improving your project management skills*. Amacom.

Siskos, Y., Grigoroudis, E., & Matsatsinis, N. F. (2016). UTA methods. In S. Greco, M. Ehrgott, & J. Figueira (Eds.), *Multiple criteria analysis: State of the art surveys* (2nd ed., pp. 315–362). Springer. doi:10.1007/978-1-4939-3094-4_9

Sommerville, J., Craig, N., & Hendry, J. (2010). The role of the project manager: All things to all people? *Structural Survey*, *82*(2), 132–141. doi:10.1108/02630801011044235

Vavra, T. G. (1997). *Improving your measurement of customer satisfaction: A guide to creating, conducting, analyzing, and reporting customer satisfaction measurement programs*. ASQC Quality Press.

Wang, Y., Liu, Y., & Wang, H. (2023). Competency model for international engineering project manager through MADM method: The Chinese context. *Expert Systems with Applications*, *212*, 118675. doi:10.1016/j.eswa.2022.118675

Woodruff, R. B., & Gardial, S. F. (1996). *Know your customer: New approaches to understanding customer value and satisfaction*. Blackwell Publishers.

Wu, T. (2022). Digital project management: Rapid changes define new working environments. *The Journal of Business Strategy*, *43*(5), 323–331. doi:10.1108/JBS-03-2021-0047

Zervaki, D. (2023). *Quality characteristics self-assessment of a project manager*. Retrieved May 1, 2023, from https://dimitrazervaki.com/project-manager-self-assessment/

ADDITIONAL READING

Anestis, G., Grigoroudis, E., Krassadaki, E., Matsatsinis, N. F., & Siskos, Y. (2006). Skills Evaluator: A multicriteria decision support system for the evaluation of qualifications and skills in information technology. *Journal of Multi-Criteria Decision Analysis*, *14*(1-3), 21–34. doi:10.1002/mcda.398

Carbone, T. A., & Gholston, S. (2004). Project manager skill development: A survey of programs and practitioners. *Engineering Management Journal*, *16*(3), 10–16. doi:10.1080/10429247.2004.11415252

Doikos, P., & Maglara, E. (2017). *Practical guide for managing EU programs*. Stamouli.

El-Sabaa, A. (2001). The skills and career path of an effective project manager. *International Journal of Project Management*, *19*(1), 1–7. doi:10.1016/S0263-7863(99)00034-4

Goodwin, E. S. C. (1993). Skills required of effective project managers. *Journal of Management Engineering*, *9*(3), 217–226. doi:10.1061/(ASCE)9742-597X(1993)9:3(217)

Grigoroudis, E., & Siskos, Y. (2002). Preference disaggregation for measuring and analysing customer satisfaction: The MUSA method. *European Journal of Operational Research, 143*(1), 148–170. doi:10.1016/S0377-2217(01)00332-0

Grigoroudis, E., Siskos, Y., & Saurais, O. (2000). TELOS: A customer satisfaction evaluation software. *Computers & Operations Research, 27*(7-8), 799–817. doi:10.1016/S0305-0548(99)00119-7

Ipsilantis, P. G., Samaras, G., & Mplanas, N. (2008). A multicriteria satisfaction analysis approach in the assessment of operational programmes. *International Journal of Project Management, 26*(6), 601–611. doi:10.1016/j.ijproman.2007.09.003

Kessler, S. (1996). *Measuring and managing customer satisfaction: Going for the gold.* ASQC Quality Press.

Krassadaki, E., Grigoroudis, E., Matsatsinis, N. F., & Siskos, Y. (2002). The evaluation of studies and training in information technology: A multicriteria approach. *Operational Research: An International Journal, 2*(3), 321–338. doi:10.1007/BF02936388

Loufrani-Fedida, S., & Missonier, S. (2015). The project manager cannot be a hero anymore! Understanding critical competencies in project-based organizations from a multilevel approach. *International Journal of Project Management, 33*(6), 1220–1235. doi:10.1016/j.ijproman.2015.02.010

Massnick, F. (1997). *The customer is CEO: How to measure what your customers want –and make sure they get it.* Amacom.

Meredith, J. R., & Mantel, S. J. (2006). *Project management: A managerial approach.* Wiley & Sons.

Siskos, Y., Grigoroudis, E., Krassadaki, E., & Matsatsinis, N. F. (2007). A multicriteria accreditation system for information technology skills and qualifications. *European Journal of Operational Research, 182*(2), 867–885. doi:10.1016/j.ejor.2006.07.017

Siskos, Y., Grigoroudis, E., Zopounidis, C., & Saurais, O. (1998). Measuring customer satisfaction using a collective preference disaggregation model. *Journal of Global Optimization, 12*(2), 175–195. doi:10.1023/A:1008262411587

Sunindijo, R. Y. (2014). Project manager skills for improving project performance. *International Journal of Business Performance Management, 16*(1), 67–83. doi:10.1504/IJBPM.2015.066041

KEY TERMS AND DEFINITIONS

Customer Satisfaction: The consumer's fulfillment response; it is a judgment that a product or service feature, or the product or service itself, provided (or is providing) a pleasurable level of consumption-related fulfillment, including levels of under- or over-fulfillment.

Multicriteria Analysis: Methods, models and approaches that aim to aid the decision-makers to handle semi-structured decision problems with multiple criteria; it handles problems where the rational solution does not preexist but constitutes an objective of research usually through an interactive process.

MUSA Method: A multicriteria decision analysis method for measuring and analyzing customer satisfaction based on the principles of ordinal regression and using linear programming techniques.

Operational Programs: Programs that implement the priorities and targets agreed between the EU Commission and the national or regional managing authorities through investment priorities and specific objectives.

Project Management: The use of specific knowledge, skills, tools and techniques to achieve specific project objectives and deliver an added value outcome to users.

Project Manager: Organized, goal-oriented professional who are responsible for the planning, execution and managing of people, resources, and project objectives.

Compilation of References

Abdelkhalek, H. A., Refaie, H. S., & Aziz, R. F. (2020). Optimization of time and cost through learning curve analysis. *Ain Shams Engineering Journal, 11*(4), 1069–1082. doi:10.1016/j.asej.2019.12.007

Adam, A., Josephson, P. E. B., & Lindahl, G. (2017). Aggregation of factors causing cost overruns and time delays in large public construction projects: Trends and implications. *Engineering, Construction, and Architectural Management, 24*(3), 393–406. doi:10.1108/ECAM-09-2015-0135

Adama, O. (2018). Urban imaginaries: Funding mega infrastructure projects in Lagos, Nigeria. *GeoJournal, 83*(1), 257–274. doi:10.100710708-016-9761-8

Agyekum-Mensah, G., & Knight, A. D. (2017). The professionals' perspective on the causes of project delay in the construction industry. *Engineering, Construction, and Architectural Management, 24*(5), 828–841. doi:10.1108/ECAM-03-2016-0085

Al mnaseer, R., Al-Smadi, S., & Al-Bdour, H. (2023). Machine learning-aided time and cost overrun prediction in construction projects: application of artificial neural network. *Asian Journal of Civil Engineering, 24*(7), 2583–2593. doi:10.1007/s42107-023-00665-7

Alaimo, L. S., Ciommi, M., Vardopoulos, I., Nosova, B., & Salvati, L. (2022). The Medium-Term Impact of the COVID-19 Pandemic on Population Dynamics: The Case of Italy. *Sustainability, 14*(21), 13995. doi:10.3390/su142113995

Alkaraan, F., Elmarzouky, M., Hussainey, K., & Venkatesh, V. G. (2023). Sustainable strategic investment decision-making practices in UK companies: The influence of governance mechanisms on synergy between industry 4.0 and circular economy. *Technological Forecasting and Social Change, 187*, 122187. Advance online publication. doi:10.1016/j.techfore.2022.122187

Alsugair, A. M., Al-Gahtani, K. S., Alsanabani, N. M., Alabduljabbar, A. A., & Almohsen, A. S. (2023). Artificial Neural Network Model to Predict Final Construction Contract Duration. *Applied Sciences (Basel, Switzerland), 13*(14), 8078. Advance online publication. doi:10.3390/app13148078

Alturayeif, N., Luqman, H., & Ahmed, M. (2023). A systematic review of machine learning techniques for stance detection and its applications. *Neural Computing & Applications, 35*(7), 5113–5144. doi:10.100700521-023-08285-7 PMID:36743664

Alvarenga, J. C., Branco, R. R., Guedes, A. L. A., Soares, C. A. P., & Silva, W. S. e. (2020). The project manager core competencies to project success. *International Journal of Managing Projects in Business*, *13*(2), 277–292. doi:10.1108/IJMPB-12-2018-0274

Amel-Zadeh, A., & Serafeim, G. (2018). Why and how investors use ESG information: Evidence from a global survey. *Financial Analysts Journal*, *74*(3), 87–103. doi:10.2469/faj.v74.n3.2

Amoatey, C., Ameyaw, Y., Adaku, E., & Famiyeh, S. (2015). Analysing delay causes and effects in Ghanaian state housing construction projects. *International Journal of Managing Projects in Business*, *8*(1), 198–214. doi:10.1108/IJMPB-04-2014-0035

Ampese, L. C., Sganzerla, W. G., Di Domenico Ziero, H., Mudhoo, A., Martins, G., & Forster-Carneiro, T. (2022). Research progress, trends, and updates on anaerobic digestion technology: A bibliometric analysis. *Journal of Cleaner Production*, *331*, 130004. Advance online publication. doi:10.1016/j.jclepro.2021.130004

Andersen, B., Samset, K., & Welde, M. (2016). Low estimates – high stakes; underestimation of costs at the front-end of projects. *International Journal of Managing Projects in Business*, *1*(1), 171–193. doi:10.1108/IJMPB-01-2015-0008

Antoniou, F., Aretoulis, G., Giannoulakis, D., & Konstantinidis, D. (2023). Cost and Material Quantities Prediction Models for the Construction of Underground Metro Stations. *Buildings*, *13*(2), 382. doi:10.3390/buildings13020382

Antoniou, F. (2021). Delay risk assessment models for road projects. *Systems*, *9*(3), 1–17. doi:10.3390ystems9030070

Antoniou, F., & Aretoulis, G. (2019). A multi-criteria decision-making support system for choice of method of compensation for highway construction contractors in Greece. *International Journal of Construction Management*, *19*(6), 492–508. doi:10.1080/15623599.2018.1452103

Antoniou, F., Aretoulis, G. N., Konstantinidis, D. K., & Kalfakakou, G. P. (2013). An empirical study of researchers' and practitioners' views on compensating major highway project contractors. *International Journal of Management and Decision Making*, *12*(4), 351–375. doi:10.1504/IJMDM.2013.056883

Antoniou, F., Konstantinidis, D., & Aretoulis, G. N. (2016). Application of the multi attribute utility theory for the selection of project procurement system for Greek highway projects. *International Journal of Management and Decision Making*, *15*(2), 83–112. doi:10.1504/IJMDM.2016.077761

Antoniou, F., Konstantinidis, D., Aretoulis, G., & Xenidis, Y. (2018a). Preliminary construction cost estimates for motorway underpass bridges. *International Journal of Construction Management*, *18*(4), 321–330. doi:10.1080/15623599.2017.1358076

Antoniou, F., & Marinelli, M. (2020). Proposal for the Promotion of Standardization of Precast Beams in Highway Concrete Bridges. *Frontiers in Built Environment*, *6*(July), 1–16. doi:10.3389/fbuil.2020.00119

APM. (2016). *APM body of knowledge*. Retrieved from https://www.apm.org.uk/Body of Knowledge

Apooja, A., Herrala, M., Pekuri, A., & Haappasalo, H. (2013). The characteristics of and cornerstones for creating integrated team. *International Journal of Managing Projects in Business*, *6*(4), 695–713. doi:10.1108/IJMPB-09-2012-0056

Arabiat, A., Al-Bdour, H., & Bisharah, M. (2023). Predicting the construction projects time and cost overruns using K-nearest neighbor and artificial neural network: A case study from Jordan. *Asian Journal of Civil Engineering*, *24*(7), 2405–2414. doi:10.100742107-023-00649-7

Aretoulis, G. N. (2018). Gender Based Perception of Successful Construction of Project Managers' Attributes. *Social Sciences (Basel, Switzerland)*, *7*(7), 112. doi:10.3390ocsci7070112

Aretoulis, G. N. (2019). Neural network models for actual cost prediction in Greek public highway projects. *International Journal of Project Organisation and Management*, *11*(1), 41–64. doi:10.1504/IJPOM.2019.098712

Aretoulis, G. N., Angelides, D. C., Kalfakakou, G. P., Fotiadis, G. S., & Anastasiadis, K. I. (2006). A prototype system for the prediction of final cost in construction projects. *Operations Research*, *6*(3), 323–332. doi:10.1007/BF02941260

Aretoulis, G. N., Papathanasiou, J., & Antoniou, F. (2019). PROMETHEE-based ranking of project managers based on the five personality traits. *Kybernetes*, *49*(4), 1083–1102. doi:10.1108/K-10-2018-0551

Bakti, E. S., Majid, M. Z. B. A., Zin, R. M., & Trigunarsyah, B. (2011). Constructability improvement in seawater intake structure. *Engineering, Construction, and Architectural Management*, *18*(6), 595–608. doi:10.1108/09699981111180908

Baldi, F., & Pandimiglio, A. (2022). The role of ESG scoring and greenwashing risk in explaining the yields of green bonds: A conceptual framework and an econometric analysis. *Global Finance Journal*, *52*, 100711. Advance online publication. doi:10.1016/j.gfj.2022.100711

Basak, S., & Makarov, D. (2014). Strategic Asset Allocation in Money Management. *The Journal of Finance*, *69*(1), 179–217. doi:10.1111/jofi.12106

Baudrit, C., Taillandier, F., Tran, T. T. P., & Breysse, D. (2019). Uncertainty Processing and Risk Monitoring in Construction Projects Using Hierarchical Probabilistic Relational Models. *Computer-Aided Civil and Infrastructure Engineering*, *34*(2), 97–115. doi:10.1111/mice.12391

Bax, K., Sahin, Ö., Czado, C., & Paterlini, S. (2023). ESG, risk, and (tail) dependence. *International Review of Financial Analysis*, *87*, 102513. doi:10.1016/j.irfa.2023.102513

Belany, P., Hrabovsky, P., & Kolkova, Z. (2021). Combination of lighting retrofit and life cycle cost analysis for energy efficiency improvement in buildings. *Energy Reports*, *7*, 2470–2483. doi:10.1016/j.egyr.2021.04.044

Berg, M., & Karlsen, J. (2014). How project managers can encourage and develop positive emotions in project teams. *International Journal of Managing Projects in Business*, *7*(3), 449–472. doi:10.1108/IJMPB-01-2013-0003

Berrone, P., Ricart, J. E., Duch, A. I., Bernardo, V., Salvador, J., Peña, J. P., & Planas, M. R. (2019). EASIER: An evaluation model for public-private partnerships contributing to the sustainable development goals. *Sustainability (Basel)*, *11*(8), 2339. Advance online publication. doi:10.3390u11082339

Bilal, M., Oyedele, L., Kusimo, H., Owolabi, H., Akanbi, L., Ajayi, A., Akinade, O., & Davilla Delgado, M. (2019). Investigating profitability performance of construction projects using big data: A project analytics approach. *Journal of Building Engineering*, *26*, 100850. doi:10.1016/j.jobe.2019.100850

Binhadab, N., Breen, M., & Gillanders, R. (2021). Press freedom and corruption in business-state interactions. *Economic Systems*, *45*(4), 100922. Advance online publication. doi:10.1016/j.ecosys.2021.100922

Björnfot, A. (2008). An engineering perspective on Lean Construction theory. *Proceedings of IGLC16: 16th Annual Conference of the International Group for Lean Construction*, 15–26.

Bogus, S., Migliaccio, G., & Jin, R. (2013). Study of the relationship between procurement duration and project performance in design-build projects: Comparison between water/wastewater and transport sectors. *Journal of Management Engineering*, *29*(4), 382–391. doi:10.1061/(ASCE)ME.1943-5479.0000165

Boussabaine, A., & Kirham, R. (2008). *Whole Life-Cycle Costing: Risk and Risk Responses*. Blackwell Publishing.

Bowenkamp, R. D., & Kleiner, B. H. (1987). How to be a successful project manager. *Industrial Management & Data Systems*, *87*(3/4), 3–6. doi:10.1108/eb057468

Bromilow, F. J., & Pawsey, M. R. (1987). Life cycle cost of university buildings. *Construction Management and Economics*, *5*(4), S3–S22. doi:10.1080/01446193.1987.10462089

Brown, M. (1998). *Successful project management* (2nd ed.). Hodder & Stoughton Ltd.

Brown, T. J. (2007). *The handbook of program management*. McGraw-Hill.

Bull, J. W. (2003). *Life Cycle Costing for Construction*. John Wiley and Sons. doi:10.4324/9780203487723

Burke, R. (2013). *Project management: Planning and control techniques* (5th ed.). Jon Wiley and Sons Ltd.

Burnett, M. (2009). Using Competitive Dialogue in EU Public Procurement – Early Trends and Future Developments. *EIPAScope*, 17–22.

Cambrea, D. R., Paolone, F., & Cucari, N. (2023). Advisory or monitoring role in ESG scenario: Which women directors are more influential in the Italian context? *Business Strategy and the Environment*, bse.3366. doi:10.1002/bse.3366

Carvalho, M. M. D., & Rabechini, R. Junior. (2015). Impact of risk management on project performance: The importance of soft skills. *International Journal of Production Research*, *53*(2), 321–340. doi:10.1080/00207543.2014.919423

Çevikbaş, M., & Işık, Z. (2021). An overarching review on delay analyses in construction projects. *Buildings*, *11*(3), 109. Advance online publication. doi:10.3390/buildings11030109

Chou, J. S., Yang, I. T., & Chong, W. K. (2009). Probabilistic simulation for developing likelihood distribution of engineering project cost. *Automation in Construction*, *18*(5), 570–577. Advance online publication. doi:10.1016/j.autcon.2008.12.001

Chua, D. K. H., Loh, P. K., Kog, Y. C., & Jaselskis, E. J. (1997). Neural networks for construction project success. *3rd Singapore International Conference on Intelligent Systems (SPICIS 97)*, 317–328. 10.1016/S0957-4174(97)00046-8

Connaughton, J. N., & Green, S. D. (1996). *Value management in construction: a client's guide*. CIRIA.

Creedy, G. D., Skitmore, M., & Wong, J. K. W. (2010). Evaluation of Risk Factors Leading to Cost Overrun in Delivery of Highway Construction Projects. *Journal of Construction Engineering and Management*, *136*(5), 528–537. doi:10.1061/(ASCE)CO.1943-7862.0000160

Cruz, C. A., & Matos, F. (2023). ESG Maturity: A Software Framework for the Challenges of ESG Data in Investment. *Sustainability (Basel)*, *15*(3), 2610. doi:10.3390u15032610

D'Hondt, C., Merli, M., & Roger, T. (2021). What drives retail portfolio exposure to ESG factors? *Finance Research Letters*. Advance online publication. doi:10.1016/j.frl.2021.102470

Dalcher, D. (2012). The nature of project management. *International Journal of Managing Projects in Business*, *5*(4), 643–660. doi:10.1108/17538371211268960

DasGupta, R. (2022). Financial performance shortfall, ESG controversies, and ESG performance: Evidence from firms around the world. *Finance Research Letters*, *46*, 102487. Advance online publication. doi:10.1016/j.frl.2021.102487

de Araújo, M. C. B., Alencar, L. H., & de Miranda Mota, C. M. (2017). Project procurement management: A structured literature review. *International Journal of Project Management*, *35*(3), 353–377. doi:10.1016/j.ijproman.2017.01.008

Department of Trade and Industry. (2011). *Strategy for broad-based black economic empowerment*. Retrieved from http://www.thedti.gov.za

Derbe, G., Li, Y., Wu, D., & Zhao, Q. (2020). Scientometric review of construction project schedule studies: Trends, gaps and potential research areas. *Journal of Civil Engineering and Management*, *26*(4), 343–363. doi:10.3846/jcem.2020.12317

Dhaval, P. (2019). Development of Prediction Models for Claim Cause Analyses in Highway Projects. *Journal of Legal Affairs and Dispute Resolution in Engineering and Construction, 11*(4), 4519018. doi:10.1061/(ASCE)LA.1943-4170.0000303

Dhillon, B. S. (2009). *Life Cycle Costing for Engineers.* CRC Press.

Di Giuseppe, E., Massi, A., & D'Orazio, M. (2017). Probabilistic Life Cycle Cost Analysis of Building Energy Efficiency Measures: Selection and Characterization of the Stochastic Inputs through a Case Study. *Procedia Engineering, 180*, 491–501. doi:10.1016/j.proeng.2017.04.208

Diamantas, V., Kirytopoulos, K., & Leopoulos, V. (2007). Project's duration prediction: Traditional tools or simulation. *World Review of Entrepreneurship, Management and Sustainable Development, 3*(3), 317–333. doi:10.1504/WREMSD.2007.014049

Dimitriadis, A. (2019). *Project management.* New Technologies Publications.

Dutka, A. (1995). *AMA handbook of customer satisfaction: A complete guide to research, planning and implementation.* NTC Business Books.

Eccles, R. G., Serafeim, G., & Krzus, M. P. (2011). Market interest in nonfinancial information. *The Bank of America Journal of Applied Corporate Finance, 23*(4), 113–127. doi:10.1111/j.1745-6622.2011.00357.x

Eccles, R. G., Serafeim, G., Seth, D., & Ming, C. C. Y. (2013). The Performance Frontier: Innovating for a Sustainable Strategy: Interaction. *Harvard Business Review, 91*(7), 17–18.

Eghbali-Zarch, M., Tavakkoli-Moghaddam, R., Dehghan-Sanej, K., & Kaboli, A. (2022). Prioritizing the effective strategies for construction and demolition waste management using fuzzy IDOCRIW and WASPAS methods. *Engineering, Construction, and Architectural Management, 29*(3), 1109–1138. doi:10.1108/ECAM-08-2020-0617

Eriksson, P. E., & Westerberg, M. (2011). Effects of cooperative procurement procedures on construction project performance: A conceptual framework. *International Journal of Project Management, 29*(2), 197–208. doi:10.1016/j.ijproman.2010.01.003

Ernzen, J. J., & Schexnayder, C. (2000). One Company's Experience with Design/Build: Labor Cost Risk and Profit Potential. *Journal of Construction Engineering & Management, 126*(1), 10–14.

European Commission. (2014). Guide to Cost-benefit Analysis of Investment Projects: Economic appraisal tool for Cohesion Policy 2014-2020. Publications Office of the European Union. https://doi.org/ doi:10.2776/97516

European Court of Auditors. (2014). *2014 Activity Report.* doi:10.2865/67808

Fathi, E. A., Taher, S. E. D., & Mahfouz, S. Y. (2020). Value engineering analysis of RC roadway bridges assimilating environmental impact. *HBRC Journal, 16*(1), 207–226. doi:10.1080/16874048.2020.1794348

Fisher, E. (2011). What practitioners consider to be the skills and behaviours of an effective people project manager. *International Journal of Project Management*, *29*(8), 994–1002. doi:10.1016/j.ijproman.2010.09.002

Fowler, F. J. (1993). *Survey research method.* SAGE Publications.

Fregonara, E., Ferrando, D. G., & Pattono, S. (2018). Economic-environmental sustainability in building projects: Introducing risk and uncertainty in LCCE and LCCA. *Sustainability (Basel)*, *10*(6), 1901. doi:10.3390u10061901

Galletta, S., Goodell, J. W., Mazzù, S., & Paltrinieri, A. (2023). Bank reputation and operational risk: The impact of ESG. *Finance Research Letters*, *51*, 103494. Advance online publication. doi:10.1016/j.frl.2022.103494

Gangi, F., Meles, A., Daniele, L. M., Varrone, N., Salerno, D., & Salerno, D. (2021). ESG criteria in alternative Investments. *The Evolution of Sustainable Investments and Finance: Theoretical Perspectives and New Challenges*, 59-99.

Georgiadou, M. C. (2014). Future-proofed energy design approaches for achieving low-energy homes: Enhancing the code for sustainable homes. *Buildings*, *4*(3), 488–519. doi:10.3390/buildings4030488

Georgiadou, M. C., Hacking, T., & Guthrie, P. (2012). A conceptual framework for future-proofing the energy performance of buildings. *Energy Policy*, *47*, 145–155. doi:10.1016/j.enpol.2012.04.039

Gerth, R., Boqvist, A., Bjelkemyr, M., & Lindberg, B. (2013). Design for construction: Utilizing production experiences in development. *Construction Management and Economics*, *31*(2), 135–150. doi:10.1080/01446193.2012.756142

Ghaleh, R. M. B., Pourrostam, T., Sharifloo, N. M., Sardroud, J. M., & Safa, E. (2021). Delays in the road construction projects from risk management perspective. *Infrastructures*, *6*(9), 135. Advance online publication. doi:10.3390/infrastructures6090135

Ghorbani, A. (2023). A review of successful construction project managers' competencies and leadership profile. *Journal of Rehabilitation in Civil Engineering*, *11*(1), 76–95. https://do.org/10.22075/jrce.2022.24638.1560

Gibb, A. G. F. (2001). Standardization and pre-assembly- distinguishing myth from reality using case study research. *Construction Management and Economics*, *19*(3), 307–315. doi:10.1080/01446190010020435

Giese, G., Lee, L. E., Melas, D., Nagy, Z., & Nishikawa, L. (2019). Foundations of ESG investing: How ESG affects equity valuation, risk, and performance. *Journal of Portfolio Management*, *45*(5), 69–83. doi:10.3905/jpm.2019.45.5.069

Giese, G., Nagy, Z., & Lee, L. E. (2021). Deconstructing ESG ratings performance: Risk and return for E, S, and G by time horizon, sector, and weighting. *Journal of Portfolio Management*, *47*(3), 94–111. doi:10.3905/jpm.2020.1.198

Giuffrida, M., Jiang, H., & Mangiaracina, R. (2021). Investigating the relationships between uncertainty types and risk management strategies in cross-border e-commerce logistics. *International Journal of Logistics Management, 32*(4), 1406–1433. doi:10.1108/IJLM-04-2020-0158

Gkovedarou, M., & Aretoulis, G. N. (2017). Neural Networks and Statistical Analysis for Time and Cost Prediction Models of Urban Redevelopment Projects. *International Journal of Information Systems and Social Change, 8*(4), 37–52. doi:10.4018/IJISSC.2017100103

Globerson, S., & Zwikael, O. (2002). The impact of the project manager on project management planning processes. *Project Management Journal, 33*(3), 58–64. doi:10.1177/875697280203300308

Goodier, C., & Gibb, A. (2007). Future opportunities for offsite in the UK. *Construction Management and Economics, 25*(6), 585–595. doi:10.1080/01446190601071821

Goodier, C., Gibb, A., Mancini, M., Turck, C., Gjepali, O., & Daniels, E. (2019). Modularisation and offsite in engineering construction: An early decision-support tool. *Proceedings of the Institution of Civil Engineers. Civil Engineering, 172*(6), 3–14. doi:10.1680/jcien.19.00015

Gorshunov, M. A., Armenakis, A. A., Harris, S. G., & Walker, H. J. (2021). Quad-qualified audit committee director: Implications for monitoring and reducing financial corruption. *Journal of Corporate Finance, 66*, 101854. Advance online publication. doi:10.1016/j.jcorpfin.2020.101854

Graham, R., & Englund, R. (2004). *Creating an environment for successful projects* (2nd ed.). Jhn Wiley and Sons.

Grigoroudis, E., & Siskos, Y. (2010). *Customer satisfaction evaluation methods for measuring and implementing service quality*. Springer. doi:10.1007/978-1-4419-1640-2

Grimsey, D., & Lewis, M. K. (2005). Are Public Private Partnerships value for money?: Evaluating alternative approaches and comparing academic and practitioner views. *Accounting Forum, 29*(4), 345–378. doi:10.1016/j.accfor.2005.01.001

Gupta, V. K., & Thakkar, J. J. (2018). A quantitative risk assessment methodology for construction project. *Sadhana - Academy Proceedings in Engineering Sciences, 43*(7), 1–16. doi:10.1007/s12046-018-0846-6

Hale, D. R., Shrestha, P. P., Gibson, G. E. Jr, & Migliaccio, G. C. (2009). Empirical Comparison of Design/Build and Design/Bid/Build Project Delivery Methods. *Journal of Construction Engineering and Management, 135*(7), 579–587. doi:10.1061/(ASCE)CO.1943-7862.0000017

Han, W., Yusof, A., Ismail, S., & Aun, N. (2012). Reviewing the notions of construction project success. *International Journal of Business and Management, 7*(1), 90–101.

Hasnain, M., Thaheem, M. J., & Ullah, F. (2018). Best Value Contractor Selection in Road Construction Projects: ANP-Based Decision Support System. *International Journal of Civil Engineering, 16*(6), 695–714. doi:10.100740999-017-0199-2

Hazini, K., Dehghan, R., & Ruwanpura, J. (2014). A heuristic method to determine optimum degree of activity accelerating and overlapping in schedule compression. *Canadian Journal of Civil Engineering*, *41*(4), 382–392. doi:10.1139/cjce-2013-0194

Heijboer, G., & Telgen, J. (2002). Choosing the open or the restricted procedure: A big deal or a big deal? *Journal of Public Procurement*, *2*(2), 12–26. doi:10.1108/JOPP-02-02-2002-B002

Henriksson, R., Livnat, J., Pfeifer, P., & Stumpp, M. (2019). Integrating ESG in portfolio construction. *Journal of Portfolio Management*, *45*(4), 67–81. doi:10.3905/jpm.2019.45.4.067

He, Q., Wang, T., Chan, A. P. C., Li, H., & Chen, Y. (2019). Identifying the gaps in project success research: A mixed bibliographic and bibliometric analysis. *Engineering, Construction, and Architectural Management*, *26*(8), 1553–1573. doi:10.1108/ECAM-04-2018-0181

Hola, B., & Schabowicz, K. (2010). Estimation of earthworks execution time cost by means of artificial neural networks. *Automation in Construction*, *19*(5), 570–579. doi:10.1016/j.autcon.2010.02.004

Holzmann, V., Zitter, D., & Peshkess, S. (2022). The expectations of project managers from artificial intelligence: A Delphi study. *Project Management Journal*, *53*(5), 438–455. doi:10.1177/87569728211061779

Honcharenko, T., Akselrod, R., Shpakov, A., & Khomenko, O. (2023). Information system based on multi-value classification of fully connected neural network for construction management. *IAES International Journal of Artificial Intelligence*, *12*(2), 593–601. doi:10.11591/ijai.v12.i2.pp593-601

Horine, M. (2017). *Absolute beginner's guide to project management* (4th ed.). Que Publishing.

HSPPA. (2015). *Award criteria during public procurement procedures Guideline 11*. Retrieved February 27, 2023, from https://www.eaadhsy.gr/sdg/dg.php?qid=1114

Hwang, B. G., & Ng, W. J. (2013). Project management knowledge and skills for green construction: Overcoming challenges. *International Journal of Project Management*, *31*(2), 272–284. doi:10.1016/j.ijproman.2012.05.004

Hwang, C. L., & Yoon, K. (1981). *Multiple Attribute Decision Making: Methods and Applications*. Springer-Verlag. doi:10.1007/978-3-642-48318-9

Ibrahim, M., Ofori, G., Morcos, M., & Egbu, C. (2020). *A conceptual risk management framework in the construction of mega housing projects in Egypt.* Urban Regeneration, University of East London. https://openresearch.lsbu.ac.uk/item/8vz06

Ibrahim, C., Costello, S., & Wilkinson, S. (2015). Key indicators influencing the management of team integration in construction projects. *International Journal of Managing Projects in Business*, *1*(1), 300–323. doi:10.1108/IJMPB-04-2014-0028

Ika, L., & Hodgson, D. (2014). Learning from international development projects: Blending critical project studies and critical development studies. *International Journal of Project Management*, *32*(7), 1182–1196. doi:10.1016/j.ijproman.2014.01.004

International Organization for Standardization. (2006*) Environmental management – Life cycle assessment – Principles and framework* (ISO No. 14040). Retrieved from https://www.iso.org/standard/37456.html

International Organization for Standardization. (2015) *Environmental management systems – Requirements with guidance for use* (ISO No. 14001). Retrieved from https://www.iso.org/standard/60857.html

International Organization for Standardization. (2017) *Building and constructed assets – Service life planning – Part 5: Life-cycle costing* (ISO No. 15686-5). Retrieved from https://www.iso.org/standard/61148.html

Ishizaka, A., & Nemery, P. (2013). *Multi-Criteria Decision Analysis Methods and Software*. John Wiley and Sons Inc. doi:10.1002/9781118644898

Jay, C. I., & Bowen, P. A. (2015). Value management and innovation: A historical perspective and review of the evidence. *Journal of Engineering. Design and Technology*, *13*(1), 123–143. doi:10.1108/JEDT-03-2013-0021

Jepson, J., Kirytopoulos, K., & London, K. (2020). Insights into the application of risk tools and techniques by construction project managers. *International Journal of Construction Management*, *20*(8), 848–866. doi:10.1080/15623599.2018.1494673

Jha, C. K. (2019). Financial reforms and corruption: Evidence using GMM estimation. *International Review of Economics & Finance*, *62*, 66–78. doi:10.1016/j.iref.2019.03.003

Jiang, W., Yang, Q., Jiang, J., Martek, I., & Gao, F. (2022). Operational Risk Management of Public–Private Partnership Infrastructure Projects: A Bibliometric Literature Review. *Buildings*, *12*(11), 1905. Advance online publication. doi:10.3390/buildings12111905

Jiang, Y., & Wu, H. (2007). A method for highway agency to estimate highway construction durations and set contract times. *International Journal of Construction Education and Research*, *3*(3), 199–216. doi:10.1080/15578770701715052

Jia, Y. L., Wang, J., Shou, W. C., Hosseini, M. R., & Bai, Y. (2023). Graph neural networks for construction applications. *Automation in Construction*, *154*, 104984. Advance online publication. doi:10.1016/j.autcon.2023.104984

JMD 126829. (2015). *Joint Ministerial Decision (JMD) 126829/ΕΥΘΥ/1217/8.12.2015-System of fiscal corrections and procedures for the recovery of sums unduly or illegally paid from resources of the NSRF 2014-2020 state budget* (Official Gazette 2784/B/21.12.2015). Retrieved May 1, 2023, from https://www.espa.gr/el/Pages/eLibraryFS.aspx?item=2332

Joint Initiative on Priority Skills Acquisition (JIPSA). (2016). *Annual Report.* Retrieved from Available at www.pmg.org.xa

Ju, X., Ferreira, F. A. F., & Wang, M. (2020). Innovation, agile project management and firm performance in a public sector-dominated economy: Empirical evidence from high-tech small and medium-sized enterprises in China. *Socio-Economic Planning Sciences*, *72*, 100779. Advance online publication. doi:10.1016/j.seps.2019.100779

Kelly, J., Male S., & Graham, D. (1993). *Value Management of Construction Projects*. Academic Press.

Kelly, J., Male, S., & Graham, D. (2014). Value Management in Design and Construction: The Economic Management of Projects (2nd ed.). Blackwell Publishing.

Kerzner, H. (2013). *Project management: A systems approach to planning, scheduling and controlling*. John Wiley & Sons.

Kifokeris, D., & Xenidis, Y. (2017). Constructability: Outline of Past, Present, and Future Research. *Journal of Construction Engineering and Management*, *143*(8), 04017035. Advance online publication. doi:10.1061/(ASCE)CO.1943-7862.0001331

Kim, M. K., McGovern, S., Belsky, M., Middleton, C., & Brilakis, I. (2016). A Suitability Analysis of Precast Components for Standardized Bridge Construction in the United Kingdom. *Procedia Engineering*, *164*(June), 188–195. doi:10.1016/j.proeng.2016.11.609

Kirytopoulos, K. (2021). *Risk Management in Projects and Organizations* (1st ed.). Kleidarithmos.

Kokkosis, A. I. (2016). *Management of projects*. Modern Publishing Publications. (in Greek)

Korinth, F., & Lueg, R. (2022). Corporate sustainability and risk management—The u-shaped relationships of disaggregated esg rating scores and risk in the German capital market. *Sustainability (Basel)*, *14*(9), 5735. doi:10.3390u14095735

Koulinas, G. K., Demesouka, O. E., Sidas, K. A., & Koulouriotis, D. E. (2021). A TOPSIS — Risk Matrix and Monte Carlo Expert System for Risk Assessment in Engineering Projects. *Sustainability*, *13*(2), 1–14. doi:10.3390u132011277 PMID:34123411

Koulinas, G. K., Xanthopoulos, A. S., Tsilipiras, T. T., & Koulouriotis, D. E. (2020). Schedule delay risk analysis in construction projects with a simulation-based expert system. *Buildings*, *10*(8), 134. Advance online publication. doi:10.3390/buildings10080134

Krejcie, R. V., & Morgan, D. W. (1970). Table for determining sample size from a given population. *Educational and Psychological Measurement*, *30*(1), 607–610. doi:10.1177/001316447003000308

Kumar, D., Alam, M., Zou, P. X. W., Sanjayan, J. G., & Memon, R. A. (2020). Comparative analysis of building insulation material properties and performance. *Renewable & Sustainable Energy Reviews*, *131*(110038), 110038. Advance online publication. doi:10.1016/j.rser.2020.110038

Lambropoulos, S. (2007). The use of time and cost utility for construction contract award under European Union Legislation. *Building and Environment*, *42*(1), 452–463. doi:10.1016/j.buildenv.2005.08.002

Lam, K. C., Hu, T., Cheung, S. O., Yuen, R. K. K., & Deng, Z. M. (2001). Multi-project cash flow optimization: Non-inferior solution through neuro-multiobjective algorithm. *Engineering, Construction, and Architectural Management*, *8*(2), 130–144. doi:10.1108/eb021176

Larsen, D. S., Van Stokkum, I. H. M., Vengris, M., Van Der Horst, M. A., De Weerd, F. L., Hellingwerf, K. J., & Van Grondelle, R. (2004). Incoherent manipulation of the photoactive yellow protein photocycle with dispersed pump-dump-probe spectroscopy. *Biophysical Journal*, *87*(3), 1858–1872. doi:10.1529/biophysj.104.043794 PMID:15345564

Law, No. 4412/2016, Pub. L. No. A 147 / 08.08.2016, 692 (2016). https://europam.eu/data/mechanisms/PP/PP Laws/Greece/1.LawNo.4412of2016_ENG,consolidated, last amended in 2020.pdf

Le Guern, S. (2013). *First fuel begins to flow through SA's new R23bn fuel pipeline.* Retrieved from www.engineeringnews.co.za

Leopoulos, V. N., Kirytopoulos, K. A., & Malandrakis, C. (2006). Risk management for SMEs: Tools to use and how. *Production Planning and Control*, *17*(3), 322–332. doi:10.1080/09537280500285136

Le, P. T., Chileshe, N., Kirytopoulos, K., & Rameezdeen, R. (2020). Investigating the significance of risks in BOT transportation projects in Vietnam. *Engineering, Construction, and Architectural Management*, *27*(6), 1401–1425. Advance online publication. doi:10.1108/ECAM-08-2019-0439

Lin, X., Mazlan, A. N., Ismail, S., Hu, L., Kasiman, E. H., & Yahya, K. (2023). Status of value management studies in construction projects: A systematic review. *Ain Shams Engineering Journal*, *14*(1), 101820. doi:10.1016/j.asej.2022.101820

Liu, X., Yang, Y., Jiang, Y., Fu, Y., Zhong, R. Y., Li, M., & Huang, G. Q. (2023). Data-driven ESG assessment for blockchain services: A comparative study in textiles and apparel industry. *Resources, Conservation and Recycling*, *190*, 106837. Advance online publication. doi:10.1016/j.resconrec.2022.106837

Loizia, P., Voukkali, I., Zorpas, A. A., Navarro Pedreño, J., Chatziparaskeva, G., Inglezakis, V. J., Vardopoulos, I., & Doula, M. (2021). Measuring the level of environmental performance in insular areas, through key performed indicators, in the framework of waste strategy development. *The Science of the Total Environment*, *753*, 141974. doi:10.1016/j.scitotenv.2020.141974 PMID:32906046

Lu, Y., & Gong, P. P., Tang, Y., Sun, S., & Li, Q. (2021). BIM-integrated construction safety risk assessment at the design stage of building projects, *Automation in Construction, 124*(103553). doi:10.1016/j.autcon.2021.103553

Lu, W., Hua, Y. Y., & Zhang, S. J. (2017). Logistic regression analysis for factors influencing cost performance of design-bid-build and design-build projects. *Engineering, Construction, and Architectural Management*, *24*(1), 118–132. doi:10.1108/ECAM-07-2015-0119

Lu, W., Tan, T., Xu, J., Wang, J., Chen, K., Gao, S., & Xue, F. (2021). Design for manufacture and assembly (DfMA) in construction: The old and the new. *Architectural Engineering and Design Management, 17*(1–2), 77–91. doi:10.1080/17452007.2020.1768505

Lu, Y., Wang, L., & Zhang, Y. (2022). Does digital financial inclusion matter for firms' ESG disclosure? Evidence from China. *Frontiers in Environmental Science, 10*, 1029975. Advance online publication. doi:10.3389/fenvs.2022.1029975

Malek, J., & Desai, T. N. (2020). A systematic literature review to map literature focus of sustainable manufacturing. *Journal of Cleaner Production, 256*, 120345. doi:10.1016/j.jclepro.2020.120345

Mao, X., Zhang, X., & AbouRizk, S. M. (2009). Enhancing Value Engineering Process by Incorporating Inventive Problem-Solving Techniques. *Journal of Construction Engineering and Management, 135*(5), 416–424. doi:10.1061/(ASCE)CO.1943-7862.0000001

Marinelli, M. (2022). A DfX-based approach for incorporating sustainability in infrastructure project planning. *Built Environment Project and Asset Management, 12*(1), 20–37. doi:10.1108/BEPAM-05-2020-0083

Marinelli, M., & Antoniou, F. (2020). Improving public works' value for money: A new procurement strategy. *International Journal of Managing Projects in Business, 13*(1), 85–102. doi:10.1108/IJMPB-04-2018-0084

Marinelli, M., & Janardhanan, M. (2022). Green cement production in India: Prioritization and alleviation of barriers using the best–worst method. *Environmental Science and Pollution Research International, 29*(42), 63988–64003. doi:10.100711356-022-20217-x PMID:35469385

Marinelli, M., Petroutsatou, K., Fragkakis, N., & Lambropoulos, S. (2018). Rethinking new public infrastructure value for money in recession times: The Greek case. *International Journal of Construction Management, 18*(4), 331–342. doi:10.1080/15623599.2017.1358131

Marks, M., & Ellis, L. (2013). Delays in major agricultural infrastructure projects in Guyana: Causes and proposed solutions. *The West Indian Journal of Engineering, 36*(1), 225–235.

Martinez, E. H., Alvear, A. M., Tommelein, I. D., & Ballard, G. (2015). Formwork standardization and production flow: Lessons from an affordable housing project in Ecuador. *Proceedings of IGLC 23 - 23rd Annual Conference of the International Group for Lean Construction: Global Knowledge - Global Solutions,* 53–62.

Masud, M. A. K., Rahman, M., & Rashid, M. H. U. (2022). Anti-Corruption Disclosure, Corporate Social Expenditure and Political Corporate Social Responsibility: Empirical Evidence from Bangladesh. *Sustainability (Basel), 14*(10), 6140. Advance online publication. doi:10.3390u14106140

McKinsey. (2016). *Bridging global infrastructure gaps.* Retrieved from https://www.mckinsey.com/industries/capital-projects-and-infrastructure/our-insights/management

McKinsey. (2017). *Reinventing Construction: A Route to Higher Productivity.* Author.

MD 137675. (2018). *Ministerial Decision (MD) 137675/EYΘY/1016/19.12.2018-Replacement of MD 110427/EYΘY/1020/20.10.2016 (Official Gazette 3521/B/01.11.16) for the legality audits of NSRF public contracts 2014-2020.* Retrieved May 1, 2023, from https://www.espa.gr/el/Pages/eLibraryFS.aspx? item=2450

Merková, M., Drábek, J., & Jelačić, D. (2013). Application of risk analysis in business investment decision-making [Primjena analize rizika u donošenju odluka o poslovnim investicijama]. *Drvna Industrija, 64*(4), 313–322. doi:10.5552/drind.2013.1317

Merrow, E. (2011). *Industrial mega-projects; Concepts, strategies, and practices for success.* Wiley and Sons.

Merrow, E. (2012). Oil and gas industry mega-projects: Our recent track record. *Oil and Gas Facilities, 1*(2), 38–42. doi:10.2118/153695-PA

Mi, X., Tang, M., Liao, H., Shen, W., & Lev, B. (2019). The state-of-the-art survey on integrations and applications of the best worst method in decision making: Why, what, what for and what's next? *Omega, 87*, 205–225. doi:10.1016/j.omega.2019.01.009

Moghayedi, A., & Windapo, A. (2022). Modelling the uncertainty of cost and time in highway projects. *Infrastructure Asset Management, 9*(2), 73–88. doi:10.1680/jinam.21.00004

Moon, S., Ha, C., & Yang, J. (2012). Structured Idea Creation for Improving the Value of Construction Design. *Journal of Construction Engineering and Management, 138*(7), 841–853. doi:10.1061/(ASCE)CO.1943-7862.0000491

Moore, D. (1996). Buildability assessment and the development of an automated design aid for managing the transfer of construction process knowledge. *Engineering, Construction, and Architectural Management, 3*(1–2), 29–46. doi:10.1108/eb021021

Moretti, L., Cantisani, G., & Di Mascio, P. (2016). Management of road tunnels: Construction, maintenance and lighting costs. *Tunnelling and Underground Space Technology, 51*, 84–89. doi:10.1016/j.tust.2015.10.027

Moret, Y., & Einstein, H. H. (2016). Construction Cost and Duration Uncertainty Model: Application to High-Speed Rail Line Project. *Journal of Construction Engineering and Management, 142*(10), 05016010. doi:10.1061/(ASCE)CO.1943-7862.0001161

Mousa, A. A., Hussein, M., & Kineber, A. F. (2022). Value-Engineering Methodology for the Selection of an Optimal Bridge System. *Transportation Research Record: Journal of the Transportation Research Board, 2676*(4), 483–498. doi:10.1177/03611981211062154

Mousakhani, E., Yavarkhani, M., & Sohrabi, S. (2017). Selecting an appropriate alternative for a major infrastructure project with regard to value engineering approach. *Journal of Engineering. Design and Technology, 15*(3), 395–416. doi:10.1108/JEDT-12-2015-0083

Muller, R., & Jugdev, K. (2012). Critical success factors in projects. *International Journal of Managing Projects in Business, 5*(4), 757–775. doi:10.1108/17538371211269040

Munns, A. K., & Bjeirmi, B. F. (1996). The role of project management in achieving project success. *International Journal of Project Management*, *14*(2), 81–87. doi:10.1016/0263-7863(95)00057-7

Naderpour, A., Sardroud, J. M., Mo, M., & Xenidis, Y. (2019). *Uncertainty management in time estimation of construction projects : A systematic literature review and new model development.* doi:10.24200/sci.2017.4605

Naffa, H., & Fain, M. (2020). Performance measurement of ESG-themed megatrend investments in global equity markets using pure factor portfolios methodology. *PLoS One*, *15*(12), e0244225. doi:10.1371/journal.pone.0244225 PMID:33351834

Naoum, S. G., & Egbu, C. (2016). Modern selection criteria for procurement methods in construction: A state-of-the-art literature review and a survey. *International Journal of Managing Projects in Business*, *9*(2), 309–336. doi:10.1108/IJMPB-09-2015-0094

Narbaev, T., & De Marco, A. (2013). Combination of growth model and earned schedule to forecast project cost at completion. *Journal of Construction Engineering and Management*, *1*, 130–138.

National Strategic Reference Framework 2007-2013. (2007). Retrieved August 28, 2020, from https://www. certh. gr/dat/7190CCE2/file. pdf

Naumann, E., & Giel, K. (1995). *Customer satisfaction measurement and management: Using the voice of the customer*. Thomson Executive Press.

Nesheim, T., & Smith, J. (2015). Knowledge sharing in projects: Does employment arrangement matter? *Personnel Review*, *44*(2), 255–269. doi:10.1108/PR-11-2013-0203

NguyenD. A.TranD. Q.NguyenT. N.TranH. H. (2023). Modeling labor productivity in high-rise building construction projects using neural networks. *Archives of Civil Engineering, 69*(1), 675–692. https://doi.org/ doi:10.24425/ace.2023.144195

Nima, M. A., Abdul-Kadir, M. R., Jaafar, M. S., & Alghulami, R. G. (2004). Constructability Concepts in Kuala Selangor Cable-Stayed Bridge in Malaysia. *Journal of Construction Engineering and Management*, *130*(3), 315–321. doi:10.1061/(ASCE)0733-9364(2004)130:3(315)

Norouzi, G., Heydari, M., Noori, S., & Bagherpour, M. (2015). Mathematical modeling for scheduling and determining success probability of research projects considering complex-fuzzy networks. *Journal of Applied Mathematics*, 1–2. doi:10.1155/2015/809216

Noshadravan, A., Miller, T. R., & Gregory, J. G. (2017). A lifecycle cost analysis of residential buildings including natural hazard risk. *Journal of Construction Engineering and Management*, *143*(7), 04017017. doi:10.1061/(ASCE)CO.1943-7862.0001286

Obianyo, J. I., Udeala, R. C., & Alaneme, G. U. (2023). Application of neural networks and neuro-fuzzy models in construction scheduling. *Scientific Reports*, *13*(1), 8199. Advance online publication. doi:10.103841598-023-35445-5 PMID:37211564

Odedairo, B. O., & Olenloa, O. E. (2021). Scheduling of Post-Flood Recovery Project with Flexible Project Structure. *Journal of Engineering, Project, and Production Management, 11*(2), 118–126. doi:10.2478/jeppm-2021-0012

Omer, M. M., Mohd-Ezazee, N. M. A., Lee, Y. S., Rajabi, M. S., & Rahman, R. A. (2022). Constructive and destructive leadership behaviors, skills, styles and traits in BIM-based construction projects. *Buildings, 12*(12), 2068. doi:10.3390/buildings12122068

Pan, Y., & Zhang, L. (2021). Roles of artificial intelligence in construction engineering and management: A critical review and future trends. *Automation in Construction, 122*, 103517. doi:10.1016/j.autcon.2020.103517

Park, J., & Kwak, Y. H. (2017). Design-Bid-Build (DBB) vs. Design-Build (DB) in the U.S. public transportation projects: The choice and consequences. *International Journal of Project Management, 35*(3), 280–295. doi:10.1016/j.ijproman.2016.10.013

Parra Márquez, C., Crespo Márquez, A., González-Prida Díaz, V., Gómez Fernández, J.F., Kristjanpoller Rodríguez, F., Viveros Gunckel, P. (2017). Economic impact of a failure using life-cycle cost analysis. *Advanced Maintenance Modelling for Asset Management: Techniques and Methods for Complex Industrial Systems*, 213-243. doi:10.1007/978-3-319-58045-6_9

Parvaneh, F., & El-Sayegh, S. (2016). Project selection using the combined approach of AHP and LP. *Journal of Financial Management of Property and Construction, 21*(1), 39–53. doi:10.1108/JFMPC-09-2015-0034

Passas, I., Ragazou, K., Zafeiriou, E., Garefalakis, A., & Zopounidis, C. (2022). ESG Controversies: A Quantitative and Qualitative Analysis for the Sociopolitical Determinants in EU Firms. *Sustainability (Basel), 14*(19), 12879. doi:10.3390u141912879

Peng, W., & Xiong, L. (2022). Managing financing costs and fostering green transition: The role of green financial policy in China. *Economic Analysis and Policy, 76*, 820–836. Advance online publication. doi:10.1016/j.eap.2022.09.014

Petroutsatou, K., & Kantilierakis, D. (2023). Productivity Analysis and Associated Risks in Steel Structures. *Buildings, 13*(905), 1–18. doi:10.3390/buildings13040905

Petroutsatou, K., Ladopoulos, I., & Tsakelidou, K. (2022). Scientometric Analysis and AHP for Hierarchizing Criteria Affecting Construction Equipment Operators' Performance. *Sustainability (Basel), 14*(11), 6836. Advance online publication. doi:10.3390u14116836

Petroutsatou, K., Maravas, A., & Saramourtsis, A. (2021). A life cycle model for estimating road tunnel cost. *Tunnelling and Underground Space Technology, 111*, 103858. doi:10.1016/j.tust.2021.103858

Petrusheva, S., Car-Pušić, D., & Zileska-Pancovska, V. (2019). Support Vector Machine Based Hybrid Model for Prediction of Road Structures Construction Costs. *IOP Conference Series. Earth and Environmental Science, 222*, 012010. doi:10.1088/1755-1315/222/1/012010

Pewdum, W., Rujirayanyong, T., & Sooksatra, V. (2009). Forecasting final budget and duration of highway construction projects. *Engineering, Construction, and Architectural Management, 16*(6), 544–557. doi:10.1108/09699980911002566

Plebankiewicz, E., Zima, K., & Wieczorek, D. (2016). Life Cycle Cost Modelling of Buildings with Consideration of the Risk. *Archives of Civil Engineering, 62*(2), 149–166. doi:10.1515/ace-2015-0071

PMI. (2008). A guide to the project management body of knowledge (PMBOK Guide) (4th ed.). Project Management Institute.

PMI. (2017). *A guide to the Project Management Body of Knowledge (PMBOK guide)* (P. M. Institute, Ed.; 6th ed.). Project Management Institute Newton Square.

PMI. (2019). *The Standard for Risk Management in Portfolios, Programs and Projects*. Project Management Institute.

PMI. (2021). *A Guide to the Project Management Body of Knowledge (PMBOK® Guide)* (7th ed.). Project Management Institute.

Podgórska, M., & Pichlak, M. (2019). Analysis of project managers' leadership competencies: project success relation: What are the competencies of polish project leaders? *International Journal of Managing Projects in Business, 12*(4), 869–887. doi:10.1108/IJMPB-08-2018-0149

Prater, J., Kirytopoulos, K., & Ma, T. (2017). Optimism bias within the project management context: A systematic quantitative literature review. *International Journal of Managing Projects in Business, 10*(2), 370–385. doi:10.1108/IJMPB-07-2016-0063

Project Management Institute. (2013). *A guide to project management body of knowledge*. PMI.

Project Management Institute. (2013). *Project management body of knowledge*. Project Management Institute.

Ragazou, K., Passas, I., & Garefalakis, A. (2022). It Is Time for Anti-Bribery: Financial Institutions Set the New Strategic "Roadmap" to Mitigate Illicit Practices and Corruption in the Market. *Administrative Sciences, 12*(4), 1–25. doi:10.3390/admsci12040166

Rasheed, N., Shahzad, W., Khalfan, M., & Rotimi, J. O. B. (2022). Risk Identification, Assessment, and Allocation in PPP Projects: A Systematic Review. *Buildings, 12*(8), 1109. Advance online publication. doi:10.3390/buildings12081109

Ren, Z., Shen, G. Q., & Xue, X. L. (2013). Failure Caused by Inappropriate Construction Methods: An Expensive Lesson. *Journal of Management Engineering, 29*(1), 25–34. doi:10.1061/(ASCE)ME.1943-5479.0000117

Rezaei, J. (2015). Best-worst multi-criteria decision-making method. *Omega, 53*, 49–57. doi:10.1016/j.omega.2014.11.009

Rezaei, J. (2016). Best-worst multi-criteria decision-making method: Some properties and a linear model. *Omega, 64*, 126–130. doi:10.1016/j.omega.2015.12.001

Richman, L. (2011). *Improving your project management skills*. Amacom.

Roe, P. (2014). *Factors which contribute to successful projects*. Retrieved from www.apm.org.uk

Rostami, A., Sommerville, J., Wong, I. L., & Lee, C. (2015). Risk management implementation in small and medium enterprises in the UK construction industry. *Engineering, Construction, and Architectural Management, 22*(1), 91–107. doi:10.1108/ECAM-04-2014-0057

Roy, P. P., Rao, S., & Zhu, M. (2022). Mandatory CSR expenditure and stock market liquidity. *Journal of Corporate Finance, 72*, 102158. Advance online publication. doi:10.1016/j.jcorpfin.2022.102158

Ruffle, B., Henderson, J., Murphy-Hagan, C., Kirkwood, G., Wolf, F., & Edwards, D. A. (2018). Application of probabilistic risk assessment: Evaluating remedial alternatives at the Portland Harbor Superfund Site. *Integrated Environmental Assessment and Management, 14*(1), 63–78. doi:10.1002/ieam.1999 PMID:29105341

Sabbaghi, O. (2022). The impact of news on the volatility of ESG firms. *Global Finance Journal, 51*, 100570. Advance online publication. doi:10.1016/j.gfj.2020.100570

Sahu, A. K., Padhy, R. K., Das, D., & Gautam, A. (2021). Improving financial and environmental performance through MFCA: A SME case study. *Journal of Cleaner Production, 279*, 123751. Advance online publication. doi:10.1016/j.jclepro.2020.123751

Salling, K. B., & Leleur, S. (2011). Transport appraisal and Monte Carlo simulation by use of the CBA-DK model. *Transport Policy, 18*(1), 236–245. doi:10.1016/j.tranpol.2010.08.007

Salvatierra-Garrido, J., & Pasquire, C. (2011). Value theory in lean construction. *Journal of Financial Management of Property and Construction, 16*(1), 8–18. doi:10.1108/13664381111116043

Savvides, S. (1994). Risk analysis in investment appraisal. *Project Appraisal, 9*(1), 3–18. doi:10.1080/02688867.1994.9726923

Sawyer, M. (2012). *Vico software integrating construction*. Retrieved from www.vicosoftware.com

Sekaran, U., & Bougie, R. (2019). *Research methods for business: A skill buildding approach*. John Wiley and Sons.

Shaffie, S. S., & Jaaman, S. H. (2016). Monte Carlo on Net Present Value for Capital Investment in Malaysia. *Procedia: Social and Behavioral Sciences, 219*, 688–693. doi:10.1016/j.sbspro.2016.05.052

Shaheen, S. M., Antoniadis, V., Shahid, M., Yang, Y., Abdelrahman, H., Zhang, T., Hassan, N. E. E., Bibi, I., Niazi, N. K., Younis, S. A., Almazroui, M., Tsang, Y. F., Sarmah, A. K., Kim, K. H., & Rinklebe, J. (2022). Sustainable applications of rice feedstock in agro-environmental and construction sectors: A global perspective. *Renewable & Sustainable Energy Reviews*, *153*, 111791. Advance online publication. doi:10.1016/j.rser.2021.111791

Shu, H., & Tan, W. (2023). Does carbon control policy risk affect corporate ESG performance? *Economic Modelling*, *120*, 106148. Advance online publication. doi:10.1016/j.econmod.2022.106148

Sieglinde, F. (2016, September 19). *Life-Cycle Cost Analysis (LCCA)*. Whole Building Design Guide. https://www.wbdg.org/resources/life-cycle-cost-analysis-lcca

Siemonsma, H., van Nus, W., & Uyttendaele, P. (2012). Awarding of port PPP contracts: The added value of a competitive dialogue procedure. *Maritime Policy & Management*, *39*(1), 63–78. doi:10.1080/03088839.2011.642314

Singhania, D. M., & Saini, D. N. (2022). Systems approach to environment, social and governance (ESG): Case of Reliance industries. *Sustainable Operations and Computers*, *3*, 103–117. doi:10.1016/j.susoc.2021.11.003

Siskos, Y., Grigoroudis, E., & Matsatsinis, N. F. (2016). UTA methods. In S. Greco, M. Ehrgott, & J. Figueira (Eds.), *Multiple criteria analysis: State of the art surveys* (2nd ed., pp. 315–362). Springer. doi:10.1007/978-1-4939-3094-4_9

Smith, M., Bevacqua, A., Tembe, S., & Lal, P. (2021). Life cycle analysis (LCA) of residential ground source heat pump systems: A comparative analysis of energy efficiency in New Jersey. *Sustainable Energy Technologies and Assessments*, *47*(101364), 101364. Advance online publication. doi:10.1016/j.seta.2021.101364

Sommerville, J., Craig, N., & Hendry, J. (2010). The role of the project manager: All things to all people? *Structural Survey*, *82*(2), 132–141. doi:10.1108/02630801011044235

Stamatiadis, N., Sturgill, R., & Amiridis, K. (2017). Benefits from Constructability Reviews. *Transportation Research Procedia*, *25*, 2889–2897. doi:10.1016/j.trpro.2017.05.275

Tam, C. M. (2000). Design and Build on a complicated redevelopment project in Hong Kong: The Happy Valley Racecourse Redevelopment. *International Journal of Project Management*, *18*(2), 125–129. doi:10.1016/S0263-7863(99)00012-5

Tamimi, N., & Sebastianelli, R. (2017). Transparency among S&P 500 companies: An analysis of ESG disclosure scores. *Management Decision*, *55*(8), 1660–1680. doi:10.1108/MD-01-2017-0018

Tan, G. E., Ong, T. B., Ong, C. Y., & Choong, K. K. (2014). Development and standardisation of new precast concrete open spandrel arch bridge system. *Engineering for Progress, Nature and People*, 799–806. doi:10.2749/222137814814066960

Tang, P., & Bittner, R. B. (2014). Use of Value Engineering to Develop Creative Design Solutions for Marine Construction Projects. *Practice Periodical on Structural Design and Construction, 19*(1), 129–136. doi:10.1061/(ASCE)SC.1943-5576.0000184

Tawiah, P. A., & Russell, A. D. (2008). Assessing Infrastructure Project Innovation as a Function of Procurement Mode. *Journal of Management Engineering, 24*(3), 173–186. doi:10.1061/(ASCE)0742-597X(2008)24:3(173)

The Standish Group. (2014). *CHAOS*. The Standish Group. Retrieved from https://www.projectsmart.co.uk/white-papers/chaos-report.pdf

TILOS. (2012). *TILOS linear project*. Retrieved from www.tilos.org

Titirla, M., & Aretoulis, G. (2019). Neural network models for actual duration of Greek highway projects. *Journal of Engineering. Design and Technology, 17*(6), 1323–1339. doi:10.1108/JEDT-01-2019-0027

Titirla, M., Larbi, W., & Aretoulis, G. (2021). Prediction methods for the actual duration of greek highway projects. *WSEAS Transactions on Business and Economics, 18*, 1389–1396. doi:10.37394/23207.2021.18.128

Torvatn, T., & de Boer, L. (2017). Public procurement reform in the EU: Start of a new era? *IMP Journal, 11*(3), 431–451. doi:10.1108/IMP-09-2015-0056

Transnet. (2014). *Market demand strategy*. Retrieved from www.Transnet.net

Transnet. (2015). *Sustainability Report*. Retrieved from www.transnet.net

Transnet. (2017). *Transnet sustainability report 2017*. Retrieved from www.transnet net

Tsz Wai, C., Wai Yi, P., Ibrahim Olanrewaju, O., Abdelmageed, S., Hussein, M., Tariq, S., & Zayed, T. (2021). A critical analysis of benefits and challenges of implementing modular integrated construction. *International Journal of Construction Management, 23*(4), 656–668. doi:10.1080/15623599.2021.1907525

Tziralis, G., Kirytopoulos, K., Rentizelas, A., & Tatsiopoulos, I. (2009). Holistic Investment Assessment: Optimization. *Risk Appraisal and Decision Making. MDE. Managerial and Decision Economics, 30*(6), 393–403. doi:10.1002/mde.1458

Umit Dikmen, S., & Sonmez, M. (2011). An artificial neural networks model for the estimation of formwork labour. *Journal of Civil Engineering and Management, 17*(3), 340–347. doi:10.3846/13923730.2011.594154

Vagdatli, T., & Petroutsatou, K. (2021). CBA and probabilistic risk analysis tool for non-revenue generating infrastructure projects. The case of Greece. *Case Studies on Transport Policy, 9*(1), 103–124. doi:10.1016/j.cstp.2020.10.004

Varajao, J., Dominguez, C., Ribeiro, P., & Paiva, A. (2014). Critical success aspects in project management: similarities and differences between the construction and software industry. *Technical Gazette*, 586-587.

Vardopoulos, I. (2018). Multi-Criteria Decision-Making Approach for the Sustainable Autonomous Energy Generation through Renewable Sources. Studying Zakynthos Island in Greece. *Journal of Environment and Sustainable Development*, *7*(1), 52. Advance online publication. doi:10.5296/emsd.v7i1.12110

Vardopoulos, I. (2019). Critical sustainable development factors in the adaptive reuse of urban industrial buildings. A fuzzy DEMATEL approach. *Sustainable Cities and Society*, *50*, 101684. Advance online publication. doi:10.1016/j.scs.2019.101684

Vardopoulos, I., Falireas, S., Konstantopoulos, I., Kaliora, E., & Theodoropoulou, E. (2018). Sustainability assessment of the agri-environmental practices in Greece. Indicators' comparative study. *International Journal of Agricultural Resources, Governance and Ecology*, *14*(4), 368–399. doi:10.1504/IJARGE.2018.098024

Vardopoulos, I., Konstantopoulos, I., Zorpas, A. A., Limousy, L., Bennici, S., Inglezakis, V. J., & Voukkali, I. (2021). Sustainable metropolitan areas perspectives through assessment of the existing waste management strategies. *Environmental Science and Pollution Research International*, *28*(19), 24305–24320. Advance online publication. doi:10.100711356-020-07930-1 PMID:32072414

Vavra, T. G. (1997). *Improving your measurement of customer satisfaction: A guide to creating, conducting, analyzing, and reporting customer satisfaction measurement programs*. ASQC Quality Press.

Vose, D. (2008). Risk Analysis – A Quantitative Guide (3rd ed.). John Wiley and Sons.

Wang, N., Chang, Y. C., & El-Sheikh, A. A. (2012). Monte Carlo simulation approach to life cycle cost management. *Structure and Infrastructure Engineering*, *8*(8), 739–746. doi:10.1080/15732479.2010.481304

Wang, Y., Liu, Y., & Wang, H. (2023). Competency model for international engineering project manager through MADM method: The Chinese context. *Expert Systems with Applications*, *212*, 118675. doi:10.1016/j.eswa.2022.118675

Waziri, B. S., Jibrin, A. T., & Kadai, B. (2014). Functional duration models for highway construction projects in Nigeria. *Arid Zone Journal of Engineering, Technology and Environment*, *10*, 13–23.

Welde, M., & Dahl, R. E. (2021). Cost escalation in road construction contracts. *Transportation Research Record: Journal of the Transportation Research Board*, *2675*(9), 1006–1015. doi:10.1177/03611981211005462

Wells, H. (2012). How effective are project management methodologies: An explorative evaluation of their benefits in practice. *Project Management Journal*, *43*(2), 43–58. doi:10.1002/pmj.21302

Westney, R. E. (1997). *The Engineer's cost handbook: tools for managing project costs*. CRC Press. doi:10.1201/9780203910016

Woodruff, R. B., & Gardial, S. F. (1996). *Know your customer: New approaches to understanding customer value and satisfaction.* Blackwell Publishers.

World Bank. (2015). *Capacity building in Africa.* World Bank.

Wu, T. (2022). Digital project management: Rapid changes define new working environments. *The Journal of Business Strategy, 43*(5), 323–331. doi:10.1108/JBS-03-2021-0047

Xaba, M. (2011). *Root cause analysis of major capital projects at Transnet freight rail.* UNISA.

Yang, J., Baeg, H., & Moon, S. (2014). Utilization of contradiction for creating design alternatives in construction value engineering. *KSCE Journal of Civil Engineering, 18*(2), 355–364. doi:10.100712205-014-0284-x

Zervaki, D. (2023). *Quality characteristics self-assessment of a project manager.* Retrieved May 1, 2023, from https://dimitrazervaki.com/project-manager-self-assessment/

Zhang, N., Zhang, Y., & Zong, Z. (2023). Fund ESG performance and downside risk: Evidence from China. *International Review of Financial Analysis, 86.*

Zhang, J. P., Liu, L. H., & Coble, R. J. (2002). Hybrid intelligence utilization for construction site layout. *Automation in Construction, 11*(5), 511–519. doi:10.1016/S0926-5805(01)00071-1

Zhang, J., & El-Diraby, T. E. (2006). Constructability Analysis of the Bridge Superstructure Rotation Construction Method in China. *Journal of Construction Engineering and Management, 132*(4), 353–362. doi:10.1061/(ASCE)0733-9364(2006)132:4(353)

Zhang, L., & Fan, W. (2013). Improving performance of construction projects: A project manager's emotional intelligence approach. *Engineering, Construction, and Architectural Management, 20*(2), 195–207. doi:10.1108/09699981311303044

Zhao, N., & Ying, F. (2018). Method selection: A conceptual framework for public sector PPP selection. *Built Environment Project and Asset Management, 9*(2), 214–232. doi:10.1108/BEPAM-01-2018-0018

Related References

To continue our tradition of advancing information science and technology research, we have compiled a list of recommended IGI Global readings. These references will provide additional information and guidance to further enrich your knowledge and assist you with your own research and future publications.

Abdul Razak, R., & Mansor, N. A. (2021). Instagram Influencers in Social Media-Induced Tourism: Rethinking Tourist Trust Towards Tourism Destination. In M. Dinis, L. Bonixe, S. Lamy, & Z. Breda (Eds.), *Impact of New Media in Tourism* (pp. 135-144). IGI Global. https://doi.org/10.4018/978-1-7998-7095-1.ch009

Abir, T., & Khan, M. Y. (2022). Importance of ICT Advancement and Culture of Adaptation in the Tourism and Hospitality Industry for Developing Countries. In C. Ramos, S. Quinteiro, & A. Gonçalves (Eds.), *ICT as Innovator Between Tourism and Culture* (pp. 30–41). IGI Global. https://doi.org/10.4018/978-1-7998-8165-0.ch003

Abir, T., & Khan, M. Y. (2022). Importance of ICT Advancement and Culture of Adaptation in the Tourism and Hospitality Industry for Developing Countries. In C. Ramos, S. Quinteiro, & A. Gonçalves (Eds.), *ICT as Innovator Between Tourism and Culture* (pp. 30–41). IGI Global. https://doi.org/10.4018/978-1-7998-8165-0.ch003

Abtahi, M. S., Behboudi, L., & Hasanabad, H. M. (2017). Factors Affecting Internet Advertising Adoption in Ad Agencies. *International Journal of Innovation in the Digital Economy*, *8*(4), 18–29. doi:10.4018/IJIDE.2017100102

Afenyo-Agbe, E., & Mensah, I. (2022). Principles, Benefits, and Barriers to Community-Based Tourism: Implications for Management. In I. Mensah & E. Afenyo-Agbe (Eds.), *Prospects and Challenges of Community-Based Tourism and Changing Demographics* (pp. 1–29). IGI Global. doi:10.4018/978-1-7998-7335-8.ch001

Agbo, V. M. (2022). Distributive Justice Issues in Community-Based Tourism. In I. Mensah & E. Afenyo-Agbe (Eds.), *Prospects and Challenges of Community-Based Tourism and Changing Demographics* (pp. 107–129). IGI Global. https://doi.org/10.4018/978-1-7998-7335-8.ch005

Agrawal, S. (2017). The Impact of Emerging Technologies and Social Media on Different Business(es): Marketing and Management. In O. Rishi & A. Sharma (Eds.), *Maximizing Business Performance and Efficiency Through Intelligent Systems* (pp. 37–49). Hershey, PA: IGI Global. doi:10.4018/978-1-5225-2234-8.ch002

Ahmad, A., & Johari, S. (2022). Georgetown as a Gastronomy Tourism Destination: Visitor Awareness Towards Revisit Intention of Nasi Kandar Restaurant. In M. Valeri (Ed.), *New Governance and Management in Touristic Destinations* (pp. 71–83). IGI Global. https://doi.org/10.4018/978-1-6684-3889-3.ch005

Alkhatib, G., & Bayouq, S. T. (2021). A TAM-Based Model of Technological Factors Affecting Use of E-Tourism. *International Journal of Tourism and Hospitality Management in the Digital Age*, *5*(2), 50–67. https://doi.org/10.4018/IJTHMDA.20210701.oa1

Altinay Ozdemir, M. (2021). Virtual Reality (VR) and Augmented Reality (AR) Technologies for Accessibility and Marketing in the Tourism Industry. In C. Eusébio, L. Teixeira, & M. Carneiro (Eds.), *ICT Tools and Applications for Accessible Tourism* (pp. 277-301). IGI Global. https://doi.org/10.4018/978-1-7998-6428-8.ch013

Anantharaman, R. N., Rajeswari, K. S., Angusamy, A., & Kuppusamy, J. (2017). Role of Self-Efficacy and Collective Efficacy as Moderators of Occupational Stress Among Software Development Professionals. *International Journal of Human Capital and Information Technology Professionals*, *8*(2), 45–58. doi:10.4018/IJHCITP.2017040103

Aninze, F., El-Gohary, H., & Hussain, J. (2018). The Role of Microfinance to Empower Women: The Case of Developing Countries. *International Journal of Customer Relationship Marketing and Management*, *9*(1), 54–78. doi:10.4018/IJCRMM.2018010104

Antosova, G., Sabogal-Salamanca, M., & Krizova, E. (2021). Human Capital in Tourism: A Practical Model of Endogenous and Exogenous Territorial Tourism Planning in Bahía Solano, Colombia. In V. Costa, A. Moura, & M. Mira (Eds.), *Handbook of Research on Human Capital and People Management in the Tourism Industry* (pp. 282–302). IGI Global. https://doi.org/10.4018/978-1-7998-4318-4.ch014

Arsenijević, O. M., Orčić, D., & Kastratović, E. (2017). Development of an Optimization Tool for Intangibles in SMEs: A Case Study from Serbia with a Pilot Research in the Prestige by Milka Company. In M. Vemić (Ed.), *Optimal Management Strategies in Small and Medium Enterprises* (pp. 320–347). Hershey, PA: IGI Global. doi:10.4018/978-1-5225-1949-2.ch015

Aryanto, V. D., Wismantoro, Y., & Widyatmoko, K. (2018). Implementing Eco-Innovation by Utilizing the Internet to Enhance Firm's Marketing Performance: Study of Green Batik Small and Medium Enterprises in Indonesia. *International Journal of E-Business Research, 14*(1), 21–36. doi:10.4018/IJEBR.2018010102

Asero, V., & Billi, S. (2022). New Perspective of Networking in the DMO Model. In M. Valeri (Ed.), *New Governance and Management in Touristic Destinations* (pp. 105–118). IGI Global. https://doi.org/10.4018/978-1-6684-3889-3.ch007

Atiku, S. O., & Fields, Z. (2017). Multicultural Orientations for 21st Century Global Leadership. In N. Baporikar (Ed.), *Management Education for Global Leadership* (pp. 28–51). Hershey, PA: IGI Global. doi:10.4018/978-1-5225-1013-0.ch002

Atiku, S. O., & Fields, Z. (2018). Organisational Learning Dimensions and Talent Retention Strategies for the Service Industries. In N. Baporikar (Ed.), *Global Practices in Knowledge Management for Societal and Organizational Development* (pp. 358–381). Hershey, PA: IGI Global. doi:10.4018/978-1-5225-3009-1.ch017

Atsa'am, D. D., & Kuset Bodur, E. (2021). Pattern Mining on How Organizational Tenure Affects the Psychological Capital of Employees Within the Hospitality and Tourism Industry: Linking Employees' Organizational Tenure With PsyCap. *International Journal of Tourism and Hospitality Management in the Digital Age, 5*(2), 17–28. https://doi.org/10.4018/IJTHMDA.2021070102

Ávila, L., & Teixeira, L. (2018). The Main Concepts Behind the Dematerialization of Business Processes. In M. Khosrow-Pour, D.B.A. (Ed.), Encyclopedia of Information Science and Technology, Fourth Edition (pp. 888-898). Hershey, PA: IGI Global. https://doi.org/ doi:10.4018/978-1-5225-2255-3.ch076

Ayorekire, J., Mugizi, F., Obua, J., & Ampaire, G. (2022). Community-Based Tourism and Local People's Perceptions Towards Conservation: The Case of Queen Elizabeth Conservation Area, Uganda. In I. Mensah & E. Afenyo-Agbe (Eds.), *Prospects and Challenges of Community-Based Tourism and Changing Demographics* (pp. 56–82). IGI Global. https://doi.org/10.4018/978-1-7998-7335-8.ch003

Baleiro, R. (2022). Tourist Literature and the Architecture of Travel in Olga Tokarczuk and Patti Smith. In R. Baleiro & R. Pereira (Eds.), *Global Perspectives on Literary Tourism and Film-Induced Tourism* (pp. 202-216). IGI Global. https://doi.org/10.4018/978-1-7998-8262-6.ch011

Barat, S. (2021). Looking at the Future of Medical Tourism in Asia. *International Journal of Tourism and Hospitality Management in the Digital Age*, *5*(1), 19–33. https://doi.org/10.4018/IJTHMDA.2021010102

Barbosa, C. A., Magalhães, M., & Nunes, M. R. (2021). Travel Instagramability: A Way of Choosing a Destination? In M. Dinis, L. Bonixe, S. Lamy, & Z. Breda (Eds.), *Impact of New Media in Tourism* (pp. 173-190). IGI Global. https://doi.org/10.4018/978-1-7998-7095-1.ch011

Bari, M. W., & Khan, Q. (2021). Pakistan as a Destination of Religious Tourism. In E. Alaverdov & M. Bari (Eds.), *Global Development of Religious Tourism* (pp. 1-10). IGI Global. https://doi.org/10.4018/978-1-7998-5792-1.ch001

Bartens, Y., Chunpir, H. I., Schulte, F., & Voß, S. (2017). Business/IT Alignment in Two-Sided Markets: A COBIT 5 Analysis for Media Streaming Business Models. In S. De Haes & W. Van Grembergen (Eds.), *Strategic IT Governance and Alignment in Business Settings* (pp. 82–111). Hershey, PA: IGI Global. doi:10.4018/978-1-5225-0861-8.ch004

Bashayreh, A. M. (2018). Organizational Culture and Organizational Performance. In W. Lee & F. Sabetzadeh (Eds.), *Contemporary Knowledge and Systems Science* (pp. 50–69). Hershey, PA: IGI Global. doi:10.4018/978-1-5225-5655-8.ch003

Bechthold, L., Lude, M., & Prügl, R. (2021). Crisis Favors the Prepared Firm: How Organizational Ambidexterity Relates to Perceptions of Organizational Resilience. In A. Zehrer, G. Glowka, K. Schwaiger, & V. Ranacher-Lackner (Eds.), *Resiliency Models and Addressing Future Risks for Family Firms in the Tourism Industry* (pp. 178–205). IGI Global. https://doi.org/10.4018/978-1-7998-7352-5.ch008

Bedford, D. A. (2018). Sustainable Knowledge Management Strategies: Aligning Business Capabilities and Knowledge Management Goals. In N. Baporikar (Ed.), *Global Practices in Knowledge Management for Societal and Organizational Development* (pp. 46–73). Hershey, PA: IGI Global. doi:10.4018/978-1-5225-3009-1.ch003

Bekjanov, D., & Matyusupov, B. (2021). Influence of Innovative Processes in the Competitiveness of Tourist Destination. In J. Soares (Ed.), *Innovation and Entrepreneurial Opportunities in Community Tourism* (pp. 243–263). IGI Global. https://doi.org/10.4018/978-1-7998-4855-4.ch014

Bharwani, S., & Musunuri, D. (2018). Reflection as a Process From Theory to Practice. In M. Khosrow-Pour, D.B.A. (Ed.), Encyclopedia of Information Science and Technology, Fourth Edition (pp. 1529-1539). Hershey, PA: IGI Global. doi:10.4018/978-1-5225-2255-3.ch132

Bhatt, G. D., Wang, Z., & Rodger, J. A. (2017). Information Systems Capabilities and Their Effects on Competitive Advantages: A Study of Chinese Companies. *Information Resources Management Journal*, *30*(3), 41–57. doi:10.4018/IRMJ.2017070103

Bhushan, M., & Yadav, A. (2017). Concept of Cloud Computing in ESB. In R. Bhadoria, N. Chaudhari, G. Tomar, & S. Singh (Eds.), *Exploring Enterprise Service Bus in the Service-Oriented Architecture Paradigm* (pp. 116–127). Hershey, PA: IGI Global. doi:10.4018/978-1-5225-2157-0.ch008

Bhushan, S. (2017). System Dynamics Base-Model of Humanitarian Supply Chain (HSCM) in Disaster Prone Eco-Communities of India: A Discussion on Simulation and Scenario Results. *International Journal of System Dynamics Applications*, *6*(3), 20–37. doi:10.4018/IJSDA.2017070102

Binder, D., & Miller, J. W. (2021). A Generations' Perspective on Employer Branding in Tourism. In V. Costa, A. Moura, & M. Mira (Eds.), *Handbook of Research on Human Capital and People Management in the Tourism Industry* (pp. 152–174). IGI Global. https://doi.org/10.4018/978-1-7998-4318-4.ch008

Birch Freeman, A. A., Mensah, I., & Antwi, K. B. (2022). Smiling vs. Frowning Faces: Community Participation for Sustainable Tourism in Ghanaian Communities. In I. Mensah & E. Afenyo-Agbe (Eds.), *Prospects and Challenges of Community-Based Tourism and Changing Demographics* (pp. 83–106). IGI Global. https://doi.org/10.4018/978-1-7998-7335-8.ch004

Biswas, A., & De, A. K. (2017). On Development of a Fuzzy Stochastic Programming Model with Its Application to Business Management. In S. Trivedi, S. Dey, A. Kumar, & T. Panda (Eds.), *Handbook of Research on Advanced Data Mining Techniques and Applications for Business Intelligence* (pp. 353–378). Hershey, PA: IGI Global. doi:10.4018/978-1-5225-2031-3.ch021

Boragnio, A., & Faracce Macia, C. (2021). "Taking Care of Yourself at Home": Use of E-Commerce About Food and Care During the COVID-19 Pandemic in the City of Buenos Aires. In M. Korstanje (Ed.), *Socio-Economic Effects and Recovery Efforts for the Rental Industry: Post-COVID-19 Strategies* (pp. 45–71). IGI Global. https://doi.org/10.4018/978-1-7998-7287-0.ch003

Borges, V. D. (2021). Happiness: The Basis for Public Policy in Tourism. In A. Perinotto, V. Mayer, & J. Soares (Eds.), *Rebuilding and Restructuring the Tourism Industry: Infusion of Happiness and Quality of Life* (pp. 1–25). IGI Global. https://doi.org/10.4018/978-1-7998-7239-9.ch001

Bücker, J., & Ernste, K. (2018). Use of Brand Heroes in Strategic Reputation Management: The Case of Bacardi, Adidas, and Daimler. In A. Erdemir (Ed.), *Reputation Management Techniques in Public Relations* (pp. 126–150). Hershey, PA: IGI Global. doi:10.4018/978-1-5225-3619-2.ch007

Buluk Eşitti, B. (2021). COVID-19 and Alternative Tourism: New Destinations and New Tourism Products. In M. Demir, A. Dalgıç, & F. Ergen (Eds.), *Handbook of Research on the Impacts and Implications of COVID-19 on the Tourism Industry* (pp. 786–805). IGI Global. https://doi.org/10.4018/978-1-7998-8231-2.ch038

Bureš, V. (2018). Industry 4.0 From the Systems Engineering Perspective: Alternative Holistic Framework Development. In R. Brunet-Thornton & F. Martinez (Eds.), *Analyzing the Impacts of Industry 4.0 in Modern Business Environments* (pp. 199–223). Hershey, PA: IGI Global. doi:10.4018/978-1-5225-3468-6.ch011

Buzady, Z. (2017). Resolving the Magic Cube of Effective Case Teaching: Benchmarking Case Teaching Practices in Emerging Markets – Insights from the Central European University Business School, Hungary. In D. Latusek (Ed.), *Case Studies as a Teaching Tool in Management Education* (pp. 79–103). Hershey, PA: IGI Global. doi:10.4018/978-1-5225-0770-3.ch005

Camillo, A. (2021). *Legal Matters, Risk Management, and Risk Prevention: From Forming a Business to Legal Representation*. IGI Global. doi:10.4018/978-1-7998-4342-9.ch004

Căpusneanu, S., & Topor, D. I. (2018). Business Ethics and Cost Management in SMEs: Theories of Business Ethics and Cost Management Ethos. In I. Oncioiu (Ed.), *Ethics and Decision-Making for Sustainable Business Practices* (pp. 109–127). Hershey, PA: IGI Global. doi:10.4018/978-1-5225-3773-1.ch007

Chan, R. L., Mo, P. L., & Moon, K. K. (2018). Strategic and Tactical Measures in Managing Enterprise Risks: A Study of the Textile and Apparel Industry. In K. Strang, M. Korstanje, & N. Vajjhala (Eds.), *Research, Practices, and Innovations in Global Risk and Contingency Management* (pp. 1–19). Hershey, PA: IGI Global. doi:10.4018/978-1-5225-4754-9.ch001

Charlier, S. D., Burke-Smalley, L. A., & Fisher, S. L. (2018). Undergraduate Programs in the U.S: A Contextual and Content-Based Analysis. In J. Mendy (Ed.), *Teaching Human Resources and Organizational Behavior at the College Level* (pp. 26–57). Hershey, PA: IGI Global. doi:10.4018/978-1-5225-2820-3.ch002

Chumillas, J., Güell, M., & Quer, P. (2022). The Use of ICT in Tourist and Educational Literary Routes: The Role of the Guide. In C. Ramos, S. Quinteiro, & A. Gonçalves (Eds.), *ICT as Innovator Between Tourism and Culture* (pp. 15–29). IGI Global. https://doi.org/10.4018/978-1-7998-8165-0.ch002

Dahlberg, T., Kivijärvi, H., & Saarinen, T. (2017). IT Investment Consistency and Other Factors Influencing the Success of IT Performance. In S. De Haes & W. Van Grembergen (Eds.), *Strategic IT Governance and Alignment in Business Settings* (pp. 176–208). Hershey, PA: IGI Global. doi:10.4018/978-1-5225-0861-8.ch007

Damnjanović, A. M. (2017). Knowledge Management Optimization through IT and E-Business Utilization: A Qualitative Study on Serbian SMEs. In M. Vemić (Ed.), *Optimal Management Strategies in Small and Medium Enterprises* (pp. 249–267). Hershey, PA: IGI Global. doi:10.4018/978-1-5225-1949-2.ch012

Daneshpour, H. (2017). Integrating Sustainable Development into Project Portfolio Management through Application of Open Innovation. In M. Vemić (Ed.), *Optimal Management Strategies in Small and Medium Enterprises* (pp. 370–387). Hershey, PA: IGI Global. doi:10.4018/978-1-5225-1949-2.ch017

Daniel, A. D., & Reis de Castro, V. (2018). Entrepreneurship Education: How to Measure the Impact on Nascent Entrepreneurs. In A. Carrizo Moreira, J. Guilherme Leitão Dantas, & F. Manuel Valente (Eds.), *Nascent Entrepreneurship and Successful New Venture Creation* (pp. 85–110). Hershey, PA: IGI Global. doi:10.4018/978-1-5225-2936-1.ch004

David, R., Swami, B. N., & Tangirala, S. (2018). Ethics Impact on Knowledge Management in Organizational Development: A Case Study. In N. Baporikar (Ed.), *Global Practices in Knowledge Management for Societal and Organizational Development* (pp. 19–45). Hershey, PA: IGI Global. doi:10.4018/978-1-5225-3009-1.ch002

De Uña-Álvarez, E., & Villarino-Pérez, M. (2022). Fostering Ecocultural Resources, Identity, and Tourism in Inland Territories (Galicia, NW Spain). In G. Fernandes (Ed.), *Challenges and New Opportunities for Tourism in Inland Territories: Ecocultural Resources and Sustainable Initiatives* (pp. 1-16). IGI Global. https://doi.org/10.4018/978-1-7998-7339-6.ch001

Delias, P., & Lakiotaki, K. (2018). Discovering Process Horizontal Boundaries to Facilitate Process Comprehension. *International Journal of Operations Research and Information Systems, 9*(2), 1–31. doi:10.4018/IJORIS.2018040101

Denholm, J., & Lee-Davies, L. (2018). Success Factors for Games in Business and Project Management. In *Enhancing Education and Training Initiatives Through Serious Games* (pp. 34–68). Hershey, PA: IGI Global. doi:10.4018/978-1-5225-3689-5.ch002

Deshpande, M. (2017). Best Practices in Management Institutions for Global Leadership: Policy Aspects. In N. Baporikar (Ed.), *Management Education for Global Leadership* (pp. 1–27). Hershey, PA: IGI Global. doi:10.4018/978-1-5225-1013-0.ch001

Deshpande, M. (2018). Policy Perspectives for SMEs Knowledge Management. In N. Baporikar (Ed.), *Knowledge Integration Strategies for Entrepreneurship and Sustainability* (pp. 23–46). Hershey, PA: IGI Global. doi:10.4018/978-1-5225-5115-7.ch002

Dezdar, S. (2017). ERP Implementation Projects in Asian Countries: A Comparative Study on Iran and China. *International Journal of Information Technology Project Management, 8*(3), 52–68. doi:10.4018/IJITPM.2017070104

Domingos, D., Respício, A., & Martinho, R. (2017). Reliability of IoT-Aware BPMN Healthcare Processes. In C. Reis & M. Maximiano (Eds.), *Internet of Things and Advanced Application in Healthcare* (pp. 214–248). Hershey, PA: IGI Global. doi:10.4018/978-1-5225-1820-4.ch008

Dosumu, O., Hussain, J., & El-Gohary, H. (2017). An Exploratory Study of the Impact of Government Policies on the Development of Small and Medium Enterprises in Developing Countries: The Case of Nigeria. *International Journal of Customer Relationship Marketing and Management, 8*(4), 51–62. doi:10.4018/IJCRMM.2017100104

Durst, S., Bruns, G., & Edvardsson, I. R. (2017). Retaining Knowledge in Smaller Building and Construction Firms. *International Journal of Knowledge and Systems Science, 8*(3), 1–12. doi:10.4018/IJKSS.2017070101

Edvardsson, I. R., & Durst, S. (2017). Outsourcing, Knowledge, and Learning: A Critical Review. *International Journal of Knowledge-Based Organizations, 7*(2), 13–26. doi:10.4018/IJKBO.2017040102

Edwards, J. S. (2018). Integrating Knowledge Management and Business Processes. In M. Khosrow-Pour, D.B.A. (Ed.), Encyclopedia of Information Science and Technology, Fourth Edition (pp. 5046-5055). Hershey, PA: IGI Global. doi:10.4018/978-1-5225-2255-3.ch437

Eichelberger, S., & Peters, M. (2021). Family Firm Management in Turbulent Times: Opportunities for Responsible Tourism. In A. Zehrer, G. Glowka, K. Schwaiger, & V. Ranacher-Lackner (Eds.), *Resiliency Models and Addressing Future Risks for Family Firms in the Tourism Industry* (pp. 103–124). IGI Global. https://doi.org/10.4018/978-1-7998-7352-5.ch005

Eide, D., Hjalager, A., & Hansen, M. (2022). Innovative Certifications in Adventure Tourism: Attributes and Diffusion. In R. Augusto Costa, F. Brandão, Z. Breda, & C. Costa (Eds.), *Planning and Managing the Experience Economy in Tourism* (pp. 161-175). IGI Global. https://doi.org/10.4018/978-1-7998-8775-1.ch009

Ejiogu, A. O. (2018). Economics of Farm Management. In *Agricultural Finance and Opportunities for Investment and Expansion* (pp. 56–72). Hershey, PA: IGI Global. doi:10.4018/978-1-5225-3059-6.ch003

Ekanem, I., & Abiade, G. E. (2018). Factors Influencing the Use of E-Commerce by Small Enterprises in Nigeria. *International Journal of ICT Research in Africa and the Middle East, 7*(1), 37–53. doi:10.4018/IJICTRAME.2018010103

Ekanem, I., & Alrossais, L. A. (2017). Succession Challenges Facing Family Businesses in Saudi Arabia. In P. Zgheib (Ed.), *Entrepreneurship and Business Innovation in the Middle East* (pp. 122–146). Hershey, PA: IGI Global. doi:10.4018/978-1-5225-2066-5.ch007

El Faquih, L., & Fredj, M. (2017). Ontology-Based Framework for Quality in Configurable Process Models. *Journal of Electronic Commerce in Organizations, 15*(2), 48–60. doi:10.4018/JECO.2017040104

Faisal, M. N., & Talib, F. (2017). Building Ambidextrous Supply Chains in SMEs: How to Tackle the Barriers? *International Journal of Information Systems and Supply Chain Management, 10*(4), 80–100. doi:10.4018/IJISSCM.2017100105

Fernandes, T. M., Gomes, J., & Romão, M. (2017). Investments in E-Government: A Benefit Management Case Study. *International Journal of Electronic Government Research, 13*(3), 1–17. doi:10.4018/IJEGR.2017070101

Figueira, L. M., Honrado, G. R., & Dionísio, M. S. (2021). Human Capital Management in the Tourism Industry in Portugal. In V. Costa, A. Moura, & M. Mira (Eds.), *Handbook of Research on Human Capital and People Management in the Tourism Industry* (pp. 1–19). IGI Global. doi:10.4018/978-1-7998-4318-4.ch001

Gao, S. S., Oreal, S., & Zhang, J. (2018). Contemporary Financial Risk Management Perceptions and Practices of Small-Sized Chinese Businesses. In I. Management Association (Ed.), Global Business Expansion: Concepts, Methodologies, Tools, and Applications (pp. 917-931). Hershey, PA: IGI Global. doi:10.4018/978-1-5225-5481-3.ch041

Garg, R., & Berning, S. C. (2017). Indigenous Chinese Management Philosophies: Key Concepts and Relevance for Modern Chinese Firms. In B. Christiansen & G. Koc (Eds.), *Transcontinental Strategies for Industrial Development and Economic Growth* (pp. 43–57). Hershey, PA: IGI Global. doi:10.4018/978-1-5225-2160-0.ch003

Gencer, Y. G. (2017). Supply Chain Management in Retailing Business. In U. Akkucuk (Ed.), *Ethics and Sustainability in Global Supply Chain Management* (pp. 197–210). Hershey, PA: IGI Global. doi:10.4018/978-1-5225-2036-8.ch011

Gera, R., Arora, S., & Malik, S. (2021). Emotional Labor in the Tourism Industry: Strategies, Antecedents, and Outcomes. In V. Costa, A. Moura, & M. Mira (Eds.), *Handbook of Research on Human Capital and People Management in the Tourism Industry* (pp. 73–91). IGI Global. https://doi.org/10.4018/978-1-7998-4318-4.ch004

Giacosa, E. (2018). The Increasing of the Regional Development Thanks to the Luxury Business Innovation. In L. Carvalho (Ed.), *Handbook of Research on Entrepreneurial Ecosystems and Social Dynamics in a Globalized World* (pp. 260–273). Hershey, PA: IGI Global. doi:10.4018/978-1-5225-3525-6.ch011

Glowka, G., Tusch, M., & Zehrer, A. (2021). The Risk Perception of Family Business Owner-Manager in the Tourism Industry: A Qualitative Comparison of the Intra-Firm Senior and Junior Generation. In A. Zehrer, G. Glowka, K. Schwaiger, & V. Ranacher-Lackner (Eds.), *Resiliency Models and Addressing Future Risks for Family Firms in the Tourism Industry* (pp. 126–153). IGI Global. https://doi.org/10.4018/978-1-7998-7352-5.ch006

Glykas, M., & George, J. (2017). Quality and Process Management Systems in the UAE Maritime Industry. *International Journal of Productivity Management and Assessment Technologies*, *5*(1), 20–39. doi:10.4018/IJPMAT.2017010102

Glykas, M., Valiris, G., Kokkinaki, A., & Koutsoukou, Z. (2018). Banking Business Process Management Implementation. *International Journal of Productivity Management and Assessment Technologies, 6*(1), 50–69. doi:10.4018/IJPMAT.2018010104

Gomes, J., & Romão, M. (2017). The Balanced Scorecard: Keeping Updated and Aligned with Today's Business Trends. *International Journal of Productivity Management and Assessment Technologies, 5*(2), 1–15. doi:10.4018/IJPMAT.2017070101

Gomes, J., & Romão, M. (2017). Aligning Information Systems and Technology with Benefit Management and Balanced Scorecard. In S. De Haes & W. Van Grembergen (Eds.), *Strategic IT Governance and Alignment in Business Settings* (pp. 112–131). Hershey, PA: IGI Global. doi:10.4018/978-1-5225-0861-8.ch005

Goyal, A. (2021). Communicating and Building Destination Brands With New Media. In M. Dinis, L. Bonixe, S. Lamy, & Z. Breda (Eds.), *Impact of New Media in Tourism* (pp. 1-20). IGI Global. https://doi.org/10.4018/978-1-7998-7095-1.ch001

Grefen, P., & Turetken, O. (2017). Advanced Business Process Management in Networked E-Business Scenarios. *International Journal of E-Business Research, 13*(4), 70–104. doi:10.4018/IJEBR.2017100105

Guasca, M., Van Broeck, A. M., & Vanneste, D. (2021). Tourism and the Social Reintegration of Colombian Ex-Combatants. In J. da Silva, Z. Breda, & F. Carbone (Eds.), *Role and Impact of Tourism in Peacebuilding and Conflict Transformation* (pp. 66-86). IGI Global. https://doi.org/10.4018/978-1-7998-5053-3.ch005

Haider, A., & Saetang, S. (2017). Strategic IT Alignment in Service Sector. In S. Rozenes & Y. Cohen (Eds.), *Handbook of Research on Strategic Alliances and Value Co-Creation in the Service Industry* (pp. 231–258). Hershey, PA: IGI Global. doi:10.4018/978-1-5225-2084-9.ch012

Hajilari, A. B., Ghadaksaz, M., & Fasghandis, G. S. (2017). Assessing Organizational Readiness for Implementing ERP System Using Fuzzy Expert System Approach. *International Journal of Enterprise Information Systems, 13*(1), 67–85. doi:10.4018/IJEIS.2017010105

Haldorai, A., Ramu, A., & Murugan, S. (2018). Social Aware Cognitive Radio Networks: Effectiveness of Social Networks as a Strategic Tool for Organizational Business Management. In H. Bansal, G. Shrivastava, G. Nguyen, & L. Stanciu (Eds.), *Social Network Analytics for Contemporary Business Organizations* (pp. 188–202). Hershey, PA: IGI Global. doi:10.4018/978-1-5225-5097-6.ch010

Hall, O. P. Jr. (2017). Social Media Driven Management Education. *International Journal of Knowledge-Based Organizations, 7*(2), 43–59. doi:10.4018/IJKBO.2017040104

Hanifah, H., Halim, H. A., Ahmad, N. H., & Vafaei-Zadeh, A. (2017). Innovation Culture as a Mediator Between Specific Human Capital and Innovation Performance Among Bumiputera SMEs in Malaysia. In N. Ahmad, T. Ramayah, H. Halim, & S. Rahman (Eds.), *Handbook of Research on Small and Medium Enterprises in Developing Countries* (pp. 261–279). Hershey, PA: IGI Global. doi:10.4018/978-1-5225-2165-5.ch012

Hartlieb, S., & Silvius, G. (2017). Handling Uncertainty in Project Management and Business Development: Similarities and Differences. In Y. Raydugin (Ed.), *Handbook of Research on Leveraging Risk and Uncertainties for Effective Project Management* (pp. 337–362). Hershey, PA: IGI Global. doi:10.4018/978-1-5225-1790-0.ch016

Hass, K. B. (2017). Living on the Edge: Managing Project Complexity. In Y. Raydugin (Ed.), *Handbook of Research on Leveraging Risk and Uncertainties for Effective Project Management* (pp. 177–201). Hershey, PA: IGI Global. doi:10.4018/978-1-5225-1790-0.ch009

Hawking, P., & Carmine Sellitto, C. (2017). Developing an Effective Strategy for Organizational Business Intelligence. In M. Tavana (Ed.), *Enterprise Information Systems and the Digitalization of Business Functions* (pp. 222–237). Hershey, PA: IGI Global. doi:10.4018/978-1-5225-2382-6.ch010

Hawking, P., & Sellitto, C. (2017). A Fast-Moving Consumer Goods Company and Business Intelligence Strategy Development. *International Journal of Enterprise Information Systems, 13*(2), 22–33. doi:10.4018/IJEIS.2017040102

Hawking, P., & Sellitto, C. (2017). Business Intelligence Strategy: Two Case Studies. *International Journal of Business Intelligence Research, 8*(2), 17–30. doi:10.4018/IJBIR.2017070102

Hee, W. J., Jalleh, G., Lai, H., & Lin, C. (2017). E-Commerce and IT Projects: Evaluation and Management Issues in Australian and Taiwanese Hospitals. *International Journal of Public Health Management and Ethics, 2*(1), 69–90. doi:10.4018/IJPHME.2017010104

Hernandez, A. A. (2018). Exploring the Factors to Green IT Adoption of SMEs in the Philippines. *Journal of Cases on Information Technology, 20*(2), 49–66. doi:10.4018/JCIT.2018040104

Hollman, A., Bickford, S., & Hollman, T. (2017). Cyber InSecurity: A Post-Mortem Attempt to Assess Cyber Problems from IT and Business Management Perspectives. *Journal of Cases on Information Technology, 19*(3), 42–70. doi:10.4018/JCIT.2017070104

Ibrahim, F., & Zainin, N. M. (2021). Exploring the Technological Impacts: The Case of Museums in Brunei Darussalam. *International Journal of Tourism and Hospitality Management in the Digital Age, 5*(1), 1–18. https://doi.org/10.4018/IJTHMDA.2021010101

Igbinakhase, I. (2017). Responsible and Sustainable Management Practices in Developing and Developed Business Environments. In Z. Fields (Ed.), *Collective Creativity for Responsible and Sustainable Business Practice* (pp. 180–207). Hershey, PA: IGI Global. doi:10.4018/978-1-5225-1823-5.ch010

Iwata, J. J., & Hoskins, R. G. (2017). Managing Indigenous Knowledge in Tanzania: A Business Perspective. In P. Jain & N. Mnjama (Eds.), *Managing Knowledge Resources and Records in Modern Organizations* (pp. 198–214). Hershey, PA: IGI Global. doi:10.4018/978-1-5225-1965-2.ch012

Jain, P. (2017). Ethical and Legal Issues in Knowledge Management Life-Cycle in Business. In P. Jain & N. Mnjama (Eds.), *Managing Knowledge Resources and Records in Modern Organizations* (pp. 82–101). Hershey, PA: IGI Global. doi:10.4018/978-1-5225-1965-2.ch006

James, S., & Hauli, E. (2017). Holistic Management Education at Tanzanian Rural Development Planning Institute. In N. Baporikar (Ed.), *Management Education for Global Leadership* (pp. 112–136). Hershey, PA: IGI Global. doi:10.4018/978-1-5225-1013-0.ch006

Janošková, M., Csikósová, A., & Čulková, K. (2018). Measurement of Company Performance as Part of Its Strategic Management. In R. Leon (Ed.), *Managerial Strategies for Business Sustainability During Turbulent Times* (pp. 309–335). Hershey, PA: IGI Global. doi:10.4018/978-1-5225-2716-9.ch017

Jean-Vasile, A., & Alecu, A. (2017). Theoretical and Practical Approaches in Understanding the Influences of Cost-Productivity-Profit Trinomial in Contemporary Enterprises. In A. Jean Vasile & D. Nicolò (Eds.), *Sustainable Entrepreneurship and Investments in the Green Economy* (pp. 28–62). Hershey, PA: IGI Global. doi:10.4018/978-1-5225-2075-7.ch002

Joia, L. A., & Correia, J. C. (2018). CIO Competencies From the IT Professional Perspective: Insights From Brazil. *Journal of Global Information Management, 26*(2), 74–103. doi:10.4018/JGIM.2018040104

Juma, A., & Mzera, N. (2017). Knowledge Management and Records Management and Competitive Advantage in Business. In P. Jain & N. Mnjama (Eds.), *Managing Knowledge Resources and Records in Modern Organizations* (pp. 15–28). Hershey, PA: IGI Global. doi:10.4018/978-1-5225-1965-2.ch002

K., I., & A, V. (2018). Monitoring and Auditing in the Cloud. In K. Munir (Ed.), *Cloud Computing Technologies for Green Enterprises* (pp. 318-350). Hershey, PA: IGI Global. https://doi.org/ doi:10.4018/978-1-5225-3038-1.ch013

Kabra, G., Ghosh, V., & Ramesh, A. (2018). Enterprise Integrated Business Process Management and Business Intelligence Framework for Business Process Sustainability. In A. Paul, D. Bhattacharyya, & S. Anand (Eds.), *Green Initiatives for Business Sustainability and Value Creation* (pp. 228–238). Hershey, PA: IGI Global. doi:10.4018/978-1-5225-2662-9.ch010

Kaoud, M. (2017). Investigation of Customer Knowledge Management: A Case Study Research. *International Journal of Service Science, Management, Engineering, and Technology*, *8*(2), 12–22. doi:10.4018/IJSSMET.2017040102

Katuu, S. (2018). A Comparative Assessment of Enterprise Content Management Maturity Models. In N. Gwangwava & M. Mutingi (Eds.), *E-Manufacturing and E-Service Strategies in Contemporary Organizations* (pp. 93–118). Hershey, PA: IGI Global. doi:10.4018/978-1-5225-3628-4.ch005

Khan, M. Y., & Abir, T. (2022). The Role of Social Media Marketing in the Tourism and Hospitality Industry: A Conceptual Study on Bangladesh. In C. Ramos, S. Quinteiro, & A. Gonçalves (Eds.), *ICT as Innovator Between Tourism and Culture* (pp. 213–229). IGI Global. https://doi.org/10.4018/978-1-7998-8165-0.ch013

Kinnunen, S., Ylä-Kujala, A., Marttonen-Arola, S., Kärri, T., & Baglee, D. (2018). Internet of Things in Asset Management: Insights from Industrial Professionals and Academia. *International Journal of Service Science, Management, Engineering, and Technology*, *9*(2), 104–119. doi:10.4018/IJSSMET.2018040105

Klein, A. Z., Sabino de Freitas, A., Machado, L., Freitas, J. C. Jr, Graziola, P. G. Jr, & Schlemmer, E. (2017). Virtual Worlds Applications for Management Education. In L. Tomei (Ed.), *Exploring the New Era of Technology-Infused Education* (pp. 279–299). Hershey, PA: IGI Global. doi:10.4018/978-1-5225-1709-2.ch017

Kővári, E., Saleh, M., & Steinbachné Hajmásy, G. (2022). The Impact of Corporate Digital Responsibility (CDR) on Internal Stakeholders' Satisfaction in Hungarian Upscale Hotels. In M. Valeri (Ed.), *New Governance and Management in Touristic Destinations* (pp. 35–51). IGI Global. https://doi.org/10.4018/978-1-6684-3889-3.ch003

Kożuch, B., & Jabłoński, A. (2017). Adopting the Concept of Business Models in Public Management. In M. Lewandowski & B. Kożuch (Eds.), *Public Sector Entrepreneurship and the Integration of Innovative Business Models* (pp. 10–46). Hershey, PA: IGI Global. doi:10.4018/978-1-5225-2215-7.ch002

Kumar, J., Adhikary, A., & Jha, A. (2017). Small Active Investors' Perceptions and Preferences Towards Tax Saving Mutual Fund Schemes in Eastern India: An Empirical Note. *International Journal of Asian Business and Information Management*, *8*(2), 35–45. doi:10.4018/IJABIM.2017040103

Latusi, S., & Fissore, M. (2021). Pilgrimage Routes to Happiness: Comparing the Camino de Santiago and Via Francigena. In A. Perinotto, V. Mayer, & J. Soares (Eds.), *Rebuilding and Restructuring the Tourism Industry: Infusion of Happiness and Quality of Life* (pp. 157–182). IGI Global. https://doi.org/10.4018/978-1-7998-7239-9.ch008

Lavassani, K. M., & Movahedi, B. (2017). Applications Driven Information Systems: Beyond Networks toward Business Ecosystems. *International Journal of Innovation in the Digital Economy*, *8*(1), 61–75. doi:10.4018/IJIDE.2017010104

Lazzareschi, V. H., & Brito, M. S. (2017). Strategic Information Management: Proposal of Business Project Model. In G. Jamil, A. Soares, & C. Pessoa (Eds.), *Handbook of Research on Information Management for Effective Logistics and Supply Chains* (pp. 59–88). Hershey, PA: IGI Global. doi:10.4018/978-1-5225-0973-8.ch004

Lechuga Sancho, M. P., & Martín Navarro, A. (2022). Evolution of the Literature on Social Responsibility in the Tourism Sector: A Systematic Literature Review. In G. Fernandes (Ed.), *Challenges and New Opportunities for Tourism in Inland Territories: Ecocultural Resources and Sustainable Initiatives* (pp. 169–186). IGI Global. https://doi.org/10.4018/978-1-7998-7339-6.ch010

Lederer, M., Kurz, M., & Lazarov, P. (2017). Usage and Suitability of Methods for Strategic Business Process Initiatives: A Multi Case Study Research. *International Journal of Productivity Management and Assessment Technologies*, *5*(1), 40–51. doi:10.4018/IJPMAT.2017010103

Lee, I. (2017). A Social Enterprise Business Model and a Case Study of Pacific Community Ventures (PCV). In V. Potocan, M. Üngan, & Z. Nedelko (Eds.), *Handbook of Research on Managerial Solutions in Non-Profit Organizations* (pp. 182–204). Hershey, PA: IGI Global. doi:10.4018/978-1-5225-0731-4.ch009

Leon, L. A., Seal, K. C., Przasnyski, Z. H., & Wiedenman, I. (2017). Skills and Competencies Required for Jobs in Business Analytics: A Content Analysis of Job Advertisements Using Text Mining. *International Journal of Business Intelligence Research, 8*(1), 1–25. doi:10.4018/IJBIR.2017010101

Levy, C. L., & Elias, N. I. (2017). SOHO Users' Perceptions of Reliability and Continuity of Cloud-Based Services. In M. Moore (Ed.), *Cybersecurity Breaches and Issues Surrounding Online Threat Protection* (pp. 248–287). Hershey, PA: IGI Global. doi:10.4018/978-1-5225-1941-6.ch011

Levy, M. (2018). Change Management Serving Knowledge Management and Organizational Development: Reflections and Review. In N. Baporikar (Ed.), *Global Practices in Knowledge Management for Societal and Organizational Development* (pp. 256–270). Hershey, PA: IGI Global. doi:10.4018/978-1-5225-3009-1.ch012

Lewandowski, M. (2017). Public Organizations and Business Model Innovation: The Role of Public Service Design. In M. Lewandowski & B. Kożuch (Eds.), *Public Sector Entrepreneurship and the Integration of Innovative Business Models* (pp. 47–72). Hershey, PA: IGI Global. doi:10.4018/978-1-5225-2215-7.ch003

Lhannaoui, H., Kabbaj, M. I., & Bakkoury, Z. (2017). A Survey of Risk-Aware Business Process Modelling. *International Journal of Risk and Contingency Management, 6*(3), 14–26. doi:10.4018/IJRCM.2017070102

Li, J., Sun, W., Jiang, W., Yang, H., & Zhang, L. (2017). How the Nature of Exogenous Shocks and Crises Impact Company Performance?: The Effects of Industry Characteristics. *International Journal of Risk and Contingency Management, 6*(4), 40–55. doi:10.4018/IJRCM.2017100103

Lopez-Fernandez, M., Perez-Perez, M., Serrano-Bedia, A., & Cobo-Gonzalez, A. (2021). Small and Medium Tourism Enterprise Survival in Times of Crisis: "El Capricho de Gaudí. In D. Toubes & N. Araújo-Vila (Eds.), *Risk, Crisis, and Disaster Management in Small and Medium-Sized Tourism Enterprises* (pp. 103–129). IGI Global. doi:10.4018/978-1-7998-6996-2.ch005

Mahajan, A., Maidullah, S., & Hossain, M. R. (2022). Experience Toward Smart Tour Guide Apps in Travelling: An Analysis of Users' Reviews on Audio Odigos and Trip My Way. In R. Augusto Costa, F. Brandão, Z. Breda, & C. Costa (Eds.), *Planning and Managing the Experience Economy in Tourism* (pp. 255-273). IGI Global. https://doi.org/10.4018/978-1-7998-8775-1.ch014

Malega, P. (2017). Small and Medium Enterprises in the Slovak Republic: Status and Competitiveness of SMEs in the Global Markets and Possibilities of Optimization. In M. Vemić (Ed.), *Optimal Management Strategies in Small and Medium Enterprises* (pp. 102–124). Hershey, PA: IGI Global. doi:10.4018/978-1-5225-1949-2.ch006

Malewska, K. M. (2017). Intuition in Decision-Making on the Example of a Non-Profit Organization. In V. Potocan, M. Üngan, & Z. Nedelko (Eds.), *Handbook of Research on Managerial Solutions in Non-Profit Organizations* (pp. 378–399). Hershey, PA: IGI Global. doi:10.4018/978-1-5225-0731-4.ch018

Maroofi, F. (2017). Entrepreneurial Orientation and Organizational Learning Ability Analysis for Innovation and Firm Performance. In N. Baporikar (Ed.), *Innovation and Shifting Perspectives in Management Education* (pp. 144–165). Hershey, PA: IGI Global. doi:10.4018/978-1-5225-1019-2.ch007

Marques, M., Moleiro, D., Brito, T. M., & Marques, T. (2021). Customer Relationship Management as an Important Relationship Marketing Tool: The Case of the Hospitality Industry in Estoril Coast. In M. Dinis, L. Bonixe, S. Lamy, & Z. Breda (Eds.), Impact of New Media in Tourism (pp. 39-56). IGI Global. https://doi.org/doi:10.4018/978-1-7998-7095-1.ch003

Martins, P. V., & Zacarias, M. (2017). A Web-based Tool for Business Process Improvement. *International Journal of Web Portals*, *9*(2), 68–84. doi:10.4018/IJWP.2017070104

Matthies, B., & Coners, A. (2017). Exploring the Conceptual Nature of e-Business Projects. *Journal of Electronic Commerce in Organizations*, *15*(3), 33–63. doi:10.4018/JECO.2017070103

Mayer, V. F., Fraga, C. C., & Silva, L. C. (2021). Contributions of Neurosciences to Studies of Well-Being in Tourism. In A. Perinotto, V. Mayer, & J. Soares (Eds.), *Rebuilding and Restructuring the Tourism Industry: Infusion of Happiness and Quality of Life* (pp. 108–128). IGI Global. https://doi.org/10.4018/978-1-7998-7239-9.ch006

McKee, J. (2018). Architecture as a Tool to Solve Business Planning Problems. In M. Khosrow-Pour, D.B.A. (Ed.), Encyclopedia of Information Science and Technology, Fourth Edition (pp. 573-586). Hershey, PA: IGI Global. doi:10.4018/978-1-5225-2255-3.ch050

McMurray, A. J., Cross, J., & Caponecchia, C. (2018). The Risk Management Profession in Australia: Business Continuity Plan Practices. In N. Bajgoric (Ed.), *Always-On Enterprise Information Systems for Modern Organizations* (pp. 112–129). Hershey, PA: IGI Global. doi:10.4018/978-1-5225-3704-5.ch006

Meddah, I. H., & Belkadi, K. (2018). Mining Patterns Using Business Process Management. In R. Hamou (Ed.), *Handbook of Research on Biomimicry in Information Retrieval and Knowledge Management* (pp. 78–89). Hershey, PA: IGI Global. doi:10.4018/978-1-5225-3004-6.ch005

Melian, A. G., & Camprubí, R. (2021). The Accessibility of Museum Websites: The Case of Barcelona. In C. Eusébio, L. Teixeira, & M. Carneiro (Eds.), *ICT Tools and Applications for Accessible Tourism* (pp. 234–255). IGI Global. https://doi.org/10.4018/978-1-7998-6428-8.ch011

Mendes, L. (2017). TQM and Knowledge Management: An Integrated Approach Towards Tacit Knowledge Management. In D. Jaziri-Bouagina & G. Jamil (Eds.), *Handbook of Research on Tacit Knowledge Management for Organizational Success* (pp. 236–263). Hershey, PA: IGI Global. doi:10.4018/978-1-5225-2394-9.ch009

Menezes, V. D., & Cavagnaro, E. (2021). Communicating Sustainable Initiatives in the Hotel Industry: The Case of the Hotel Jakarta Amsterdam. In F. Brandão, Z. Breda, R. Costa, & C. Costa (Eds.), *Handbook of Research on the Role of Tourism in Achieving Sustainable Development Goals* (pp. 224-234). IGI Global. https://doi.org/10.4018/978-1-7998-5691-7.ch013

Menezes, V. D., & Cavagnaro, E. (2021). Communicating Sustainable Initiatives in the Hotel Industry: The Case of the Hotel Jakarta Amsterdam. In F. Brandão, Z. Breda, R. Costa, & C. Costa (Eds.), *Handbook of Research on the Role of Tourism in Achieving Sustainable Development Goals* (pp. 224-234). IGI Global. https://doi.org/10.4018/978-1-7998-5691-7.ch013

Mitas, O., Bastiaansen, M., & Boode, W. (2022). If You're Happy, I'm Happy: Emotion Contagion at a Tourist Information Center. In R. Augusto Costa, F. Brandão, Z. Breda, & C. Costa (Eds.), *Planning and Managing the Experience Economy in Tourism* (pp. 122-140). IGI Global. https://doi.org/10.4018/978-1-7998-8775-1.ch007

Mnjama, N. M. (2017). Preservation of Recorded Information in Public and Private Sector Organizations. In P. Jain & N. Mnjama (Eds.), *Managing Knowledge Resources and Records in Modern Organizations* (pp. 149–167). Hershey, PA: IGI Global. doi:10.4018/978-1-5225-1965-2.ch009

Mokoqama, M., & Fields, Z. (2017). Principles of Responsible Management Education (PRME): Call for Responsible Management Education. In Z. Fields (Ed.), *Collective Creativity for Responsible and Sustainable Business Practice* (pp. 229–241). Hershey, PA: IGI Global. doi:10.4018/978-1-5225-1823-5.ch012

Monteiro, A., Lopes, S., & Carbone, F. (2021). Academic Mobility: Bridging Tourism and Peace Education. In J. da Silva, Z. Breda, & F. Carbone (Eds.), *Role and Impact of Tourism in Peacebuilding and Conflict Transformation* (pp. 275-301). IGI Global. https://doi.org/10.4018/978-1-7998-5053-3.ch016

Muniapan, B. (2017). Philosophy and Management: The Relevance of Vedanta in Management. In P. Ordóñez de Pablos (Ed.), *Managerial Strategies and Solutions for Business Success in Asia* (pp. 124–139). Hershey, PA: IGI Global. doi:10.4018/978-1-5225-1886-0.ch007

Murad, S. E., & Dowaji, S. (2017). Using Value-Based Approach for Managing Cloud-Based Services. In A. Turuk, B. Sahoo, & S. Addya (Eds.), *Resource Management and Efficiency in Cloud Computing Environments* (pp. 33–60). Hershey, PA: IGI Global. doi:10.4018/978-1-5225-1721-4.ch002

Mutahar, A. M., Daud, N. M., Thurasamy, R., Isaac, O., & Abdulsalam, R. (2018). The Mediating of Perceived Usefulness and Perceived Ease of Use: The Case of Mobile Banking in Yemen. *International Journal of Technology Diffusion*, *9*(2), 21–40. doi:10.4018/IJTD.2018040102

Naidoo, V. (2017). E-Learning and Management Education at African Universities. In N. Baporikar (Ed.), *Management Education for Global Leadership* (pp. 181–201). Hershey, PA: IGI Global. doi:10.4018/978-1-5225-1013-0.ch009

Naidoo, V., & Igbinakhase, I. (2018). Opportunities and Challenges of Knowledge Retention in SMEs. In N. Baporikar (Ed.), *Knowledge Integration Strategies for Entrepreneurship and Sustainability* (pp. 70–94). Hershey, PA: IGI Global. doi:10.4018/978-1-5225-5115-7.ch004

Naumov, N., & Costandachi, G. (2021). Creativity and Entrepreneurship: Gastronomic Tourism in Mexico. In J. Soares (Ed.), *Innovation and Entrepreneurial Opportunities in Community Tourism* (pp. 90–108). IGI Global. https://doi.org/10.4018/978-1-7998-4855-4.ch006

Nayak, S., & Prabhu, N. (2017). Paradigm Shift in Management Education: Need for a Cross Functional Perspective. In N. Baporikar (Ed.), *Management Education for Global Leadership* (pp. 241–255). Hershey, PA: IGI Global. doi:10.4018/978-1-5225-1013-0.ch012

Nedelko, Z., & Potocan, V. (2017). Management Solutions in Non-Profit Organizations: Case of Slovenia. In V. Potocan, M. Ünğan, & Z. Nedelko (Eds.), *Handbook of Research on Managerial Solutions in Non-Profit Organizations* (pp. 1–22). Hershey, PA: IGI Global. doi:10.4018/978-1-5225-0731-4.ch001

Nedelko, Z., & Potocan, V. (2017). Priority of Management Tools Utilization among Managers: International Comparison. In V. Wang (Ed.), *Encyclopedia of Strategic Leadership and Management* (pp. 1083–1094). Hershey, PA: IGI Global. doi:10.4018/978-1-5225-1049-9.ch075

Nedelko, Z., Raudeliūnienė, J., & Črešnar, R. (2018). Knowledge Dynamics in Supply Chain Management. In N. Baporikar (Ed.), *Knowledge Integration Strategies for Entrepreneurship and Sustainability* (pp. 150–166). Hershey, PA: IGI Global. doi:10.4018/978-1-5225-5115-7.ch008

Nguyen, H. T., & Hipsher, S. A. (2018). Innovation and Creativity Used by Private Sector Firms in a Resources-Constrained Environment. In S. Hipsher (Ed.), *Examining the Private Sector's Role in Wealth Creation and Poverty Reduction* (pp. 219–238). Hershey, PA: IGI Global. doi:10.4018/978-1-5225-3117-3.ch010

Obicci, P. A. (2017). Risk Sharing in a Partnership. In *Risk Management Strategies in Public-Private Partnerships* (pp. 115–152). Hershey, PA: IGI Global. doi:10.4018/978-1-5225-2503-5.ch004

Obidallah, W. J., & Raahemi, B. (2017). Managing Changes in Service Oriented Virtual Organizations: A Structural and Procedural Framework to Facilitate the Process of Change. *Journal of Electronic Commerce in Organizations, 15*(1), 59–83. doi:10.4018/JECO.2017010104

Ojo, O. (2017). Impact of Innovation on the Entrepreneurial Success in Selected Business Enterprises in South-West Nigeria. *International Journal of Innovation in the Digital Economy, 8*(2), 29–38. doi:10.4018/IJIDE.2017040103

Okdinawati, L., Simatupang, T. M., & Sunitiyoso, Y. (2017). Multi-Agent Reinforcement Learning for Value Co-Creation of Collaborative Transportation Management (CTM). *International Journal of Information Systems and Supply Chain Management, 10*(3), 84–95. doi:10.4018/IJISSCM.2017070105

Olivera, V. A., & Carrillo, I. M. (2021). Organizational Culture: A Key Element for the Development of Mexican Micro and Small Tourist Companies. In J. Soares (Ed.), *Innovation and Entrepreneurial Opportunities in Community Tourism* (pp. 227–242). IGI Global. doi:10.4018/978-1-7998-4855-4.ch013

Ossorio, M. (2022). Corporate Museum Experiences in Enogastronomic Tourism. In R. Augusto Costa, F. Brandão, Z. Breda, & C. Costa (Eds.), Planning and Managing the Experience Economy in Tourism (pp. 107-121). IGI Global. https://doi.org/doi:10.4018/978-1-7998-8775-1.ch006

Ossorio, M. (2022). Enogastronomic Tourism in Times of Pandemic. In G. Fernandes (Ed.), *Challenges and New Opportunities for Tourism in Inland Territories: Ecocultural Resources and Sustainable Initiatives* (pp. 241–255). IGI Global. https://doi.org/10.4018/978-1-7998-7339-6.ch014

Özekici, Y. K. (2022). ICT as an Acculturative Agent and Its Role in the Tourism Context: Introduction, Acculturation Theory, Progress of the Acculturation Theory in Extant Literature. In C. Ramos, S. Quinteiro, & A. Gonçalves (Eds.), *ICT as Innovator Between Tourism and Culture* (pp. 42–66). IGI Global. https://doi.org/10.4018/978-1-7998-8165-0.ch004

Pal, K. (2018). Building High Quality Big Data-Based Applications in Supply Chains. In A. Kumar & S. Saurav (Eds.), *Supply Chain Management Strategies and Risk Assessment in Retail Environments* (pp. 1–24). Hershey, PA: IGI Global. doi:10.4018/978-1-5225-3056-5.ch001

Palos-Sanchez, P. R., & Correia, M. B. (2018). Perspectives of the Adoption of Cloud Computing in the Tourism Sector. In J. Rodrigues, C. Ramos, P. Cardoso, & C. Henriques (Eds.), *Handbook of Research on Technological Developments for Cultural Heritage and eTourism Applications* (pp. 377–400). Hershey, PA: IGI Global. doi:10.4018/978-1-5225-2927-9.ch018

Papadopoulou, G. (2021). Promoting Gender Equality and Women Empowerment in the Tourism Sector. In F. Brandão, Z. Breda, R. Costa, & C. Costa (Eds.), Handbook of Research on the Role of Tourism in Achieving Sustainable Development Goals (pp. 152-174). IGI Global. https://doi.org/ doi:10.4018/978-1-7998-5691-7.ch009

Papp-Váry, Á. F., & Tóth, T. Z. (2022). Analysis of Budapest as a Film Tourism Destination. In R. Baleiro & R. Pereira (Eds.), *Global Perspectives on Literary Tourism and Film-Induced Tourism* (pp. 257-279). IGI Global. https://doi.org/10.4018/978-1-7998-8262-6.ch014

Patiño, B. E. (2017). New Generation Management by Convergence and Individual Identity: A Systemic and Human-Oriented Approach. In N. Baporikar (Ed.), *Innovation and Shifting Perspectives in Management Education* (pp. 119–143). Hershey, PA: IGI Global. doi:10.4018/978-1-5225-1019-2.ch006

Patro, C. S. (2021). Digital Tourism: Influence of E-Marketing Technology. In M. Dinis, L. Bonixe, S. Lamy, & Z. Breda (Eds.), *Impact of New Media in Tourism* (pp. 234-254). IGI Global. https://doi.org/10.4018/978-1-7998-7095-1.ch014

Pawliczek, A., & Rössler, M. (2017). Knowledge of Management Tools and Systems in SMEs: Knowledge Transfer in Management. In A. Bencsik (Ed.), *Knowledge Management Initiatives and Strategies in Small and Medium Enterprises* (pp. 180–203). Hershey, PA: IGI Global. doi:10.4018/978-1-5225-1642-2.ch009

Pejic-Bach, M., Omazic, M. A., Aleksic, A., & Zoroja, J. (2018). Knowledge-Based Decision Making: A Multi-Case Analysis. In R. Leon (Ed.), *Managerial Strategies for Business Sustainability During Turbulent Times* (pp. 160–184). Hershey, PA: IGI Global. doi:10.4018/978-1-5225-2716-9.ch009

Perano, M., Hysa, X., & Calabrese, M. (2018). Strategic Planning, Cultural Context, and Business Continuity Management: Business Cases in the City of Shkoder. In A. Presenza & L. Sheehan (Eds.), *Geopolitics and Strategic Management in the Global Economy* (pp. 57–77). Hershey, PA: IGI Global. doi:10.4018/978-1-5225-2673-5.ch004

Pereira, R., Mira da Silva, M., & Lapão, L. V. (2017). IT Governance Maturity Patterns in Portuguese Healthcare. In S. De Haes & W. Van Grembergen (Eds.), *Strategic IT Governance and Alignment in Business Settings* (pp. 24–52). Hershey, PA: IGI Global. doi:10.4018/978-1-5225-0861-8.ch002

Pérez-Uribe, R. I., Torres, D. A., Jurado, S. P., & Prada, D. M. (2018). Cloud Tools for the Development of Project Management in SMEs. In R. Perez-Uribe, C. Salcedo-Perez, & D. Ocampo-Guzman (Eds.), *Handbook of Research on Intrapreneurship and Organizational Sustainability in SMEs* (pp. 95–120). Hershey, PA: IGI Global. doi:10.4018/978-1-5225-3543-0.ch005

Petrisor, I., & Cozmiuc, D. (2017). Global Supply Chain Management Organization at Siemens in the Advent of Industry 4.0. In L. Saglietto & C. Cezanne (Eds.), *Global Intermediation and Logistics Service Providers* (pp. 123–142). Hershey, PA: IGI Global. doi:10.4018/978-1-5225-2133-4.ch007

Pierce, J. M., Velliaris, D. M., & Edwards, J. (2017). A Living Case Study: A Journey Not a Destination. In N. Silton (Ed.), *Exploring the Benefits of Creativity in Education, Media, and the Arts* (pp. 158–178). Hershey, PA: IGI Global. doi:10.4018/978-1-5225-0504-4.ch008

Pipia, S., & Pipia, S. (2021). Challenges of Religious Tourism in the Conflict Region: An Example of Jerusalem. In E. Alaverdov & M. Bari (Eds.), *Global Development of Religious Tourism* (pp. 135-148). IGI Global. https://doi.org/10.4018/978-1-7998-5792-1.ch009

Poulaki, P., Kritikos, A., Vasilakis, N., & Valeri, M. (2022). The Contribution of Female Creativity to the Development of Gastronomic Tourism in Greece: The Case of the Island of Naxos in the South Aegean Region. In M. Valeri (Ed.), *New Governance and Management in Touristic Destinations* (pp. 246–258). IGI Global. https://doi.org/10.4018/978-1-6684-3889-3.ch015

Radosavljevic, M., & Andjelkovic, A. (2017). Multi-Criteria Decision Making Approach for Choosing Business Process for the Improvement: Upgrading of the Six Sigma Methodology. In J. Stanković, P. Delias, S. Marinković, & S. Rochhia (Eds.), *Tools and Techniques for Economic Decision Analysis* (pp. 225–247). Hershey, PA: IGI Global. doi:10.4018/978-1-5225-0959-2.ch011

Radovic, V. M. (2017). Corporate Sustainability and Responsibility and Disaster Risk Reduction: A Serbian Overview. In M. Camilleri (Ed.), *CSR 2.0 and the New Era of Corporate Citizenship* (pp. 147–164). Hershey, PA: IGI Global. doi:10.4018/978-1-5225-1842-6.ch008

Raghunath, K. M., Devi, S. L., & Patro, C. S. (2018). Impact of Risk Assessment Models on Risk Factors: A Holistic Outlook. In K. Strang, M. Korstanje, & N. Vajjhala (Eds.), *Research, Practices, and Innovations in Global Risk and Contingency Management* (pp. 134–153). Hershey, PA: IGI Global. doi:10.4018/978-1-5225-4754-9.ch008

Raman, A., & Goyal, D. P. (2017). Extending IMPLEMENT Framework for Enterprise Information Systems Implementation to Information System Innovation. In M. Tavana (Ed.), *Enterprise Information Systems and the Digitalization of Business Functions* (pp. 137–177). Hershey, PA: IGI Global. doi:10.4018/978-1-5225-2382-6.ch007

Rao, Y., & Zhang, Y. (2017). The Construction and Development of Academic Library Digital Special Subject Databases. In L. Ruan, Q. Zhu, & Y. Ye (Eds.), *Academic Library Development and Administration in China* (pp. 163–183). Hershey, PA: IGI Global. doi:10.4018/978-1-5225-0550-1.ch010

Ravasan, A. Z., Mohammadi, M. M., & Hamidi, H. (2018). An Investigation Into the Critical Success Factors of Implementing Information Technology Service Management Frameworks. In K. Jakobs (Ed.), *Corporate and Global Standardization Initiatives in Contemporary Society* (pp. 200–218). Hershey, PA: IGI Global. doi:10.4018/978-1-5225-5320-5.ch009

Rezaie, S., Mirabedini, S. J., & Abtahi, A. (2018). Designing a Model for Implementation of Business Intelligence in the Banking Industry. *International Journal of Enterprise Information Systems, 14*(1), 77–103. doi:10.4018/IJEIS.2018010105

Richards, V., Matthews, N., Williams, O. J., & Khan, Z. (2021). The Challenges of Accessible Tourism Information Systems for Tourists With Vision Impairment: Sensory Communications Beyond the Screen. In C. Eusébio, L. Teixeira, & M. Carneiro (Eds.), *ICT Tools and Applications for Accessible Tourism* (pp. 26–54). IGI Global. https://doi.org/10.4018/978-1-7998-6428-8.ch002

Rodrigues de Souza Neto, V., & Marques, O. (2021). Rural Tourism Fostering Welfare Through Sustainable Development: A Conceptual Approach. In A. Perinotto, V. Mayer, & J. Soares (Eds.), *Rebuilding and Restructuring the Tourism Industry: Infusion of Happiness and Quality of Life* (pp. 38–57). IGI Global. https://doi.org/10.4018/978-1-7998-7239-9.ch003

Romano, L., Grimaldi, R., & Colasuonno, F. S. (2017). Demand Management as a Success Factor in Project Portfolio Management. In L. Romano (Ed.), *Project Portfolio Management Strategies for Effective Organizational Operations* (pp. 202–219). Hershey, PA: IGI Global. doi:10.4018/978-1-5225-2151-8.ch008

Rubio-Escuderos, L., & García-Andreu, H. (2021). Competitiveness Factors of Accessible Tourism E-Travel Agencies. In C. Eusébio, L. Teixeira, & M. Carneiro (Eds.), *ICT Tools and Applications for Accessible Tourism* (pp. 196–217). IGI Global. https://doi.org/10.4018/978-1-7998-6428-8.ch009

Rucci, A. C., Porto, N., Darcy, S., & Becka, L. (2021). Smart and Accessible Cities?: Not Always – The Case for Accessible Tourism Initiatives in Buenos Aries and Sydney. In C. Eusébio, L. Teixeira, & M. Carneiro (Eds.), *ICT Tools and Applications for Accessible Tourism* (pp. 115–145). IGI Global. https://doi.org/10.4018/978-1-7998-6428-8.ch006

Ruhi, U. (2018). Towards an Interdisciplinary Socio-Technical Definition of Virtual Communities. In M. Khosrow-Pour, D.B.A. (Ed.), Encyclopedia of Information Science and Technology, Fourth Edition (pp. 4278-4295). Hershey, PA: IGI Global. doi:10.4018/978-1-5225-2255-3.ch371

Ryan, L., Catena, M., Ros, P., & Stephens, S. (2021). Designing Entrepreneurial Ecosystems to Support Resource Management in the Tourism Industry. In V. Costa, A. Moura, & M. Mira (Eds.), *Handbook of Research on Human Capital and People Management in the Tourism Industry* (pp. 265–281). IGI Global. https://doi.org/10.4018/978-1-7998-4318-4.ch013

Sabuncu, I. (2021). Understanding Tourist Perceptions and Expectations During Pandemic Through Social Media Big Data. In M. Demir, A. Dalgıç, & F. Ergen (Eds.), *Handbook of Research on the Impacts and Implications of COVID-19 on the Tourism Industry* (pp. 330–350). IGI Global. https://doi.org/10.4018/978-1-7998-8231-2.ch016

Safari, M. R., & Jiang, Q. (2018). The Theory and Practice of IT Governance Maturity and Strategies Alignment: Evidence From Banking Industry. *Journal of Global Information Management, 26*(2), 127–146. doi:10.4018/JGIM.2018040106

Sahoo, J., Pati, B., & Mohanty, B. (2017). Knowledge Management as an Academic Discipline: An Assessment. In B. Gunjal (Ed.), *Managing Knowledge and Scholarly Assets in Academic Libraries* (pp. 99–126). Hershey, PA: IGI Global. doi:10.4018/978-1-5225-1741-2.ch005

Saini, D. (2017). Relevance of Teaching Values and Ethics in Management Education. In N. Baporikar (Ed.), *Management Education for Global Leadership* (pp. 90–111). Hershey, PA: IGI Global. doi:10.4018/978-1-5225-1013-0.ch005

Sambhanthan, A. (2017). Assessing and Benchmarking Sustainability in Organisations: An Integrated Conceptual Model. *International Journal of Systems and Service-Oriented Engineering, 7*(4), 22–43. doi:10.4018/IJSSOE.2017100102

Sambhanthan, A., & Potdar, V. (2017). A Study of the Parameters Impacting Sustainability in Information Technology Organizations. *International Journal of Knowledge-Based Organizations, 7*(3), 27–39. doi:10.4018/IJKBO.2017070103

Sánchez-Fernández, M. D., & Manríquez, M. R. (2018). The Entrepreneurial Spirit Based on Social Values: The Digital Generation. In P. Isaias & L. Carvalho (Eds.), *User Innovation and the Entrepreneurship Phenomenon in the Digital Economy* (pp. 173–193). Hershey, PA: IGI Global. doi:10.4018/978-1-5225-2826-5.ch009

Sanchez-Ruiz, L., & Blanco, B. (2017). Process Management for SMEs: Barriers, Enablers, and Benefits. In M. Vemić (Ed.), *Optimal Management Strategies in Small and Medium Enterprises* (pp. 293–319). Hershey, PA: IGI Global. doi:10.4018/978-1-5225-1949-2.ch014

Sanz, L. F., Gómez-Pérez, J., & Castillo-Martinez, A. (2018). Analysis of the European ICT Competence Frameworks. In V. Ahuja & S. Rathore (Eds.), *Multidisciplinary Perspectives on Human Capital and Information Technology Professionals* (pp. 225–245). Hershey, PA: IGI Global. doi:10.4018/978-1-5225-5297-0.ch012

Sarvepalli, A., & Godin, J. (2017). Business Process Management in the Classroom. *Journal of Cases on Information Technology, 19*(2), 17–28. doi:10.4018/JCIT.2017040102

Saxena, G. G., & Saxena, A. (2021). Host Community Role in Medical Tourism Development. In M. Singh & S. Kumaran (Eds.), *Growth of the Medical Tourism Industry and Its Impact on Society: Emerging Research and Opportunities* (pp. 105–127). IGI Global. https://doi.org/10.4018/978-1-7998-3427-4.ch006

Saygili, E. E., Ozturkoglu, Y., & Kocakulah, M. C. (2017). End Users' Perceptions of Critical Success Factors in ERP Applications. *International Journal of Enterprise Information Systems, 13*(4), 58–75. doi:10.4018/IJEIS.2017100104

Saygili, E. E., & Saygili, A. T. (2017). Contemporary Issues in Enterprise Information Systems: A Critical Review of CSFs in ERP Implementations. In M. Tavana (Ed.), *Enterprise Information Systems and the Digitalization of Business Functions* (pp. 120–136). Hershey, PA: IGI Global. doi:10.4018/978-1-5225-2382-6.ch006

Schwaiger, K. M., & Zehrer, A. (2021). The COVID-19 Pandemic and Organizational Resilience in Hospitality Family Firms: A Qualitative Approach. In A. Zehrer, G. Glowka, K. Schwaiger, & V. Ranacher-Lackner (Eds.), *Resiliency Models and Addressing Future Risks for Family Firms in the Tourism Industry* (pp. 32–49). IGI Global. https://doi.org/10.4018/978-1-7998-7352-5.ch002

Scott, N., & Campos, A. C. (2022). Cognitive Science of Tourism Experiences. In R. Augusto Costa, F. Brandão, Z. Breda, & C. Costa (Eds.), Planning and Managing the Experience Economy in Tourism (pp. 1-21). IGI Global. https://doi.org/ doi:10.4018/978-1-7998-8775-1.ch001

Seidenstricker, S., & Antonino, A. (2018). Business Model Innovation-Oriented Technology Management for Emergent Technologies. In M. Khosrow-Pour, D.B.A. (Ed.), Encyclopedia of Information Science and Technology, Fourth Edition (pp. 4560-4569). Hershey, PA: IGI Global. doi:10.4018/978-1-5225-2255-3.ch396

Selvi, M. S. (2021). Changes in Tourism Sales and Marketing Post COVID-19. In M. Demir, A. Dalgıç, & F. Ergen (Eds.), *Handbook of Research on the Impacts and Implications of COVID-19 on the Tourism Industry* (pp. 437–460). IGI Global. doi:10.4018/978-1-7998-8231-2.ch021

Senaratne, S., & Gunarathne, A. D. (2017). Excellence Perspective for Management Education from a Global Accountants' Hub in Asia. In N. Baporikar (Ed.), *Management Education for Global Leadership* (pp. 158–180). Hershey, PA: IGI Global. doi:10.4018/978-1-5225-1013-0.ch008

Sensuse, D. I., & Cahyaningsih, E. (2018). Knowledge Management Models: A Summative Review. *International Journal of Information Systems in the Service Sector, 10*(1), 71–100. doi:10.4018/IJISSS.2018010105

Seth, M., Goyal, D., & Kiran, R. (2017). Diminution of Impediments in Implementation of Supply Chain Management Information System for Enhancing its Effectiveness in Indian Automobile Industry. *Journal of Global Information Management, 25*(3), 1–20. doi:10.4018/JGIM.2017070101

Seyal, A. H., & Rahman, M. N. (2017). Investigating Impact of Inter-Organizational Factors in Measuring ERP Systems Success: Bruneian Perspectives. In M. Tavana (Ed.), *Enterprise Information Systems and the Digitalization of Business Functions* (pp. 178–204). Hershey, PA: IGI Global. doi:10.4018/978-1-5225-2382-6.ch008

Shaqrah, A. A. (2018). Analyzing Business Intelligence Systems Based on 7s Model of McKinsey. *International Journal of Business Intelligence Research, 9*(1), 53–63. doi:10.4018/IJBIR.2018010104

Sharma, A. J. (2017). Enhancing Sustainability through Experiential Learning in Management Education. In N. Baporikar (Ed.), *Management Education for Global Leadership* (pp. 256–274). Hershey, PA: IGI Global. doi:10.4018/978-1-5225-1013-0.ch013

Shetty, K. P. (2017). Responsible Global Leadership: Ethical Challenges in Management Education. In N. Baporikar (Ed.), *Innovation and Shifting Perspectives in Management Education* (pp. 194–223). Hershey, PA: IGI Global. doi:10.4018/978-1-5225-1019-2.ch009

Sinthupundaja, J., & Kohda, Y. (2017). Effects of Corporate Social Responsibility and Creating Shared Value on Sustainability. *International Journal of Sustainable Entrepreneurship and Corporate Social Responsibility, 2*(1), 27–38. doi:10.4018/IJSECSR.2017010103

Škarica, I., & Hrgović, A. V. (2018). Implementation of Total Quality Management Principles in Public Health Institutes in the Republic of Croatia. *International Journal of Productivity Management and Assessment Technologies, 6*(1), 1–16. doi:10.4018/IJPMAT.2018010101

Skokic, V. (2021). How Small Hotel Owners Practice Resilience: Longitudinal Study Among Small Family Hotels in Croatia. In A. Zehrer, G. Glowka, K. Schwaiger, & V. Ranacher-Lackner (Eds.), *Resiliency Models and Addressing Future Risks for Family Firms in the Tourism Industry* (pp. 50–73). IGI Global. doi:10.4018/978-1-7998-7352-5.ch003

Smuts, H., Kotzé, P., Van der Merwe, A., & Loock, M. (2017). Framework for Managing Shared Knowledge in an Information Systems Outsourcing Context. *International Journal of Knowledge Management, 13*(4), 1–30. doi:10.4018/IJKM.2017100101

Sousa, M. J., Cruz, R., Dias, I., & Caracol, C. (2017). Information Management Systems in the Supply Chain. In G. Jamil, A. Soares, & C. Pessoa (Eds.), *Handbook of Research on Information Management for Effective Logistics and Supply Chains* (pp. 469–485). Hershey, PA: IGI Global. doi:10.4018/978-1-5225-0973-8.ch025

Spremic, M., Turulja, L., & Bajgoric, N. (2018). Two Approaches in Assessing Business Continuity Management Attitudes in the Organizational Context. In N. Bajgoric (Ed.), *Always-On Enterprise Information Systems for Modern Organizations* (pp. 159–183). Hershey, PA: IGI Global. doi:10.4018/978-1-5225-3704-5.ch008

Steenkamp, A. L. (2018). Some Insights in Computer Science and Information Technology. In *Examining the Changing Role of Supervision in Doctoral Research Projects: Emerging Research and Opportunities* (pp. 113–133). Hershey, PA: IGI Global. doi:10.4018/978-1-5225-2610-0.ch005

Stipanović, C., Rudan, E., & Zubović, V. (2022). Reaching the New Tourist Through Creativity: Sustainable Development Challenges in Croatian Coastal Towns. In M. Valeri (Ed.), *New Governance and Management in Touristic Destinations* (pp. 231–245). IGI Global. https://doi.org/10.4018/978-1-6684-3889-3.ch014

Tabach, A., & Croteau, A. (2017). Configurations of Information Technology Governance Practices and Business Unit Performance. *International Journal of IT/Business Alignment and Governance, 8*(2), 1–27. doi:10.4018/IJITBAG.2017070101

Talaue, G. M., & Iqbal, T. (2017). Assessment of e-Business Mode of Selected Private Universities in the Philippines and Pakistan. *International Journal of Online Marketing, 7*(4), 63–77. doi:10.4018/IJOM.2017100105

Tam, G. C. (2017). Project Manager Sustainability Competence. In *Managerial Strategies and Green Solutions for Project Sustainability* (pp. 178–207). Hershey, PA: IGI Global. doi:10.4018/978-1-5225-2371-0.ch008

Tambo, T. (2018). Fashion Retail Innovation: About Context, Antecedents, and Outcome in Technological Change Projects. In I. Management Association (Ed.), Fashion and Textiles: Breakthroughs in Research and Practice (pp. 233-260). Hershey, PA: IGI Global. https://doi.org/ doi:10.4018/978-1-5225-3432-7.ch010

Tantau, A. D., & Frăţilă, L. C. (2018). Information and Management System for Renewable Energy Business. In *Entrepreneurship and Business Development in the Renewable Energy Sector* (pp. 200–244). Hershey, PA: IGI Global. doi:10.4018/978-1-5225-3625-3.ch006

Teixeira, N., Pardal, P. N., & Rafael, B. G. (2018). Internationalization, Financial Performance, and Organizational Challenges: A Success Case in Portugal. In L. Carvalho (Ed.), *Handbook of Research on Entrepreneurial Ecosystems and Social Dynamics in a Globalized World* (pp. 379–423). Hershey, PA: IGI Global. doi:10.4018/978-1-5225-3525-6.ch017

Teixeira, P., Teixeira, L., Eusébio, C., Silva, S., & Teixeira, A. (2021). The Impact of ICTs on Accessible Tourism: Evidence Based on a Systematic Literature Review. In C. Eusébio, L. Teixeira, & M. Carneiro (Eds.), *ICT Tools and Applications for Accessible Tourism* (pp. 1–25). IGI Global. doi:10.4018/978-1-7998-6428-8.ch001

Trad, A., & Kalpić, D. (2018). The Business Transformation Framework, Agile Project and Change Management. In M. Khosrow-Pour, D.B.A. (Ed.), Encyclopedia of Information Science and Technology, Fourth Edition (pp. 620-635). Hershey, PA: IGI Global. https://doi.org/ doi:10.4018/978-1-5225-2255-3.ch054

Trad, A., & Kalpić, D. (2018). The Business Transformation and Enterprise Architecture Framework: The Financial Engineering E-Risk Management and E-Law Integration. In B. Sergi, F. Fidanoski, M. Ziolo, & V. Naumovski (Eds.), *Regaining Global Stability After the Financial Crisis* (pp. 46–65). Hershey, PA: IGI Global. doi:10.4018/978-1-5225-4026-7.ch003

Trengereid, V. (2022). Conditions of Network Engagement: The Quest for a Common Good. In R. Augusto Costa, F. Brandão, Z. Breda, & C. Costa (Eds.), *Planning and Managing the Experience Economy in Tourism* (pp. 69-84). IGI Global. https://doi.org/10.4018/978-1-7998-8775-1.ch004

Turulja, L., & Bajgoric, N. (2018). Business Continuity and Information Systems: A Systematic Literature Review. In N. Bajgoric (Ed.), *Always-On Enterprise Information Systems for Modern Organizations* (pp. 60–87). Hershey, PA: IGI Global. doi:10.4018/978-1-5225-3704-5.ch004

Vargas-Hernández, J. G. (2017). Professional Integrity in Business Management Education. In N. Baporikar (Ed.), *Management Education for Global Leadership* (pp. 70–89). Hershey, PA: IGI Global. doi:10.4018/978-1-5225-1013-0.ch004

Varnacı Uzun, F. (2021). The Destination Preferences of Foreign Tourists During the COVID-19 Pandemic and Attitudes Towards: Marmaris, Turkey. In M. Demir, A. Dalgıç, & F. Ergen (Eds.), *Handbook of Research on the Impacts and Implications of COVID-19 on the Tourism Industry* (pp. 285–306). IGI Global. https://doi.org/10.4018/978-1-7998-8231-2.ch014

Vasista, T. G., & AlAbdullatif, A. M. (2017). Role of Electronic Customer Relationship Management in Demand Chain Management: A Predictive Analytic Approach. *International Journal of Information Systems and Supply Chain Management, 10*(1), 53–67. doi:10.4018/IJISSCM.2017010104

Vieru, D., & Bourdeau, S. (2017). Survival in the Digital Era: A Digital Competence-Based Multi-Case Study in the Canadian SME Clothing Industry. *International Journal of Social and Organizational Dynamics in IT, 6*(1), 17–34. doi:10.4018/IJSODIT.2017010102

Vijayan, G., & Kamarulzaman, N. H. (2017). An Introduction to Sustainable Supply Chain Management and Business Implications. In M. Khan, M. Hussain, & M. Ajmal (Eds.), *Green Supply Chain Management for Sustainable Business Practice* (pp. 27–50). Hershey, PA: IGI Global. doi:10.4018/978-1-5225-0635-5.ch002

Vlachvei, A., & Notta, O. (2017). Firm Competitiveness: Theories, Evidence, and Measurement. In A. Vlachvei, O. Notta, K. Karantininis, & N. Tsounis (Eds.), *Factors Affecting Firm Competitiveness and Performance in the Modern Business World* (pp. 1–42). Hershey, PA: IGI Global. doi:10.4018/978-1-5225-0843-4.ch001

Wang, C., Schofield, M., Li, X., & Ou, X. (2017). Do Chinese Students in Public and Private Higher Education Institutes Perform at Different Level in One of the Leadership Skills: Critical Thinking?: An Exploratory Comparison. In V. Wang (Ed.), *Encyclopedia of Strategic Leadership and Management* (pp. 160–181). Hershey, PA: IGI Global. doi:10.4018/978-1-5225-1049-9.ch013

Wang, J. (2017). Multi-Agent based Production Management Decision System Modelling for the Textile Enterprise. *Journal of Global Information Management, 25*(4), 1–15. doi:10.4018/JGIM.2017100101

Wiedemann, A., & Gewald, H. (2017). Examining Cross-Domain Alignment: The Correlation of Business Strategy, IT Management, and IT Business Value. *International Journal of IT/Business Alignment and Governance, 8*(1), 17–31. doi:10.4018/IJITBAG.2017010102

Wolf, R., & Thiel, M. (2018). Advancing Global Business Ethics in China: Reducing Poverty Through Human and Social Welfare. In S. Hipsher (Ed.), *Examining the Private Sector's Role in Wealth Creation and Poverty Reduction* (pp. 67–84). Hershey, PA: IGI Global. doi:10.4018/978-1-5225-3117-3.ch004

Yablonsky, S. (2018). Innovation Platforms: Data and Analytics Platforms. In *Multi-Sided Platforms (MSPs) and Sharing Strategies in the Digital Economy: Emerging Research and Opportunities* (pp. 72–95). Hershey, PA: IGI Global. doi:10.4018/978-1-5225-5457-8.ch003

Yaşar, B. (2021). The Impact of COVID-19 on Volatility of Tourism Stocks: Evidence From BIST Tourism Index. In M. Demir, A. Dalgıç, & F. Ergen (Eds.), *Handbook of Research on the Impacts and Implications of COVID-19 on the Tourism Industry* (pp. 23–44). IGI Global. https://doi.org/10.4018/978-1-7998-8231-2.ch002

Yusoff, A., Ahmad, N. H., & Halim, H. A. (2017). Agropreneurship among Gen Y in Malaysia: The Role of Academic Institutions. In N. Ahmad, T. Ramayah, H. Halim, & S. Rahman (Eds.), *Handbook of Research on Small and Medium Enterprises in Developing Countries* (pp. 23–47). Hershey, PA: IGI Global. doi:10.4018/978-1-5225-2165-5.ch002

Zacher, D., & Pechlaner, H. (2021). Resilience as an Opportunity Approach: Challenges and Perspectives for Private Sector Participation on a Community Level. In A. Zehrer, G. Glowka, K. Schwaiger, & V. Ranacher-Lackner (Eds.), *Resiliency Models and Addressing Future Risks for Family Firms in the Tourism Industry* (pp. 75–102). IGI Global. https://doi.org/10.4018/978-1-7998-7352-5.ch004

Zanin, F., Comuzzi, E., & Costantini, A. (2018). The Effect of Business Strategy and Stock Market Listing on the Use of Risk Assessment Tools. In *Management Control Systems in Complex Settings: Emerging Research and Opportunities* (pp. 145–168). Hershey, PA: IGI Global. doi:10.4018/978-1-5225-3987-2.ch007

Zgheib, P. W. (2017). Corporate Innovation and Intrapreneurship in the Middle East. In P. Zgheib (Ed.), *Entrepreneurship and Business Innovation in the Middle East* (pp. 37–56). Hershey, PA: IGI Global. doi:10.4018/978-1-5225-2066-5.ch003

About the Contributors

Kleopatra (Klery) Petroutsatou is Associate Professor at Aristotle University of Thessaloniki, Faculty of Engineering, Dpt. of Civil Engineering, Laboratory of Planning and Project Management. Her area of expertise is Construction Equipment, Cost and Management of Civil Engineering Projects. She holds a Diploma of Civil Engineering (Structural Division) from National University of Athens (NTUA). She holds a M.Sc. in Engineering Business Management (Hons) from University of Warwick in UK. She holds a PhD (Doctor Engineer) from Civil Engineering School of NTUA. She is reviewer in international scientific journals and conferences. She has submitted research proposals as leading coordinator in european and national research programs. She has completed two scientific programs as one of the main researchers. She has publications in international scientific journals and announcements in international conferences. She has supervised a large number of undergraduate and postgraduate thesis and she has been member of committees for PhDs awards. From 1997 until 2012, she has worked in the private and public sector as auditor and consultant in technical companies and infrastructure projects. For three years she was member of the technical team at the office of the General Secretary for Concessions of the Ministry of Public Works in Greece.

Constantin Zopounidis is Professor of Financial Engineering and Operations Research, at Technical University of Crete (Greece), Distinguished Research Professor in Audencia Business School (France), and Senior Academician of both the Royal Academy of Doctors and the Royal Academy of Economics and Financial Sciences of SpainHe is also elected President since early 2012, of the Financial Engineering and Banking Society (FEBS). He is Editor in the book series on Multiple Criteria Decision Making and Cooperative Management (Springer). He is also elected President since early 2012, of the Financial Engineering and Banking Society (FEBS). In recognition of his scientific work, he has received several awards from international research societies. Recently, in 2012 he was the recipient of the Long-lasting Research Contribution Award in the field of Financial Engineering & Decision Making by ESCP Europe. In 2013 he received the Edgeworth-Pareto prestigious Award from the International Society of Multicriteria Decision Making and in 2015 he received the Award for Outstanding Contribution to Research in Management Science and Decision Making by Audencia Business School. In 2018, the Aristotle University of Thessaloniki awarded him the title of Honorary Doctor. He has edited and authored 100 books in international publishers and more than 500 research papers in scientific journals, edited volumes, conference proceedings and encyclopaedias in the areas of finance, accounting, operations research, and management science.

* * *

Fani Antoniou is an experienced Project Manager with a demonstrated history of working in civil engineering public works projects and in the higher education industry. Skilled in Procurement, Construction, Civil Engineering, Contract Management, Claim Management and Project Planning. Strong education professional with a BEng, MSc focused in Civil Engineering from Imperial College London.

Georgios N. Aretoulis is an Associate Professor in Construction Management, since 2015, at the Civil Engineering Department of the Aristotle University of Thessaloniki, Greece. He holds a Diploma, an MSc in Environmental Protection and Sustainable Development, as well as a PhD from the Aristotle University of Thessaloniki.

Rajen Chetty was the first non-white Port engineer appointed at Durban Port in SA. He is an engineer and project manager with Transnet Capital Projects.

Alexandros Garefalakis is Chartered Accountant (Fellow of CPA), Management Accountant (CMA Diploma) and Business Consultant in numerous of companies and organizations. Also, he is a Assistant Professor at the Dept. of Business Administration and Tourism, Hellenic Mediterranean University (HMU). He holds a degree in Financial Applications, a Master degree in Accounting and Finance from University of Southampton and PhD in Accounting from Hellenic Open University. He has co-authored 2 books on Audit Accounting and Management Accounting issues. He has more than 70 publications in peer reviewed journals and participation in more than 21 national and international conferences. His areas of research interest include the quality of Narrative information of Financial Reports and business performance assessment as well as management efficiency and productivity.

Alexandros Grigoras completed his studies at the Civil Engineering Department, of the Aristotle University of Thessaloniki, Greece. He received his diploma. He currently works as a professional civil engineer in building construction and renovation.

Evangelos Grigoroudis is Professor on management of quality processes in the School of Production Engineering and Management of the Technical University of Crete, Greece (2002-). He has received distinctions from the Hellenic Operational Research Society, the Academy of Business and Administrative Sciences, the World Automation Congress, the Foundation of Ioannis and Vasileia Karayianni, the Technical University of Crete, the State Scholarships Foundation of Greece, and the IEEE TEM Society. He is Associate Editor and member of the Editorial Board of 8 and 6 scientific journals, respectively, and he acts as reviewer for more than 80 journals. He is author and/or editor of 30 books on service quality, operations management, business strategy and management, multicriteria decision aid approaches, and innovation management. He has published more than 200 papers in scientific journals, books and conference proceedings. His research interests include service quality measurement processes, customer and employee satisfaction, performance evaluation, business excellence, operational research, multicriteria decision analysis, data analysis, and marketing.

Stylianos Karatzas is a Marie Curie Postdoctoral Fellow in the Institute of Manufacturing (IfM) at the University of Cambridge. He has been an Adjunct Lecturer in the Civil Engineering Department at the University of Patras, in the field of Smart Infrastructure, Transportation, and Cities since 2018. He holds a Ph.D. in Civil Engineering from the University of Patras, which was selected and co-financed by the Greek State Scholarship Foundation and the European Union, a bachelor's degree in Electrical Engineering and Computer Science and a master's degree in Automation and Control Systems from the University of Patras (Greece), and a master's degree in Operations Management from the University of Bath (UK). He has been a research scholar in the Construction Science Department at the TEXAS A&M University (US), working in data-driven research focused on infrastructure asset management. He has worked in the industry for several technical projects in Greece and the UAE. He is currently coordinating several European Horizon research projects with a total of more than €25m funding received. He has supervised over 20 theses and he has more than 40 publications in peer-reviewed Journals and refereed conferences proceedings.

Stratos Kartsonakis is a PhD student at the Technical University of Greece. He holds an MSc in Technology and Operations Management from the University of Groningen, while he obtained his bachelor's degree in production engineering and management from the Technical University of Crete. During his studies he has coauthored research papers in scientific journals and books, while he has presented his work in multiple international conferences and symposiums. His research interests include multicriteria decision analysis, operational research, decision support systems, customer and employee evaluation and data analysis.

Dimitra N. Korakaki is graduate of the Physics Department of the National and Kapodistrian University of Athens (NKUoA), Greece. She has completed three (3) postgraduate programs: 1. "Quality Control and Environmental Management" (Department of Environmental Engineering, Technical University of Crete) with a scholarship, 2. "Museum Studies" (Departments of History and Archaeology, and Geology and Geoenvironment (NKUoA) and 3. "Master's in Business Administration with specialization: Public Administration Executives" (School of Production Engineering and Management, TUC). Today she is a permanent employee in the Ministry of Culture and Sports. She was employed in the Administrative Authority of the Operational Program "Digital Convergence". For the last seven years she has been teaching part-time in Higher Educational Institutions of Crete.

Marina Marinelli is an Assistant Professor in Engineering Project Planning and Management at the School of Civil Engineering, National Technical University of Athens (NTUA), and an Honorary Lecturer with the School of Engineering, University of Leicester, U.K. She has received an MEng in Civil Engineering (NTUA, 2006), an MSc degree in Structural Engineering (NTUA, 2007) and a PhD degree in Construction Management (NTUA, 2012). She has published over 35 articles in reputed journals and conferences in various areas including public contracts management, digital construction, lean engineering and sustainability strategies. She has supervised over 80 MSc theses in construction / engineering management and teaches relevant undergraduate and postgraduate modules. She is a fellow of the UK's Higher Education Academy (FHEA).

Vannie Naidoo is a full time staff member at the University of KwaZulu-Natal, South Africa, in the Faculty of Management and Law. Her field of teaching is in management, corporate strategy, project management, marketing, project management research methodology and entrepreneurship. The research areas pursued by Prof. Naidoo are in the areas of management, management, marketing, service marketing, entrepreneurship and social media and e-learning or learning with new technologies. She has presented papers at international conferences throughout the world and has written on various issues in management and marketing in journal articles and books.

Ioannis Passas is a Researcher, Adjunct Lecturer and Ph.D. in Accounting at the Department of Business Administration & Tourism of the Hellenic Mediterranean University where he teaches accounting courses at undergraduate and postgraduate level. He also teaches at the Department of Accounting and Finance of the Neapolis University of Paphos at the postgraduate program Forensic Accounting. He holds a Bachelor of Business Administration from the International Hellenic University and a Master of Business Administration in Hospitality and Tourism from the Hellenic Mediterranean University. He is also a Certified Internal Control Auditor (CICA), a Certified Control Specialist (CCS) by the Institute of Internal Auditors (IIC), a Certified Management Accountant (CMA) by the Institute of Chartered Accountants and a Certified Internal Auditor by the State of Greece. His main research interests focus on the scientific fields: ESG, Management Commentary, Disclosure Narrative information, Multiple Criteria Decision-Making in Management Accounting, Strategic decisions, Fraud, Auditing, Quality of Financial Statements, Accounting, and Operational Research.

Index

P

R

S

T

U

V

www.ingramcontent.com/pod-product-compliance
Lightning Source LLC
LaVergne TN
LVHW081325300926
849161LV00008B/1875